COUNTERING INDUSTRIAL ESPIONAGE

Countering Industrial Espionage

by

Peter A Heims

Published by
20th Century Security Education Ltd.,
293 Kingston Road,
Leatherhead,
Surrey,
England.

© 1982 PETER HEIMS
ISBN 0 905961 03 X

Printed by Bookmag, Henderson Road, Inverness.

Contents

Appendices

Foreword

I have known Peter Heims for more years than I care to remember. During that time I have seen his stature and reputation grow from a small-time (but respected) operator to that of a national name, frequently quoted as a security authority in the press.

Now comes this book — a triumphal mark and manifestation of years of experience, innovation and devotion to the job.

It is more than a dozen years since I wrote what I believe to have been the first book on industrial espionage. Hard though it is to say it, I will admit that this new book marks a considerable advance on any previous work on the subject.

I particularly like the wealth of case histories and the classifying of the lessons to be learnt from them. There is also a frightening catalogue of modern listening and seeing devices, many of them of microscopic dimensions and macroscopic performance.

I hope this book will be read widely by industrial and commercial management. It ought to convince them that information is not only the newest and a most sought after value form but if their firms are to survive, they must guard the most sensitive information like the crown jewels.

One word of warning: this book may be used by the privacists (to coin a word) as material for constructing and enforcing stringent privacy laws. Care must be taken to ensure that such laws, which while having no effect on the criminal who is breaking the law anyway, do not further handicap those whose job it is to bring criminals to justice.

Peter Hamilton
Author of Espionage, Subversion and Terrorism in an Industrial Society.

Preface

Industrial espionage has been with us ever since Boadicea sent her agents to discover how the Romans made their chariots. She made a few improvements and turned the stolen knowledge to devastating effect against her enemies.

Since then, and especially in the past fifty years, industrial espionage has become a vast international industry. The prizes at stake make the Great Train Robbery look like a casual pick-pocket operation.

Peter Heims is one of the world's leading experts on the subject. He has a long and successful record of investigation into industrial espionage of all kinds, a detailed knowledge of the complicated technology involved, and wide experience of methods of protection and prevention.

He has succeeded in distilling his vast knowledge and experience in this book. It is written with a refreshing lack of jargon, in a way that even a layman could understand.

I recommend it to industrialists, security officers, journalists, in fact to all who have a concern with this growing problem.

Lord Ted Willis

Introduction

For over two decades I have been operating as a private investigator, security consultant and — increasingly, in recent years — as a consultant on industrial espionage.

Security has always been concerned with such bread-and-butter problems as the protection of premises, safeguards against fraud and theft, the vetting of staff and the transport of valuables. But these things, in security terms, are elementary when compared with the wider, and increasing problem of industrial espionage, which has grown alarmingly both in this country and abroad, particularly in the United States of America.

The problem first assumed magnitude in the late fifties, and has gained momentum ever since. Indeed, thirteen years ago the (British) Institute of Directors found it necessary to sponsor a booklet warning industry of the menace in its midst, indicating some of the main hazards and suggesting a few elementary precautions against them.

Since those days new techniques have been devised by those who steal, and later exploit or sell, other people's secrets. Such piracy can be not only damaging, but ruinous to businesses whose formulae, production sequences, processes, organisation and plans are often rendered useless as a result of dishonest disclosure or theft.

Businesses generally, and authorities in particular, have been very slow to respond to the warnings repeated over many years. I have "swept" many a boardroom for hidden bugs, and have sometimes been struck by the timidity with which the managements have received the information that their most secret discussions have been eavesdropped upon; they are fearful of losing face by taking legal action against the culprits, who move on to other fields and make a nuisance of themselves elsewhere. In any case, the taking of legal action in itself may have its own self-defeating hazards, since the giving of evidence in support of one's case can involve the disclosure of the very industrial secrets for the protection of which the legal action is being taken. The obvious answer to such an anachronism is to prevent rather than cure — to take appropriate action and precautions for the safeguarding of industrial secrets.

My original intention was to produce a textbook for the use of security experts and top executives, but the subject, I decided, required a broader and more general treatment, by which some understanding of the scope and nature of the problem can be gained by anybody, specialist or non-specialist. Even the typist and the photocopier, by learning not to be too slap-happy in disposing of used carbon ribbons or imperfect photocopies, need to be aware of their responsibilities to their employers — even if only from motives of self-interest, since, if the company is ruined by the theft of its valuable know-how, the jobs of everyone may be in jeopardy.

I hope, therefore, that I shall have achieved my aim, and that if any reader feels otherwise he will tell me in what respects future editions can be improved or amended; I welcome such correspondence, so much so that, in these inflationary days, I am even willing to refund postage.

In the course of compilation and research I have been indebted to many good friends who have helped to clear up doubtful points, or assist with research, or comment upon such sections of my book on which they happen to be specialists. Not all are acknowledged here, and those who are not may accept this assurance that the omission of their name is dictated by space and not ingratitude; but I owe particular thanks to Dennis Bardens, Vince Carratu, Peter Clements, Mike Comer, Dektor Counterintelligence and Security, Inc., John Ellen, Peter Hamilton, Hal Lipset, Sir David McNee, QPM, Tim Matthews, Louis Moreau and Desmond Trenner.

I hope, too, that in its own way this book may provide ammunition for those who, like myself, want to see the security industry cleansed of miscreants and doubtful characters who, as the law stands at present, can operate as security consultants or guards, since any man who chooses can set up in such a business; clearly crime cannot be countered by the employment of those with criminal or dishonest tendencies. I have long worked for legislation to stop this loophole, and shall continue to do so until the glaring anomaly is ended.

Peter Heims

Part I — The Threat

CHAPTER 1

Defining and Assessing the Risk

In May, 1980, two French customs inspectors had the surprise of their lives.

It is the duty of customs officials to implement the customs laws and to prevent those who would break them. It is equally their job to seize contraband, and to arrest smugglers and others who defy the regulations.

Indeed, they were attempting to do this when, to their amazement and dismay, they found themselves arrested by the Swiss authorities.

The French officials were about to pay £5,000 for a list of French nationals having secret bank accounts in Switzerland. Presumably, had such a list been disclosed, the French authorities would have checked on whether, say, Monsieur A's deposits in Switzerland tallied with his returns of income which he had made in France, and whether he had complied with French regulations affecting the transfer of his capital.

The Swiss authorities regarded this attempt to procure a list of depositors which was confidential to the bank as industrial espionage, for the stealing of commercial secrets by foreigners is an offence under Swiss law.

It is rare for governments to concern themselves with the ever-growing problem of industrial espionage. Yet this is a menace which has grown tremendously during the last thirty years (although it existed long before then) and is now prevalent throughout the industrial world.

For over twenty-five years I have made a special study of counter-industrial espionage and run a business in which experts on different aspects of it pool their energies and knowledge. The art of this kind of spying, and the means of thwarting the wrong-doers, has, over the years, become more and more complex, and the technical devices used by both sides more sophisticated.

Industrial secrets are a form of property, often more solid as assets than the buildings and machinery or even the money in the bank. They are more often than not the basis of the company's whole existence. To lose the details of some secret process, or the plans of an invention, or the marketing plans of some proposed new product, be it a new kind of cornflakes or a revolutionary new aeroplane, can be irretrievable disaster.

The purpose of this book is to give you some idea of the extent of this modern menace, the methods followed by industrial spies, and the means by which valuable industrial secrets may be protected.

As a start, I will define the problem. Next, I will show how real and extensive that problem is. After that, I propose to show the many forms which industrial espionage can take, and the specific means by which this danger can be met.

*   *   *

WHAT IS 'INDUSTRIAL ESPIONAGE'?
My own definition is: the 'stealing' of 'secrets'.

I have put both words in quotes. The end result of industrial espionage amounts to theft, but is usually a more complicated affair than merely putting your hand into somebody's pocket. The 'stealing' is more often than not a long-drawn-out process, too. As for 'secrets' — they can be anything you do not wish disclosed. The secret may be an intention to put on the market a new kind of chocolate bar, or to devise some new application of laser which would give an army the edge on their enemies in the field.

Secrets in industry are a vital asset, the loss of which may prove disastrous. A carefully-planned sales campaign, built up over months, may have to be scrapped because a rival has been told of your intentions and strategy — may even have stolen the march on you and grabbed the very market you proposed to satisfy. A pharmaceutical formula which has taken a team of specialists years to produce, and cost millions of pounds in research, will, if lost to a rival, be exploited by them for profit with none of the burden of investment.

Another definition: The seeking, obtaining and transmitting through secret means or false pretences of industrial or commercial information for industrial, commercial, political or subversive political purposes.

The *New Law Journal* of April 24, 1980, says:
Industrial espionage can be described as the gaining of industrial or commercial intelligence by illegal, surreptitious or other undesirable means.

According to the very reliable *Guinness Book of Records*, industrial espionage 'represents the greatest robbery of all time.'

A principal of one of the world's leading firms of industrial investigators has defined it this way: 'Industrial espionage is basically the obtaining of restricted information from a company for gain.'

Sir Richard Powell, a former Director-General of The Institute of Directors, has said that 'Industrial espionage is a serious subject, far more serious than we suspect . . .'

Peter Hamilton, a noted security consultant and author, has described industrial espionage as 'a part of the family tree of what may be termed the dark forces of our civilisation.' And he adds a more formal definition: 'Industrial espionage is espionage undertaken with the object of obtaining industrial information which will be of economic or political advantage.'

It is a comparatively new term which gained currency in England in the sixties, when Management Investigation Services held a one-day seminar — a series of five lectures for 40 specialist listeners — in a London hotel.

A further (and inaccurate) description was added by a judge in the course of a court hearing in England in 1971: 'Industrial espionage is a crime.' In fact, and unfortunately, although punishable illegalities may be committed *in the course of* industrial espionage (such as the theft of papers, or trespass) it is not, in itself, a crime. Lastly, a definition from Mr Alan Campbell, Q.C.: 'A black market in information.'

I do not wish, at this point, to enlarge on the legal aspects of industrial espionage. The essential fact, and the reason for this book being written at all, *is that it exists*, that because of the casual and complacent attitude of many managements, it has grown to alarming proportions and is growing still at an ever-accelerating rate.

And, since it is not a crime, it is 'bottom of the pops' so far as the police are concerned. This is not their fault; they have their hands full in fighting crime of every description. It follows from this that it behoves every owner of property to take reasonable steps to look after it. As Sir Robert Mark, former Commissioner of the Metropolitan Police, London, put it: 'It therefore becomes essential to convince every citizen that he must assume the primary responsibility for protecting his own property' (including, by inference, the protection of industrial information).

To do this, a knowledge of the law — what is permissible under it, and what is not — and specific background information on how spies operate, the sort of people they might be, and the very many technical aspects of the whole area of information, is required. Such a combination of knowledge is unlikely to be found in untrained people. Fighting industrial espionage has produced, of necessity, a new breed of highly-trained experts who have a strong sense of professionalism and who have to be constantly on the alert to keep up-to-date on current strategy and techniques, and on changing trends.

It is for the benefit of those engaged in this specialised field that this work is primarily intended, although industrial executives may well profit from it as one aspect of the overall industrial scheme, and a field of interest which they cannot afford to ignore if their companies are to enjoy to full measure the benefits which their investment, imagination and efforts should bring.

*   *   *

INDUSTRIAL ESPIONAGE AND COMPETITIVE INTELLIGENCE:
Industrial Espionage gives the culprits an unfair advantage over their competitors. They may appropriate to themselves formulae, methods, processes and plans on which their rivals may have spent, and often have spent, million of pounds. They may bring ruin to their rivals and unemployment to their rivals' employees.

And yet, you may ask, isn't it common sense to keep abreast of what your competitors are doing? Isn't competition between people engaged in the same occupation as necessary as it is inevitable?

The answer is: yes, competition is necessary. It is inevitable. It is legitimate. Within certain bounds you are entitled to discover what new processes your competitors are employing, to what degree they are increasing their staff, or diversifying their products, or seeking new markets, or devising new sales techniques. Between industrial spying and industrial intelligence there may be presumed to be a dividing line — but where can that line be drawn? It is not so simple to define. There is, in fact, a 'grey area' between the black and the white, and where black merges into grey and white into grey is often a matter of personal judgement and decision. There is no general concensus of opinion, no universally accepted standard.

The reason for this is that attitudes, whether legal, public or industrial, towards industrial espionage differ from country to country.

Let me give a simple, though one of the least dramatic, examples of what I consider to be industrial espionage:

In 1968 two companies were in a highly competitive relationship. This is quite usual.

Both were in the field of synthetic resins.

A 51-year-old employee of Revertex, of Harlow, Essex, stole from his employers a file containing log sheets — revealing their secret process for making their product. The information was the product of costly and extensive research and concerned not only processes, but grades of material made by the firm.

The employee contacted his firm's principal rival, offering to sell them (i.e. Vinyl Products, of Carshalton, Surrey) his log book of 'formulations' used by Revertex.

Vinyl, as proud of its integrity as of its products, had not the slightest interest in being party to a deception, but, with a view to bringing this industrial nuisance to book, and in the general interest, led him along. They pretended to be interested, but got in touch with Revertex, who called in the police.

Acting on the instructions of the dishonest employee of Revertex (he had, in fact, been in their employ for 27 years), Vinyl placed an advertisement in the personal column of *The Daily Telegraph*.

It said: "V.P. Still interested. Please contact C."

"C" was a member of Vinyl sales staff who, in due course, received a telephone call during which a rendezvous was made outside Selfridge's Store in Oxford Street, London. "C" turned up as arranged, and so did the police.

The story ended at Bow Street Magistrates' Court. The culprit had been arrested in the act of handing over the stolen documents. Ironically he was merely charged with stealing a folder valued at 7s.6d.(37½p) and for this offence, to which he pleaded guilty, he was fined £100.

It was merely the physical possession of the firm's *folder* which constituted the theft. Yet, to the firm, the greatest hazard was the potential loss of their trade secrets, the very basis of that firm's activity and existence.

The rival firm to whom the secrets were offered proved an ethical concern; the results of industrial espionage are seldom as inocuous as this, because this particular spy was an amateur, and nowadays there are more professionals at the game than there are amateurs.

That case, which is far less spectacular than most, illustrates one vital point of policy; in the protection of company secrets, prevention of their theft is better than the detection and punishment of culprits. It is not even an instance of prevention being better than cure, for there frequently is no cure. Damage caused by disloyal employees, or failure to frustrate in time the conspiracy of a competitor, can be irretrievable. It is useless to lock the door after the horse has bolted.

It must be said again, for the point is basic to this whole subject: protection against industrial espionage is up to you in my opinion. It is *not* the business of the police, who have neither the time nor the necessary organisation to cope with this sector of crime prevention.

Criminologists the world over are agreed that industrial espionage exists on a vast scale, offering this class of spies rewards often exceeding those which they might earn in the world of 'orthodox' spying — i.e., in the service of one country spying upon another. Mr Vincent Carratu, a former Scotland Yard Fraud Squad detective, has said that industrial espionage is costing British industry millions of pounds a year. He sounded this warning in the *C.B.I. Review Spring 1975* (organ of the Confederation of British Industries): 'unless internal security is given the priority it deserves in a company's affairs, many companies will be forced out of business.'

A warning that there are more spies at work in industry, and that they are both capable and well organised, was sounded as early as 1963 by the already quoted Sir Richard Powell.

Sir Richard sounded the warning that what was politely described as industrial intelligence had become industrial espionage. Whereas every manufacturer considered it his right to take apart a competitor's product and see how it was made and what made it sell, the whole business had become "much more aggressive." Unethical methods, he declared, were on the increase, and he instanced some of the methods which, once unthinkable by respectable firms, were rapidly becoming accepted as the norm:

1. Bribing suppliers of components to tell them what other firms are ordering — especially when it seems to be for new products;
2. Luring away the top technicians and managerial chiefs of a rival's company, where these are known to have access to secret information;

3. Getting dupes or planting spies to strike up friendship with those having knowledge of trade secrets and secret processes or plans;
4. Planting spies in factories and offices, or even — as domestic servants — in the homes of important directors of companies;
5. Sending specialists having the necessary technical background to exhibitions, where they ask questions far more searching and technical than would normally be the case.

Sir Richard Jackson, a former head of Interpol, has described industrial espionage as an international threat which is worrying the authorities in many countries, particularly France, Germany and America.

UNETHICAL — OR LEGITIMATE?

Counter-industrial espionage, whether conducted by large concerns specialising in combatting this social nuisance (since, legally at least, it cannot always be called a crime), or by individual private investigators, is reasonable and necessary.

Those making security a career, however, will soon discover that industrial espionage and intelligence merge one into the other.

What is unethical, and what is legitimate? Who decides? And — if ever there is any concensus of professional opinion on standards — how can such standards be enforced?

Let us take a few obvious cases of such spying.

Kenneth Ian Rees, of Edmonton, London, stole heart-drug secrets worth £1,000,000 from a chemical works at Enfield. Merck & Co., the American parent company, flew three representatives to Britain with authority to spend £10,000 in recovering the secrets. Private detectives got to the bottom of the matter after much clever investigative work, and, as a result, the secrets were recovered and the culprit given a six-months jail sentence.

In 1968 BOAC discovered that its computerised seat reservation system which had cost it £3 million to develop, was being offered cut-price to rival airlines. Although one executive was fired and the resignation of three others demanded, no legal action was taken.

In both the foregoing cases deliberate dishonesty was a factor. But does keeping abreast of new trends in design, marketing, manufacture and information on staff availability, the salaries of a handful of exceptionally-talented specialists, the development of new technologies relevant to your business necessarily involve dishonesty?

Of course not. But there are grey areas, neither black nor white, in which the security expert has to be guided by his own conscience.

As regards legitimate intelligence, it is possible to assemble facts drawn from a wide variety of public sources and, by correct interpretation *of these combined sources*, draw inferences which might well surprise your rival by their accuracy. The question of two and two making four is basic to all information gathering — including industrial intelligence.

Let me give a hypothetical case.

You are in the business of making spare parts for, say, the aerospace industry.

You note that your rival is advertising in technical journals for extra staff, but your information on the extent of his business (partly culled from files held at Companies House) does nothing to explain his search for extra staff. Your curiosity is aroused.

At a trade association meeting you see a director of the rival company having a drink with a friend. You catch a snatch of conversation; he is going to some African state.

Why, you wonder. He hasn't mentioned Zambia, from which his company get most of their copper shipments. Have they found a substitute for copper in their electrical circuits? Or are they making some new part which requires no copper — branching out into some important new development?

All this might disturb you. If he has found a substitute for copper in the manufacture of the parts you both make, maybe he can undercut you to such an extent that you will be denied future contracts. For want of the right information (intelligence) your business could well be threatened.

At this point you might decide to commission a private investigator to report on what is going on. How far can he legitimately go before crossing the invisible boundary line between competitive intelligence and industrial espionage?

In the course of lecturing to management, here and abroad, it is my custom to list the many methods open to an investigator when seeking industrial information about his client's competitor. I will list them here:—

    1.   Published material, and public documents such as court records.

2. Disclosures made by competitor's employees, and obtained without subterfuge.
3. Market surveys and consultant's reports.
4. Financial reports, and broker's research surveys.
5. Trade fairs, exhibits, and competitor's brochures.
6. Analysis of competitor's products.
7. Reports of own salesmen and purchasing agents.
8. Legitimate employment interviews with people who worked for competitor.
9. Camouflaged questioning and 'drawing out' of competitor's employees at technical meetings.
10. Direct observation under secret conditions.
11. False job interviews with competitor's employee (i.e. where there is no real intent to hire).
12. False negotiations with competitor for licence.
13. Hiring a professional investigator to obtain a specific piece of information.
14. Hiring an employee away from the competitor to get specific know-how.
15. Trespassing on competitor's property.
16. Bribing competitor's supplier or employee.
17. Planting your agent on competitor's payroll.
18. Eavesdropping on competitors (e.g. via wire-tapping).
19. Theft of drawings, samples, documents and similar property.
20. Blackmail and extortion.

This list was compiled by Dr Worth Wade, a Philadelphia Management Consultant and published in the American journal *CHEMICAL ENGINEERING* on 23rd May, 1966. Of these various methods of becoming informed about competitors, Dr Wade considers the first seven methods usually ethical and legal and the remaining thirteen are in descending order of ethics or legality. The order may be affected by the means employed.

On many occasions, I have put these various methods to my audience and invited them to raise their hands when they think the line between competitive intelligence and industrial espionage has been crossed.

In England they start to go up to 8, with the majority voicing their opinion at No. 13. In the U.S.A., where competition is perhaps tougher and counter-measures against industrial espionage need to be tougher too, hands do not get raised until No. 10 is reached, or even after that.

There are industrialists in all countries who pull no punches, but, considering them collectively and comparing countries, it would seem that American businessmen are slightly more unscrupulous than their British counterparts.

What these tests, by a show of hands, make clear to an audience is that, even within a small group, there are widely differing opinions, proving that, in practice, the decision is a matter for individual conscience.

Naturally, I am asked, as a private investigator, where I would draw the line.

This is what I would find acceptable, and what I would not find acceptable, in my opinion.

If I was hired by a company to follow a competitor's salesman, to report at all the addresses that he called at and report on everyone he saw, I would accept this as a legitimate investigation.

If I was told that, on a pretext, I should make friends with this salesman, get him drunk, and pump him for information with a view to getting a client's name and address list, that I would look upon as industrial espionage.

If I was hired by a company which wanted me to undertake a surveillance outside a competitor's works, report on everyone who went inside, to report on all the vehicles that called there, even to the extent of taking a photograph, I would accept that as a legitimate investigation.

If, however, I was asked to gain access under a pretext to the company premises, to locate a specific item of plant or machinery, to photograph or draw it, to describe it and so on, that I would look upon as being industrial espionage.

There are varying degrees of susceptibility to these listed techniques of information gathering. Many people would not go as far as I am prepared to do in my profession; others would go much further.

Yet there are exceptions to every rule, the exception, too, being a matter of personal judgement and individual conscience. What does the counter industrial espionage agent do when requested to investigate an alleged case of infringed patent? Investigation, including access to the culprit's premises, or plant, or workshop, or offices, might establish a dangerous breach of the patents law. The security expert might ask himself; "Is my client truthfully stating his case? Is he genuinely worried about his patent being stolen or infringed? Or has he concocted an imagined breach of patent, as a cover for his real intentions — to get a detailed report of what his rival is doing?" I mention this to show that, while there must be standards of ethics which investigators and counter-industrial espionage experts ought never to violate, too great a rigidity of thought would make them unsuitable for their job. Every case of industrial espionage poses its own problems.

In all businesses, everything starts with *decisions*.

There are the decisions which lead to the incorporation of a company, agreement on the range of its proposed activities; acceptance of the scale of those activities; the choice of a site or sites; the purchase, hire or construction of plant and machinery; the passing of architectural and building plans; information on the size and geographical distribution of potential customers; knowledge of the sources of the raw materials, services and technical skills required for production; comparative costs of all these requirements on the basis of their different sources, and information on the best ways of recruiting and retaining the best kind of skills, on terms which are as economic as possible, yet get the edge on rivals in the same field in competition for the best skills.

Much of this information is still needed when the company is operative and much more besides. A company must know what its rivals are doing. Are their goods better in quaiity? More speedily delivered? Cheaper? Are they gaining or losing customers?

If rivals are *gaining* customers — at whose expense? Are they winning over the subject's customers and, if so, for what reasons and by what methods?

Let me take, as a single instance, the last question. The company A engaged in competitive intelligence might be making some product in very general use — say, a breakfast cereal. If observation on the rival company's salesman revealed that they were supplying an increasing number of their rival's (A's) former customers, the question would be, *why*? Is company B selling more cheaply? Have they added some extra ingredient to their breakfast food which makes it more palatable, but without revealing that they have done so? Has company B managed to get hold of a list of company A's customers? Is company B enjoying the fruits of a little quiet sabotage, perhaps a whispering campaign implying that somebody nearly choked on a piece of glass found in company A's package?

If all this sounds like excessive suspicion, I can assure the reader that it is entirely characteristic of what does go on in the industrial

world today. Even the suspicion of damaging accusations spread for
the purposes of capturing a rival's trade is not so fanciful; it has
actually happened. So has actual sabotage, such as putting foreign
bodies in food products, or leaving a part loose in machinery. But
more of sabotage later.

Clearly, decisions makers must have information on which to
make their decisions. But, on the executive level, important decisions have to be made all the time, and the need for competitive
intelligence is a constant one.

Example: You read in a trade paper that a firm in the same field as
yours is moving to another town. Such a move, you know, involves a
great upheaval and would not be undertaken except for cogent
reasons. What those reasons may be could affect your own business,
and you would therefore like to be informed. Is firm B moving
because premises are cheaper to obtain, or because they need more
room than is available where they are at the moment? Are they
moving to be nearer a better supply of labour, or labour which is
more dependable or cheaper? Are they moving to be nearer
supporting services, or sources of supply of parts or raw materials?

All that presupposes that company B is moving to somewhere
else in the same country. A move to another country, or the opening
of a branch there, could pose a threat to company A. Perhaps the
country to which their rivals are moving their works is also an
important market for company A. The move by their rivals might
result in the loss of that foreign market altogether.

It is natural, then, and legitimate, to wish to know who your
competitors are, who their principal executives are, what sort of
salaries they get, what their turnover is, what their profits are, and
details concerning potential mergers, contractions, expansions,
staff reductions, staff increases, planned sales drives and sales
methods.

There are innumerable sources of *legitimate* information available to companies wishing to keep abreast of changing social trends,
new market developments, laws affecting their business, ethnic and
political changes likely to affect their business, labour conditions
which could affect their own staff relations (and those of their rivals,
of course), proceedings of trade associations, statutory bodies and
scientific and professional organisations; the general press; the
technical periodicals, company brochures, annual reports and published advertisements. Such information, gathered and co-
ordinated, can throw a searching light on a company's policies,

plans and fortunes.

Even in the 'ordinary' world of intelligence, information freely available to the public constitutes, probably, four-fifths of the flow of information.

The amount of money spent by British firms on business intelligence has been variously estimated, but there is clearly no precise way of establishing the real figure. In 1959 Harvard University did some research on the extent of industrial intelligence and espionage, and estimated the expenditure of about 113 million dollars. In the two ensuing decades industrial spying has grown to such a degree that industrial espionage and industrial intelligence have both grown accordingly.

In the U.K., appreciation of the true nature of the menace of industrial spying came long after spies had dug themselves in and improved their techniques of information-theft. Mr James Callaghan, when Home Secretary, warned senior executives in industry as far back as 1968 that they treated industrial espionage too casually, and allocated insufficient staff and funds to combat it effectively.

Of course, competitive industrial intelligence can be highly successful and yet completely ethical. The larger the concern, the fiercer the competition for the services of the handful of "top dogs" — the small number of top-level experts whose know-how is essential to prosperity. Thus, in the late sixties, there was fierce rivalry for talented senior executives between Fords and BMC/Leyland Group. The British company lost their Vice-President to Ford of Europe, while BMC secured the services of their new European head from the Ford Staff. Hot on top of this conquest, BMC then gained from Ford their Cortina stylist, the head of their spare parts division (who became senior executive director), their production controller, and organisational and planning expert, their commercial vehicle design engineer, their purchasing expert and their director of finance.

Quite an exodus! Clearly, such a number of key men would have to be approached first, so that their identities, their salaries and their duties with Ford would need to have been ascertained in the first place; the question of how each individual approach was made is another matter. The whole operation, of its very nature, had to be based on information which, I am quite satisfied to know, was acquired quite legitimately. It is equally obvious that to tempt so many key people from a rival company could be ascribed to routine industrial strategy and commercial intelligence, not industrial espionage.

In 1967, however, the Rt. Hon. Antony Wedgwood Benn, M.P., then Minister of Technology, took a very angry view when the boot was on the other foot — when the American Westinghouse company attempted to lure away from the United Kingdom Atomic Energy Authority (U.K.A.E.A.) some of the top British technicians engaged in the development of the fast-breeder reactor at Dounreay. There were angry accusations of underhand methods, which Westinghouse were at a loss to understand. They had tried without success to get licences from the United Kingdom at the price they thought fair, and sought, as seemed to them the only sensible alternative, to secure the services of the experts who could satisfy their needs in some other way. Again, they used industrial intelligence. I have no evidence that they ever attempted to go beyond that legitimate mandate.

Management Investigations Limited, which is a specialist company in defence against industrial espionage, reported in *MIS Newsletter No. 7* a case where the "brain-drain" bore unmistakable evidence of espionage.

The Personnel Manager of a large company near London, making everyday consumer goods in a highly competitive market, came to them with a problem. One of their employees had reported — a month after the event — that he had received a confidential letter addressed to his home from a personnel consultant organisation (head-hunters) seeking staff on behalf of a client.

The employee was flattered to note that his correspondent seemed remarkably clued up on his background, qualifications, and salary.

This opening approach to the employee was very attractively presented, promising more money, better prospects and enviable, superior research facilities. He responded to the bait. Most people want to better themselves. All are entitled to.

The employee had been told that he would not need to change his place of residence, and that the "client" was a British company. He attended for interview as requested, out of office hours. Encouraged by the prospect of securing a better life-style for himself and his family, and being anxious to sell himself, he talked freely of his work and the important part he had played in new development projects.

At this point the "personnel consultant" seemed to lose interest. He had questioned the applicant at considerable length and in some depth, but so far revealed nothing of the details of the job he purported to be offering. On some flimsy excuse he terminated the interview, with only vague promises of a second; "don't call us — we'll call you" sort of thing. The applicant became suspicious and reported the matter to his employers.

Subsequent enquiries by Management Investigations revealed that three of the man's colleagues had been similarly approached and interviewed, with the same unsatisfactory results. The interviewing "firm" had occupied their premises in the West End of London for only a few days. Their notepaper looked impressive, but a check at Companies House (then in London) proved the company to be non-existent. One of the interviewing officers bore a striking resemblance to a technical executive employed by the competitor.

The conclusion drawn was that the competitor, at comparatively little cost and probably with outside assistance, had staged this cunning operation to obtain information of their rival's development plans. They had, by a combination of espionage and false pretences, stolen some information from their rival in business.

CHAPTER 2

Industrial Espionage — The Menace Grows

Industrial espionage is everywhere growing at an alarming rate.

It is growing in scope, in diversity of subject, and in the extravagent sophistication of its methods and equipment.

A company can no more afford to ignore security precautions, including those aimed specifically at preventing the loss of its secrets by industrial espionage, than it can ignore the insurance of its assets and properties.

The anamolous thing is that information *as such* cannot be insured, nor its theft accepted as a crime unless the Official Secrets Act applies . I have instanced in the foregoing chapter how a dishonest employee offered industrial secrets worth a million pounds for a trivial sum, and failed only because he chose as his potential buyer a company having high ethical standards, and one which disdained to take a mean advantage of a rival. Even so, the man's only legal offence was in stealing a cardboard file of negligible value.

The growing awareness, from the sixties onwards, that industrial espionage was rapidly increasing, has been amply confirmed by the number and variety of cases from all over the world, and by the increased awareness of large sections of industry of the menace in their midst.

Although hundreds of cases are investigated every year in Britain and elsewhere, this in no way indicates the true extent of industrial spying. What is read about is the mere tip of the iceberg. In the very nature of their calling, spies are not often caught. In this respect industrial spies — the professional sort, as distinct from amateurs, such as dishonest employees who see in their abuse of trust a chance to make easy money — are not so different from their more "orthodox" counterparts. They have the same toughness of mind and body, the same swift initiative, opportunism, social adaptability and armoury of forged documents, passports and identity documents and "James Bond" type of eavesdropping equipment.

It is this growth of industrial espionage, and the skill of the *professional* spies engaged in it, which has induced big companies to appoint *professional* crime-busters or intelligence men to their security staff, or at least engage or contract with top-level security firms which are frequently run by men who have worked in governmental security services or intelligence services.

When Imperial Chemicals, a vast concern with a turnover of £1,355 million and capital assets of £1,581 million, appointed a new security advisor in 1972 it did not appoint a retired Scotland Yard detective, as so often happens. Instead, it picked Sir Martin Furnival Jones, 61, a career MI5 man for 17 years and, from 1965 until his retirement, Director General of the Security Services.

In the United States the spread of business spying has made the big companies turn professional in their counter-measures. The protection of vital information is no longer an extra in the routine of the old-type security officer, with his absorption with passes, guard-dogs and routine physical surveillance of premises. Counter-industrial espionage is a game played for high stakes, with no punches pulled on either side. Thus, in the United States, many large corporations employ former agents of the Central Intelligence Agency (CIA), National Security Agency, the Federal Bureau of Investigation (FBI) and similar bodies as security directors.

Americans have often been puzzled by the seeming reluctance of British business executives to treat security of information as a top priority. In the Armed Forces, Government service or the employ of companies engaged in secret work, employees are bound by the Official Secrets Act. This Act is so worded that anything not specifically authorised for disclosure is an official secret, and its unauthorised disclosure a *criminal* offence.

Norman Jaspan Associates, one of the U.S.A.'s top counter-industrial espionage companies, with over 500 employees and a worldwide roster of 300 clients, consider the United Kingdom a fertile hunting-ground for business spies. Britain is so highly industrialised, and has initiated so many new discoveries and techniques in all fields of industry, as it is still doing, that, as Mr Jaspan puts it: "Nowhere else in the world has the smart commercial spy such a fantastic field to work in."

The areas most at risk, according to Robert McCrie, editor and publisher of the *Security Letter*, a confidential bi-weekly newsletter on corporate security published in New York, include the toy trade, petrochemicals, real estate development, and high technology industries such as chemicals, pharmaceuticals, electronics and plastics. Other experts would add such subjects as fashions, cosmetics, oil and mineral exploration, and financial institutions.

In fact, any company can be a target. I can no better illustrate this point than by the following random choice of industrial espionage cases.

In 1937 a former pottery works manager stole five books containing secret *recipes of mixture for pottery ware*. The stolen books belonged to Messrs. Clementsons (Potters and Millers) Ltd., of Hanley.

In 1936 the chief confectioner of Messrs. J.S. Fry, makers of confectionery and chocolates, was fined £50 at Bristol for corruptly offering for £5,000 to Messrs. Rowntree of York (also chocolate makers) a process for the manufacture of *a special chocolate bar*. The proposal was refused. Instead, a letter of warning was sent to Messrs. Fry, the writer traced and legal action taken.

The Times of 13 February 1938 reported a case in which British Industrial Plastics Ltd., were awarded £15,000 damages because of the unauthorised disclosure of *a secret process*.

These interesting pre-World War Two cases underline the variety of attempts to sell industrial secrets even then. In those days, too, there were wide-awake firms which realised they should take careful steps to prevent the leakage of trade secrets on which their businesses were founded. The makers of Drambuie, the famous liqueur said to be based on a formula given by Bonnie Prince Charlie, do part of the mixing in top-secret conditions, and very few people are allowed to know the precise formula for it. Once this became known, the unique drink might be made by other companies and the value of the product lost.

A paper making secret is closely guarded, and has been for a century or more, by the Oxford University Press. Very few share the secret of making Oxford India paper. About 110 years ago there came into the possession of an Oxford graduate a small quantity of thin, tough, opaque paper which he allowed to be used for printing a few copies of the Bible, one of which was presented to Queen Victoria. The University tried hard to reproduce this paper or trace its origin, without success. The quest had been abandoned when one of the Bibles came by accident to the notice of Sir Henry Frowde, manager of the London branch of OUP and, by experiments, he hit on the correct process, and issued an Oxford Indian Paper voume in 1875. It was agreed to keep the process secret, to be shared by only three living persons at the same time. Workmen engaged in the manufacture of this special paper now are sworn to secrecy, and permitted to become familiar with only one stage of the process.

So there we have an example of a very security-minded Victorian, foreseeing by over a century the wholesale pillage of commercial secrets which prevails today.

An attempt was made to sell the trade secrets of a *mail order firm*. In 1957 a trainee at Littlewoods Mail Order stores tried to sell some information about his firm to a rival concern. He wrote an anonymous letter saying that he had access to Littlewood's confidential information, which he was prepared to sell. He asked the advertising manager of Kay and Company, of Worcester, to put an advertisement in a Liverpool paper if interested. The manager immediately informed Littlewoods and, with their co-operation, sent registered letters containing £75 to the disloyal employee. The culprit was fined £25.

Industrial spies were responsible for the theft of a *secret wallpaper Printing process* from Printers and Finishers Ltd., who brought a case against Holloway and others which went to appeal before the Master of the Rolls, Mr Justice Harman and Lord Justice Donovan in October, 1960. A former works manager had taken the defendants over the factory and removed documents relating to a secret flock printing process. There was difficulty in presenting the case, because the plantiffs did not want to be specific about the secrets which they claimed were stolen, since they might disclose more than was known already! Mr Justice Donovan commented: "I do not know whether that is not the inevitable result of a secrets action."

He added "That might be the consequence of legal action in *some* cases but it is not inevitable. There are circumstances in which patent actions may be heard in camera and therefore, no one would know about the secrets. This is particularly so in American actions. It is often the case that the discovery of documents is limited to the experts; indeed I know personally of one case, handled by my own solicitor, where even the lawyers were not allowed to see the disclosed documents, they were seen by the patent experts."

That remark is very perceptive and appropriate today: it is better to guard trade secrets zealously, and vet staff properly, than become involved in a "protective" court action after your secrets have been stolen or infringed.

Industrial spying in *the world of fashion* has flourished for over half a century. Women wishing to wear something unique are willing to pay a high price for it, but copying the design devalues it. It also hits the *haute couture* designer, who is generally not concerned with mere production but with a select clientele of high-paying customers.

The late Sir Norman Hartnell, who designed many dresses for members of the British Royal Family, found that his design for Princess Margaret's wedding gown had been "leaked" to a New York newspaper. The design had been one of the most closely-guarded secrets for years. Only a handful of people, apart from Sir (then Mr) Norman Hartnell had seen it. Yet *Women's Wear Daily*, an American trade journal, carried a sketch and a full description of the wedding gown. I am delighted that the security precautions of Emmanuel's seem to have been more successful.

An international fashion espionage gang was believed to be behind the ransacking of a Hammersmith studio, when the autumn collection styles were stolen from the house of Yuki. His was the sixth such studio to be the subject of such a raid that year (1976). The 24 evening dresses stolen, all of pure silk, were to have been introduced to world buyers at the Ritz Hotel. They were worth £300 each, but the potential income from prospective buyers was £100,000.

Fortunes are spent, and made, in the fashion trade. Long ago, spies posing as potential buyers, or even as journalists, would seek to have a preview of new fashions and, if the owner was off guard for a moment, make a hurried sketch or sneak a quick photograph. But industrial espionage in the fashion world has since become highly organised and international in scope.

Tom Tullet, the *Daily Mirror's* crime editor, conducted an investigation into fashion spies' methods and scope in 1976. The trail, he wrote, led from London to Paris and thence to East Europe, North Africa, Hong Kong, Japan, and America. The police, he revealed, had evidence showing that stolen dresses were shipped out to Rumania, Yugoslavia, Morocco and Hong Kong, where the clothes were unpicked and used as patterns for the making of vast quantities of cheap copies.

Sometimes the motive is not to copy the new fashion on a vast scale, but to trade the exclusive design to another *haute couture* personality, who thus secures a design without the huge expense of paying a team of designers.

Tom Tullet found that unscrupulous manufacturers have been known to "plant spies in a designer's office to steal ideas at an early design stage." One well-educated woman working for a Chinese racketeer secured some of a magazine's notepaper, inveigled herself into the fashion show and photographed the whole collection. The designs were then printed in a brochure which went all over the world. Those industrial spies made a fortune from that operation alone, and have repeated the same thieving formula many times since.

In that year alone many top designers were hit by raiders acting for industrial spies. Jane Cattlin had a collection of thirty new dresses stolen from a locked room at the London Fashion Fair; Ann Buck, another designer, found that her London studio had been raided, though, fortunately, she had moved out her exclusive designs. Japanese designer Shuji Tojo had his entire collection stolen in London, including production orders which he was waiting to deliver. That it was the work of experienced fashion spies was proved by the fact that they took all the *new* designs and left the old. Nobody but an expert would have known which was which. A number of T-shirts, exclusively designed, was stolen from a messenger delivering them to Chelsea.

A Philadelphia lawyer, Sam Dash, described in an authoritative book, *The Eavesdroppers*, the growth of the electronic spying system in the U.S.A., more frightening, he maintained, than the nightmare described by George Orwell in his novel *1984*. He also described to an English journalist, Evelyn Irons, of an ingenious piece of industrial spying in a Californian funeral parlour.

"The undertaker was losing so much business to a rival that he placed a microphone in a coffin in his showroom. Sure enough, he heard one of his salesmen telling bereaved clients that they could get a similar coffin from the other undertaker 50 dollars cheaper. The salesman was fired on the spot."

An undertaker's parlour may seem to you and me an unlikely spot for industrial espionage. That happened in the sixties. It is still happening. Years later, according to the *Daily Mirror* of Tuesday, October 26, 1976 a variation of the same trick was being enacted in France. What Don Cooligan, the *Mirror's* correspondent in Paris, described as "the world's strangest espionage network" was another instance of "poaching" corpses from rival undertakers. The worst-hit victim was funeral director Madame Helen Brison, who operates the biggest concern of its kind in the Perignan area of Southern France. "We were," she told him, "losing a death a day."

So often, when her staff answered a call for her services, they were told "It's too late, another firm came along and they're looking after the arrangements now."

These coincidences were so numerous that Mme. Brison suspected spying — and she was right! Investigations revealed the reason for the dramatic falling-off of trade. A microphone had been installed in the ceiling of Mme. Brison's office, leading to a small radio transmitter. And her telephone was tapped. Detectives discovered that the tappers could not only hear her taking orders, but even divert incoming calls to other numbers. The spies had established a whole network of illegal links with hospitals, mortuaries and undertakers' parlours. The "intelligence" they sought was the addresses of the bereaved; but that intelligence, obtained illegally, was worth a great deal of money to them.

Chocolate, fashions, funerals . . . who would imagine that spies would operate in those fields? Who indeed, except intelligent business executives and those versed in the art of security; for spies of any kind are out to make money (though I accept that some spies acting for their governments are sometimes more tempted by patriotism and the admiration of their fellows, than by money alone). Money made by industrial espionage is a less risky business than spying on behalf of a nation. In many countries, including Britain, it is not an offence to steal information. The offence would lie, if at all, in the methods employed in securing the information; fraud, theft of documents, files or other records, or breaking and entering. Even then the offence would lie in the actual value of the paper, or file, that was misappropriated, not the value of the information in it, when used by a rival.

One of the most spectacular thefts of information in the history of industrial espionage was the theft of antibiotic cultures and formulae from the research laboratories of the huge Cyanamid Corporation of America. Dr Sidney Fox, who headed a research team, stole samples of special moulds used for grading the antibiotics Tetracylin, Aureomycin and Ledermycin. He enlisted the collusion of John Cancelarich, a chemical engineer and graduate of New York University. In the basement of Dr Fox's house, borrowed secret reports were microfilmed.

Dr Fox left Cyanamid in 1959 and set up a company Kim Laboratories, which was a front for the industrial spying operations.

On a visit to Milan, Dr Fox sold some of Cyanamid's secrets for $55,000. By 1961 Fox and his network of conspirators had stolen secrets which had cost Cyanamid $30,000,000 in research and development, and entailed for them loss of sales in the region of $100 million.

Six of the culprits received prison sentences, and others suspended sentences, following their trial in New York. But an enormous lot of damage had been done. The Italian companies had been flooding the medical world with cut-price antibiotics produced as a result of this industrial spying. Many countries, including Britain, bought vast quantities of these pirated drugs, which they would otherwise have had to purchase from the rightful owners.

One side-effect of this case was that seven States in the U.S.A. passed laws making the theft of technological and research secrets an offence. So there was spying in the world of *pharmaceuticals*.

In 1979 Cyril Stein, chief of the powerful Ladbroke's gambling organisation, described a spying operation designed to lure big punters away from rival casinos to his own casinos as "a James Bond exercise." He told a hearing that he knew nothing of the scheme; he did not consider it unlawful, but knew nothing of the operation.

Private detectives had noted the numbers of the limousines outside the rivals' casinos. Their owners were traced through a corrupt use of the national police computer, and they were then approached to transfer their patronage to Ladbrokes. The Playboy Club, whose customers were being stolen in this way and the Metropolitan Police opposed — successfully — the renewal of the gaming licences for the four Ladbrokes casinos. Industries spies had moved into the world of *gambling*.

Industrial espionage has even been experienced in the *television* industry. On Sunday 25th October, 1981 in the evening I.T.V. screened the latest edition of the well known saga "The Four Feathers" produced in 1978 featuring Beau Bridges, Robert Powell and Jane Seymour. I.T.V. however, was upstaged by B.B.C.1 which at 1.55 p.m. the same day had shown "Storm Over The Nile" which was produced in 1955, and at that time was the latest edition of Alexander Corder's original 1939 epic "The Four Feathers". This, incidentally, was the best of the three various versions.

Was it a coincidence that this happened, or had industrial espionage been committed by someone working for I.T.V. leaking the news to B.B.C. television that "The Four Feathers" was to be shown on Sunday the 25th October, 1981.

Even *blood*, a British made prototype machine for automatic blood grouping was stolen in mid-September 1981 from the National Blood Transfusion Centre in Edgware. The machine was valued at £100,000 and was recovered by Customs officers in America. The police suspected some form of industrial espionage because of the machine's advance technique.

Next, *paint*, an unlikely subject for an industrial spy? In 1965 a factory spy tried to sell secrets stolen from a London paint manufacturer. The employee had contacted Mr Harold Day, a scientist employed by a rival company. In that spirit of honest rivalry which is, unhappily, becoming more and more a thing of the past, Mr Day refused to contemplate benefitting from stolen secrets and, on police advice, merely pretended to play along with the thief. The two men met with Scotland Yard detectives and private detectives listening in an adjoining room by means of hidden microphones. The 20-year-old Irishman was arrested and charged before Barking magistrates, the prosecuting counsel saying "I hope this will not be the beginning when courts will have to deal with this sort of thing. At the moment it is not an offence to steal another man's secrets. But it is an offence to steal the paper on which they are written."

I have so far been talking of industrial espionage as though the gamekeeper never turns poacher. Well, he sometimes does. It is inevitable that he should do so because, despite the campaign for stringent rules of admission to the profession of private investigator, and the need for a system of proper registration of private detectives, any one who chooses can set up as a private detective in the United Kingdom.

One need not, therefore, be unduly surprised that industrial espionage is sometimes committed by those who profess to fight it.

There was, for instance, a Californian detective who had chalked up many a success in combatting espionage. But he pulled off a profitable piece of spying of his own. The Coca Cola Company had for years refused to divulge its annual sales volume. Many rival firms were anxious to discover this. Throughout these years the information they sought was freely available in the files of the Securities and Exchange Commission, where valuable and, otherwise, private statistics and confidential information were kept. It is a statutory obligation of companies to file such reports, which are intended for the protection and information of the American public and stockholders. Yet executives of rival companies either did not know, or did not remember, this simple fact. As a result, the wily detective sold to several companies information about Coca-Cola which he had merely — and legally — extracted from the Securities and Exchange Commission's files.

A formidable struggle between the two American industrial giants, Telex and IBM ended in Telex Corporation having to be paid damages of $259 million for illegal monopoly practices while, in return, Telex was ordered to return IBM documents, destroy information in its possession, refrain from using or soliciting IBM secrets, and not to employ ex-IBM employees without court approval for two years. They were also order to pay IBM $22 million for industrial espionage.

If $22 million seems a heavy sum to pay for the offence of industrial espionage, I should point out that, compared with the "advantages gained by misappropriation of IBM trade secrets" it was a very light penalty. The damage actually done by the stealing of trade secrets is not easy to assess. For one thing, nobody, not even a court, has any means of knowing the extent to which the once-secret information has been circulated, or to whom, or with what result. It is a bit like trying to stop an epidemic by tracing a few known carriers who have started travelling about and been lost track of. You may find *them*, but it will be a virtually impossible task to trace everyone with whom they have been in contact.

INDUSTRIAL ESPIONAGE BY GOVERNMENTS

It is clear that business ethics have been slipping over the last twenty years, and equally clear that, while small-time dishonesty is fairly prevalent, large companies and consortiums are equally given to spying on their competitors. Security consultants and private investigators are no longer surprised to find major companies resorting to spying tactics and the corruption of their rivals' employees to a degree that would have been unthinkable years ago.

Just as the line of demarcation between industrial intelligence and industrial espionage is vague and indefinable, so is the distinction (once quite clear) between business spying and spying by governments.

Governments, of course, have always spied one upon the other. All to some degree are two-faced; one's own spies are 'agents.' The enemy's spies are well, spies. One's own activities are assumed to be necessary and innocuous; those of the opponent unnecessary and evil.

Governmental spying includes, inevitably, commercial spying too. Defence and offence demand a constant flow of information, only a small proportion of which is achieved by dramatic adventures of the James Bond type, even though the real happenings in the spy world do out-do fiction at times in their complex and bizarre horror. The fact is that governments want to know what sort of aeroplanes, missiles and weapons are being made, what new features are being introduced, and so on.

Many commercial activities have a wartime potentiality. Keeping abreast of another country's commercial and industrial activities is to some extent achieved by what may with due respect be called "official" spies — diplomats whose stated object is to observe and report in their specific fields, such as that of Air Attache or Naval Attache.

There have been numerous, and dramatic cases, in which such diplomats have overstepped certain limits and been declared *persona non grata* — a diplomatic phrase which means, in plain English, "Clear out!" They are invariably replaced by others who do just the same sort of thing. Everybody knows that, but the convention of "holier than thou" has to be maintained.

The collection of industrial information, including secrets, is not confined to diplomats. Those "official" spies, so often seen at army, naval and air displays, are only one type of information gatherer. Their efforts are supported by an invisible army of agents. In the commercial field, for example, they are supported by trade missions, whose members are frequently spies.

Communist countries do not have independent companies. The State owns all industrial concerns, and if those concerns want to steal trade secrets from their foreign rivals (not necessarily in the arms field, but in any sphere of production) they will resort to methods similar to those of industrial spies in other countries, but having behind them all the resources of a powerful state which does not have to account to its populace for its expenditure in any field — least of all in the field of intelligence, "commercial" or otherwise.

It must not be forgotten, either, that Communist states (and other States, not necessarily Communist, which are dictatorial in structure and have one-party governments) are not solely concerned with keeping abreast of developments in the field of arms and armaments; they want international trade too, for the sake of foreign currency by which they buy such raw materials, equipment and food as they need from outside. If they can capture an increased proportion of world trade by stealing their competitors' secrets they will do so.

Nowhere is the theoretical dividing line between espionage and 'industrial' espionage so vague and indefinable as in the sphere of governmental industrial espionage.

The world has been geared for war for thirty-seven years — ever since the nominal end of the Second World War. It is doubtful if, legally speaking, even that war is at an end, for peace was never proclaimed. Even if it had been, the reality of the matter is that 1945 saw a world divided by different frontiers and a totally changed balance of power. In the new grouping, no great power trusted any other. Each watched the other with increasingly efficient surveillance including, in due course, the detailed 'outer-space' spying from satellites encircling the earth. Each sought hard to keep abreast of or acquire the industrial secrets, of the others.

"Industrial" secrets, in this sense, are the secrets of aggression, defence, or survival. Everything required for offence and defence must be manufactured. Guns, missiles, aeroplanes, communications equipment, rockets, ground-to-air missiles and other types, tanks, gun-carriers, aircraft carriers, war gases and methods of protection against them, and computers of all kinds, sizes and complexity — all are a matter of interest to the great nations, and not a few not-so-great nations too. Putting it simply, everyone is spying on everyone else. That all countries deny spying themselves is irrelevant, since all have been caught at it, at some time or another. Nor do the different terms, the "double standard" attitude which makes them describe their own spies as "agents" and other people's "agents" as "spies", make the slightest difference.

The point is that spying as part of a power game makes industrial spying on a vast scale inevitable, since everyone strives to be as informed as possible on what the other side is making, how they do it, and what features of the process or construction are new. To keep abreast of the opposition, and then streak ahead with secrets of your own which you protect efficiently, is the ambition of evey contestant.

A catalogue of the various attempts, successful or otherwise, made by various governments or their agents, would fill several books, and I will content myself with instancing just a few of them.

Vincent Carratu is quoted as saying that there are at least twenty professional groups or firms, six of them in Britain, engaged in industrial spying. It has been pointed out that industrial espionage is becoming more professional and sophisticated, and that there is increasing evidence of the involvement of foreign governments. The Russians have for years maintained a vast network of skilled informers and spies to wrest industrial secrets for use in their own State-run factories. This was one of the principal reasons for the British decision to expel 105 Russian officials in September, 1951.

Computer circuitry, affecting as it does a wide range of industrial processes, and itself a vast receptacle of scientific, industrial and often secret information, is prime target. Computers are, of course, also a modern form of electronic archives, and for this reason too the computer secrets of the west are of lively interest to the Soviet Union.

The K.G.B. (State Security) and GRU (Military Intelligence) of the U.S.S.R., as well as the comparable services of their numerous satellite countries such as Czechoslovakia, Hungary and Poland, collect industrial secrets through an intricate network of "orthodox" spies, industrial "advisers", paid or unpaid informers, diplomats, journalists or businessmen. I include journalists because, by the Soviet Union's own admission, they are government servants; when TASS, the official government news agency, was sued in a British court, it was pleaded successfully that it could not be sued on the ground of diplomatic immunity. Much of the past and current industrial espionage is carried out by the East German MFS (*Ministerium für Staatssicherheit* or Ministry for State Security) because they can come and go more easily and move around with more familiarity in the West. This was proved by the successful *Operation Brunhilde* spy ring with its vast shopping list of industrial secrets, including details of the Concorde aircraft and its engines. The theft of these secrets has proved of crucial importance in the balance of power. Although the Russians, prior to the theft of the West's secrets, lagged far behind the West, they streaked ahead of Britain and France and were the first to get a supersonic airliner in flight.

The MFS recruited a retired Swiss-born chemical engineer, Paul Soupert, who was living in Brussels and had applied for a teaching post in Eastern Germany. On visits to East Berlin he was given basic espionage training and a few items of cloak-and-dagger equipment including a book with a secret pocket in the cover and a briefcase with a secret compartment.

This operation started in 1957. Within a few years Soupert was acting as courier in a ring of 20 agents including Poles, Rumanians, Czechs and East Germans. From them he collected 35mm films which he hid in a toothpaste tube or small cigar tin. These he would later transfer to a sponge which he hid in the first class toilet on the Ostend-Warsaw express. The sponges were removed by MFS agents when the train stopped in East Berlin.

Eventually, Belgian Surete agents put Soupert under surveillance, and from the autumn of 1961 tailed his contacts to Britain, France and Germany. He was arrested in 1964, "turned" (induced to become a double agent) and under an operation named "Air Bubble" rounded up most of the ring's conspirators. They were tried mostly in camera during 1966 and 1967. In large projects very many different firms are involved before the business of assembly can be attempted. Thus, details of a project can be obtained by infiltrating companies whose activities are seemingly remote from the original project.

As part of *Operation Brunhilde*, for example, Kodak Limited was penetrated by the spy ring; Kodak was microfilming Concorde blueprints and carrying out X-ray and spectroscopic photography on the aircraft. Two Kodak employees were charged with corruptly accepting money from Soupert for information on emulsions, wetting agents, anti-static and anti-halo-aterials and other secret processes employed by Kodak. At the Old Bailey in London, in March 1965, they were acquitted without presenting their defence after Soupert admitted Kodak paid him £5,000 to give evidence.

A leading member of the *Brunhilde*, an East German called Herbert Steinbrecher, obtained many valuable industrial secrets, particularly about precision machinery and chemical processes, on 20 spying forays into Western Europe between 1959 and 1964. He was arrested in Paris carrying films of documents on Concorde's transonic acceleration, deceleration transfer, fuel and boom problems, and was sentenced to 12 years imprisonment. Others received sentences ranging from 12 to 20 years imprisonment.

That the Soviet K.G.B. (Committee for State Security) spies extensively on Western industry has been known for years. However, the ambitious network, and the constant movement of its operators under a variety of assumed names, makes constant vigilance (and active measures) necessary if the *degree* of industrial secrets protection is to be kept at a minimum. I am not being pessimistic, but merely realistic, in assuming that the seepage or theft of valuable industrial secrets cannot be wholly eliminated. But I believe it can, and should be, minimised.

According to the usually well-informed *International Intelligence*

Report, published in the U.S.A., the powerful State Committee for Science and Technology, whose chief is the former KGB chief in Geneva, Dmitry Mikolaievitch Pronskiy, draws up a list of potential industrial secrets which the Soviet Union desires to steal. The extent to which this is done, and the methods pursued, are well known to Western Intelligence services — which is not the same thing as saying that they are, in a satisfactory proportion of cases, anticipated or prevented.

There has been a stream of East German defectors from the East German Ministry of State Security (MFS), including Lieutenant Werner Stiller, formerly employed in their economic espionage department. According to Stiller, in one year alone, industrial espionage conducted by the MFS against private corporations and Government departments in West Germany had saved East Germany more than 300 million deutschmarks — about £40 million which would otherwise have needed to be expended on research and development costs. A haul of information on that scale, and of that level of practical importance, is equal to robbing a bank of £40 million worth of bullion! As a matter of fact, it is worth far more, for whereas bullion merely increases its value, according to the whims of inflation and fluctuating market values, *information* concerning industrial processes and formulae is of increasing value, since it is applied to continuous profitable use.

East Germany recruits a special type of industrial spy, known euphemistically as "officer on special duties" (Offizier im besonderen Einsatz) — usually selected undergraduates who undergo special training, particularly in the fields of nuclear energy, electronics and communications. In the manner of 'ordinary' spies, they are given false identities and supporting documentation and then sent off to infiltrate into Western Companies, where their skill and convincing cover stories enable them to work their way up into positions of extreme confidence.

International Intelligence Report has described the typical case of Mr Peter Klages, who was recruited by the MFS in 1970 while studying computer science:

> He had been "spotted" by a Professor who singled him out not only for his useful technical knowledge, but for his fierce commitment to the Communist cause; Mr Klages had been a leading activist among student members of the ruling Socialist Unity Party (SED).
>
> After exhaustive tests, Mr Klages signed a formal contract pledging

to devote all his efforts "to the service of the Party as a scout for peace".

After training in all aspects of spy work, he was despatched to West Berlin, where he successfully presented himself as a political refugee, claiming that his mother had just been arrested on charges of "anti-state activities."

It took Mr Klages several years to work his way into the ideal job as assistant to the head of research in a well-known West German computer company. After six years in the MFS he received orders to start gutting this corporation of its most closely-guarded secrets. For two years this hard-working young technician regarded by his colleagues as amiable but abnormally shy, worked overtime night after night, gathering up blueprints that he would smuggle back to his modest, one-room flat to photograph for the MFS. By the time he was caught red-handed, there was little left to steal.

Little left to steal. This classic case of industrial espionage, linked to 'conventional' State espionage because industrial monopoly is an integral part of the entire State monopoly, underlines the basic truth of effective security: it is a meagre satisfaction, if any at all, to have caught spies, industrial or otherwise, for they will soon be replaced by other spies who will have to be detected and caught in turn. It is useful to arrest spies and so halt their activities temporarily, but it does not restore the quality of secrecy to those secrets already stolen. Too often it is a case of locking the stable door after the horse has bolted. The treachery of the nuclear physicists Klaus Fuchs and Alan Nunn May enabled the Soviet Union to make its own atom bomb, thus altering the whole balance of power in the world and leading to the nuclear race.

Not all industrial spies, even those serving a State, such as the Soviet Union or one of its satellites, are selected from within that State. The recruitment of indigenous industrial spies goes on all the time, the emphasis being on journalists (whose work, necessarily, requires them to be asking questions in all fields of activity on almost any subject, and whose profession, therefore, is an ideal cover) and market researchers, whose work might be described as that of professional nosey-parkers. Women secretaries are a special target for recruitment by the MFS, and their involvement with industrial espionage, perhaps not surprisingly, is often the sequel to a sexual relationship established by the industrial spy as a means of gaining the confidence of the secretary. Few industrial secrets are not within the reach of top-level secretaries. In fact, 43 per cent of MFS recruitments of home-based industrial spies were, according to MFS defectors, female secretaries.

That the difference between industrial spies and spies in general is not very great, and in some cases indistinguishable, is shown by the fact that, in 1969, the East German lawyer Wolfgang Vogel, who arranged many East-West spy swaps, including Peter and Helen Kroger and Gerald Brooke, and Gordon Lonsdale for Greville Wynne, arranged for Marianne Bammler, Renee Krannick and Herbert Steinbrecher to be exchanged for three French agents, Philippe Thiers, Patrice Dougat and Henry Baumgarten, who were serving prison sentences in East Germany — an exchange of industrial spies for military spies. This transaction underlines the warning of Peter Hamilton, who has spent most of his working life in the security and intelligence worlds, that, since an all-out "hot" war would destroy civilisation, the industrial era would become the new battlefield where nations and ideologies will struggle for economic supremacy and industrial espionage would assume a new import-ance.

Peter Hamilton's warning was sounded as long ago as 1967 in his book, *Espionage and Subversion in an Industrial Society* (Hutch-inson, London, 1967). His prediction that industrial espionage would assume an importance greater even than military and politic-al espionage, has been more than amply fulfilled.

In Britain, according to Derek Humphry and David May, writing in the *Sunday Times* of the Russians who are gathering vital defence, political *and commercial information* about Britain — and other parts of the world — by listening to microwave, telephone and telex traffic which is leaving London via the Post Office Tower (since re-named the Telecommunications Tower). Using sophisti-cated interception equipment, the Russians are feeding the record-ings into computers, which may be in Russia.

> "By means of 'trigger' words and phrases, the important information is sifted out. From masses of tiny factual details and bits of comment contained in the messages, the Russians build up a picture of our military and diplomatic intentions, get advance information on bank-ing and share deals and tips about the prices of grain and important commodities."

The use of high-frequency radio signals for the transmission of telephone conversations and other forms of electronic communica-tions have made all this material more vulnerable to interception than the older-methods of underground cabls or overhead lines. "Most of Britain's long-distance telephone, telex and computer data traffic travels over microwave radio links, beamed between more than 200 Post Office towers throughout Britain, roughly 35 miles apart. Russian eavesdropping is greatly helped by the proximity of at least two of their main London buildings to key microwave routes from the hub of the network at London's Post Office Tower off Tottenham Court Road, which beams thousands of telephone and telegraph circuits from London in four main directions."

America has known for a long time that its telephone and telex communications are monitored (eavesdropped) from Soviet embassies, but of course the U.S.A.'s National Security Agency does the same thing.

In 1964, Vladimir I. Solomatin, a Soviet "trade representative" was expelled from Britain for trying to obtain specifications and samples of electronic equipment banned for export to the Soviet Bloc. In 1968 West Germany found that Josef Eitzenberger, who was working on an "unbreakable" code for the use of NATO, and on highly secret navigational systems for German aircraft, was a KGB agent.

In 1970 Yuri Ivanovitch Ryabov and Yuri Mamontov, two Soviet "trade officials" were seized by the Argentine police as they picked up microfilm of industrial secrets. In 1969 Japanese authorities arrested an Indonesian exchange student for stealing Japanese industrial secrets; he had studied in Russia, where he was recruited as in industrial spy into the KGB.

Hong Kong has long been a clearing house for industrial (and other) espionage, and indications are that neither the vigilance of the authorities or occasional arrests and expulsions have eliminated this form of piracy. The London *Daily Mirror* of May 15, 1980, in what is described as the "Secrets Scandal" alleged serious loopholes in the operation of the Government Communication Headquarters. Top-secret papers have vanished from a key base. A former employee declared that "dozens of documents" were missing. In this case the spying is assumed to have been by the Chinese. Staff going to Little Sai Wan were often booked into a hotel where sex services were freely available.

The *New Statesman* of 23rd May 1980 which published detailed accounts of corruption and lax security arrangements in Hong Kong, mentioned the Lee Garden Hotel as GCHQ's temporary accommodation for its top security employees in Hong Kong, "and the site of the most blatant call girl racket among the colony's luxury hotels."

A spectacular recent effort to break the data bank of IBM operating in Frankfurt am Main, Western Germany, had a rather strange twist to it. To all appearances, here was a gang of industrial spies out to crack IBM's secrets concerning computers. But it may not have been as simple as that. Perhaps in this instance the Soviet Bloc was taking counter-measures against American industrial espionage. Russia is certainly very active, and successfully active, in this field, but she has by no means a monopoly.

Jim Hougan, in *Spooks* (W.H. Allen, London, 1979) says that the gang had been operating for years without making a mistake.

> "Then, in 1974, they made an outrageous offer to a small mail-order house. In return for camera-ready layout plans of an IBM 370 computer, the group would pay DM 25,000 (about £4,000). Alerted to the extraordinary offer, U.S. and West German agents placed the group under round-the-clock surveillance. Bursting into the office of a small commercial firm in Frankfurt, they found two of the men bent over IBM 370 maintenance manuals, each page of which was being photographed."

The gang had thus far spent DM 1,000,000 on the operation, "a fabulous sum for an industrial espionage operation."

Jim Hougan found this whole episode puzzling. Why had the ring spent all that money when they could have bought it at a fraction of the cost? Why hadn't the group rented one of the computers. Stranger still, an IBM 370 computer was already in operation in Hungary and was "therefore certainly available to the KGB."

It seemed that the industrial spies must have been looking for something common to all computers in the series. There seemed two possibilities: (1) that the feature which enables this computer to detect faults and errors and disturbances such as unauthorised entries might be sought; "unauthorised entries" could include efforts to introduce into it false information, or extract data without authority. But environmental faults would also be detected, a factor in computer operation in which the USSR lags behind the United States. And, (2) it has been suggested that NASA and the CIA "have developed a novel means of bugging computers: by monitoring the noise the computer makes while operating, the spooks are able to 'read' the machine's contents" This contingency is opposed by feeding false programmes into the machine (a confusing factor for all concerned, friend or foe) or preventing the "eavesdropping" on the computer's operation by a series of architectural baffles.

However, there is a startling theory that the computer itself can be a spy. IBM has a virtual monopoly on advanced data-processing equipment, a monopoly that is worldwide. Tom Metchling, former executive assistant to IBM chief Tom Watson, commented, "IBM considers itself an extension of the U.S. government — and it is." An internal mechanism capable of monitoring all functioning aspects of an IBM 370 computer might also be able to transmit from within the computer all information flowing through it. On this supposition, Jim Hougan thinks it possible that the German ring was engaged in *counter*-intelligence on behalf of the KGB, seeking to identify the mechanism responsible for data-processing leakages from behind the Iron Curtain.

CHAPTER 3

The Professionals

If we are to counter effectively the piratical activities of the industrial spy, we must first ask: what sort of person is he likely to be?

Before considering the different categories of industrial spy, however, we must accept one unshakeable premise; industrial spies *do* exist. They are not a James Bond fantasy. Indeed, some of the situations in which they find themselves, and the intrigues and counter-intrigues that develop in the world of industrial espionage put fiction in the shade.

That *professional* spies exist was the reason for the publication, in 1968 by the Institute of Directors, of a handbook intended to warn their members of the danger and urge them to protect their information. It was indeed, as the then Director-General of the Institute of Directors put it, an "almost frightening" guide to this newly-developed, sophisticated form of dishonesty.

The general principles expounded in that useful booklet are still valid, as are most of the counter-measures listed. Yet almost all the equipment of surveillance and counter-surveillance has been immeasurably improved and miniaturised since 1968. The professional industrial spy, like his government-employed counterpart, the 'orthodox' spy, has at his disposal a bewildering and marvellous range of gadgetry and apparatus which makes his theft of secret information more sudden, more surprising, and more deadly.

The industrial spy — the professional sort — will be basically a loner. He will have plenty of social and other connections, but is unlikely to be thought a mysterious sort of man. If he were, his usefulness would be very limited indeed. Clearly, he must have enough personality to convince clients that he is worth employing, or commissioning; he needs enough physical health and vitality to get around on his own steam without being unduly dependent upon others. He will need courage and resource. He will be capable of making quick, and often uncomfortable decisions — things do not always go according to plan. He had probably served in one or other of the disciplined forces, although not invariably. If he has, he will probably have kept inside contacts and sometimes has access to information which is officially secret but is disclosed to him under an 'old pal's act'.

The industrial spy usually has two, and more often three, languages in which he is perfect. A broken accent will not help him if he wants to pass himself off as a citizen of some other country.

To some degree, he is mechanically self-reliant, too. He will probably have a more than rudimentary knowledge of electronics, since, if his tape-recorder fails in some vital operation, he will not necessarily find somebody to repair it, and more often than not will be using an expensive and sophisticated type which would make him an object of interest.

Like any good serviceman, he will know how to read maps, orientate himself, get along with different telephone systems, and drive a variety of cars. He may not be an athelete, still less a hero, but he will need to be capable of self-defence, probably of the unarmed combat type, since the carrying of arms is not only illegal in most industrial countries (though not in the U.S.A.) but also something that would arouse immediate suspicion.

Above all, his life-style and background must be a perfect "cover." He must be pursuing some calling which can be expected to pay him enough to account for his standard of living; the "front" must be absolutely convincing — not merely to ordinary people, but more particularly to any who might be curious, probing or hostile. If he is a plumber, then his plumbing had better be up to standard, and he will need to operate as a plumber. If he is a public relations officer, a market research director or a freelance journalist (all callings which involve access to much information in many fields) he will need to know the techniques of public relations, the administrative mechanics of market research, or — in the case of the journalist — to really know how to write on a wide variety of topics (unless he is a specialist writer, which would limit his field of activities somewhat).

One industrial spy, who uses the nom-de-plume or nom-de-guerre which ever you prefer of Louis Moreau and had earned over £30,000 a year for many years by his undercover work, has even written a handbook, *So You Want to be an Industrial Spy* for the benefit of those who want to make a professional job of it.

Louis Moreau says flatly that anyone with sufficient enterprise and know-how can make £30,000 a year tax-free. Qualifications? You need, he says, to be without scruples regarding matters such as commercial blackmail, tax evasion and crushing the weaker under-foot. It is not, he says, a career for "a callow youth, a sensitive girl or someone with a conscience and a reasonable code of behaviour towards his fellow humans."

You must, he insists, be content to be a lone wolf, trusting nobody except the person acting for you in your "cover" organisations while you are away on assignments. Inevitably he or she will discover what the industrial spy is doing, so there, at least, there has to be absolute trust.

In the pleasant, sun-lit luxury of a Mediterranean holiday resort I talked to our industrial spy, who had been undoubtedly one of the most successful and resourceful. He is now a retired spy.

He was easy in manner, in his early fifties, obviously well-educated and with a creditable record of service in the Royal Navy leaving with the rank of Lieut Commander. His work with public relations firms, newspapers and magazines gave him a wide circle of contacts on all levels of society, and particularly in industry.

At one time he was employed to travel the country selling training films to management. In the course of visiting 65 towns and being entertained by sales managers in companies large and small, he was forcibly struck by the inability of most such managers to exercise the slightest discretion in discussing their company's affairs. Without effort, without even drawing them on, he would be regaled with details of their manufacturing processes, their apprehension as to competitors in their markets, their hopes for new processes, econo-mies and designs, and their plans for expansion and development.

He realised how interested most of the management he encoun-tered would be to be informed of their competitors' plans. If they were so informed, he reasoned, they could take offensive and defensive action. They could submit quotations knowing them to be below those of their competitors; they could copy processes and designs; they could use the same — and hitherto secret — sales techniques and systems of work-flow or organisation of their com-petitors. Aggressively, they could spread rumours around of their competitors' inferior quality of goods, or financial instability.

So Louis Moreau decided to become an industrial spy. He was surprised to find how easy and profitable it was.

I asked him how he found his clients. Clearly, you would not approach some executive head-on and ask: "Do you need an industrial spy? I am a very good one." The executive would realise that anybody so unable to keep a secret like that could not safely be entrusted with *his* secrets!

In every case, he assured me, he would make his initial contact with the client company at topmost level, and none other. His argument here was that to start an upward climb from lower rank, ascending to contact with the Chairman or Managing Director, is to inform people below those top executives, who would — to save face with their subordinates — have to adopt an "on no account would I consider that sort of thing" attitude.

To make this initial contact successfully, the spy needs to have presence and personality; he must also either be an expert, or have done sufficient "homework" to have gained a good rudimentary grasp of, the subject. Approaching the chief of a big oil company, in a state of ignorance on anything concerned with oil wells, oil refineries and petro-chemicals would obviously be a waste of time.

He found that telling the secretary of the big man that he had something the top man would like to know, was often effective. Over lunch he would talk of his new conceptions of, and techniques in, "market intelligence". He would not himself imply that this was a euphemism, a cover-phrase for industrial spying. Mixed up in his conversation there would be a few tit-bits of trade intelligence and information about the man's business and that of his rivals, to show that he was well informed and knew something of the background to the rivalry between his company and its competitors.

Once he had established contact with the Chairman or Managing Director, and directed the conversation to the need for "aggressive market research" or "positive intelligence organisation" he would come to the point: what would they most like to know, what did they most need to know, about the activities of their main competitors?

He would then offer to spy for them, on financial terms very favourable to himself, and under conditions of secrecy as strict as those that would prevail in the field of ordinary espionage. There would be no direct contact between them. He would receive *carte blanche* for expenses through a public relations company, whose contract was under the jurisdiction of, say, an advertising manager who would not be made privy to the reasons for the unusual financial arrangement. He would have an office, a car and a secretary at the company's expense.

This industrial spy charged the equivalent of £120 a day for his services, (this was in the '60s) to which could be added his fairly considerable expenses both in the United Kingdom and abroad. His was the "good" life in true James Bond style — a round of fast cars, compliant women, lush hotels, impersonations, furtive photography, clandestine recordings of conversations and the tailing of suspects.

Moreau has achieved a certain immortality in a novel which has been written about his exploits but, so far, unpublished. With the probable exception of some of the descriptions of mayhem, it can be taken as a true account of what transpires in the world of industrial espionage with which he is so familiar in the novel. He is commissioned by an international electronics firm to find out what their principal rivals are doing; they have some secret project afoot which would leave the British firm standing. The firm has works in France and Portugal. Moreau returns to his office, tidies up his existing work and commissions, and tells his secretary that he will be away for a while. He plans to go to France and then 'play it by ear' but before leaving discovers that somebody — he does not yet know who — is watching *him*:

> Jill told him during the course of the day, that when he was out earlier, a Post Office man had called and said he had come in response to a complaint about a fault on the telephone. Jill said he had examined the telephone in Louis' office and tinkered a bit, and then looked at her Plan 7 unit. Louis was surprised, because there had been nothing wrong with the telephone for months, apart from a few wrong STD numbers, which was normal.
>
> He unscrewed the cap of his own telephone handset and looked underneath his own telephone and found nothing out of the ordinary, so he unscrewed the four screws holding on the baseplate and looked inside. All seemed normal. Then he looked at Jill's telephone. He unscrewed the handset transmitter cap and there, instead of the usual GPO microphone was a thicker unit with a short length of aerial wire attached to it.
>
> "Jill," he said, "that was no GPO man. We've had a 'bug' planted on us."

An ordinary telephone subscriber would, of course, have complained to the police or the post office, or both. Moreau, being a professional, did neither, recognising immediately what it was about, and being sufficiently trained to turn the situation to his own advantage. He did not detach the 'bug' right away. It had been planted to transmit to somebody — within a few hundred metres radius — whatever was said in his office. If he removed it, whoever was spying on him would know that they had been detected. Better he decided to leave it where it was, and transmit misleading information, so that he could get away to France and follow his industrial spying assignment without anyone knowing where precisely he had gone.

First, he told his secretary to hold a long, gossipy, conversation on the telephone with some friend of her choice. Next, he went outside the building and looked around until he found a parked car, with two men inside, one of them listening through a hearing aid.

Now he knew that he was under observation. He had noted the number and appearance of the car, and the look of the occupants.

Fortunately, he had booked his air passage before this discovery, and could fool the opposition by talking on the telephone of a projected visit to *Germany*. In order that this might make sense to his surreptitious listeners, he discussed a projected, and fictitious, visit to Germany, and sent his secretary round to the airline company, ostensibly to buy the tickets and confirm the booking. As he anticipated, she was followed by the same men who had been listening to the short-wave transmissions from the 'bug'.

When the author continues his story in France, the real nature of the professional industry spy becomes apparent. He lies his way into the offices of the chief of the electronics firm near Paris, by posing as an inspector of the French railway system, come to investigate a report of late delivery — safe enough alibi in France, as in Britain! With a firm so large, and with consignments going all over the country and for export, some complaint of non-delivery or delay would be inevitable, and even a 'cleared-up' complaint might still be followed up in error by some railway employee who had not been told that the problem had been resolved.

Moreau gets to the chief, but not before he has taken delivery of a new Citroen (at the expense of his client), visited the Surete in order to note the number on a police car, visited a supplier of blank number plates and adhesive letters, and so substituted a false number plate for his own.

This is the sort of detail one would expect a conventional spy to attend to, but it is less generally known that an industrial spy would go to equal trouble and show equal audacity.

Once inside the French firm's laboratory, however, Moreau tells the chief "in strict confidence" that he is not, in fact, from the railway company but from the Surete, the French police force:

> He pulled out the 'eye' of the Surete Nationale: "Monsieur, it is only to you that I can reveal my true identity."

The little director looked startled, put his hands up and held his head for a moment, and said, "I knew it, I knew it, I should have sent it by my lorry and not by rail, but all the lorries were out of commission and the item was badly needed. I did not realise that the Surete would be involved so quickly."

Louis said: "I am here to help. You must now give me the fullest details. No-one outside this office must know who I am, and I will not tell my superiors about the circumstances just yet. I should explain that I come from a special section of the Surete that deals with the manufacturers on secret government work — the Cinquieme Escadrille."

The industrial spy, Moreau, was tempting providence, for, since his guess that some package might have gone astray in transit, thus providing him with an excuse to gain entry and probe for information on the nature of the package's contents, there was now a real chance that a genuine inspector of the railway department might come. However, being knowledgeable in the ways of monopolies and bureaucracies, he knew they were seldom swift to act. The man he is seeing is thankful for the enforced promise of secrecy, having presumably done something against standing orders in despatching the package in the way he did.

"Yes, yes, certainly," said Director Lagrange, whose name Louis had noticed on the door as he went in, "you are, of course, aware of what we are making here?"

"Of course," said Louis, "but I want descriptions and despatch details, so that I can put in hand the most urgent priority for tracing the package . . ."

The Professor reveals the nature of the invention, tells him what the package looks like, and the route by which it was despatched. By a whole series of subterfuges, Louis follows the trail, impersonating other officials, until he traces and photographs the apparatus.

After that, the plot thickens. Louis finds himself dogged by another industrial spy on the same trail for information; he finds that the French woman journalist who both assists and comforts him is, in fact, in French intelligence. An ordinary person, unaware of how industrial espionage had developed and spread during recent years, might consider the novel far-fetched and contrived. I know that it merely states the facts and methods of industrial espionage without running into the libel risk of mentioning specific people. The methods outlined, particularly the forging of documents and passes and the impudent impostures, are truly part of the stock-in-trade of the industrial spy.

In the end, Moreau secures the information his sponsors require, even secret plans in Portugal, the latter having been obtained by posing as a representative of the British Patent Office.

I did not ask Moreau how much of his narrative was true and how much invented. The offensive and counter-offensive methods described in his book have all been used at one time or another, and his descriptions of listening devices and other surveillance apparatus are technically accurate. At many points in his narrative he might have been discovered; at one point the British Intelligence Service contacted him, having watched his activities with some interest, since the apparatus on which he was seeking information was of importance in the battle between the big powers to devise the perfect means of destroying space satellites.

In the handbook which Louis Moreau wrote for would-be industrial spies, he is meticulous in setting forth the means of "producing results and getting paid."

> When you get the fully detailed brief from your sponsor, write it down in front of him and read it back aloud, saying something like this: 'I want to get it quite clear between us, *this* is what you want me to find out'. Then get a date by which he wants the information and agree it between you.

After appointing an industrial spy to steal a rival's secrets, the top executive may begin to worry as to whether he has done the right thing — whether, in fact, he can trust the industrial spy he has engaged. Supposing the spy approaches the other side, and says, 'I've been paid to spy on you. My sponsors have had to trust me sufficiently to tell me what information they require urgently, and what that information means to them. Now if *you* knew what was going on, you would be better able to defend yourselves . . .' In other words, the spy may turn double-agent, getting a second retaining fee.

There is, says the author, a need for a formal, though secret, contract with sponsors. The payment of substantial funds has to make some sort of financial sense to executives and accountants, and for Inland Revenue purposes is "absorbed" in the expenses accounts of the sponsor's advertising agency.

Moreau's do-it-yourself industry-spy guide contains detailed and accurate information on "audio-visual equipment and suppliers," showing where the apparatus for eavesdropping, interception and surveillance can be obtained. His book is both a study in cynicism and a reminder that the ever-present danger of industrial espionage can be ignored by companies only at their peril.

In the wrong hands, Moreau's book could be a potential danger, but, luckily, I insured against this by buying his whole stock, (he also published it) restricting its sales to management, who, by reading it, can be put on their guard by the tips, from an expert, of what industrial spies do!

The manner in which an industrial spy may operate was revealed with considerable detail in 1971. In many cases of spying of this kind, the injured party fails to seek redress. The company which has lost its important technical or trading secrets to a thief, presumably a thief acting on behalf of a hostile company, is reluctant to admit its inefficiency in guarding its most valuable property. They may fear loss of promotion within their company if the truth comes out; they may worry about publicity attendant upon court proceedings; they may think their share value may be hit by revelations of the loss of manufacturing or design secrets hitherto exclusive to themselves.

Strange as it is, many firms will not protect themselves or pursue a culprit with the energy and promptitude that mere survival demands. It is ironic that a company will often spend endless man-hours and commit itself to expensive security and legal proceedings to punish, say, the theft of a large packet of paper-clips or the erosion of its stationery stock, but will remain mute and ineffectual when its very life-blood is drained away.

British Titan Products, however, which became the target of a professional, albeit rather clumsy, industrial spy, was the exception to this unhappy rule, and acted with coolness and intelligence when it learned that a planned attempt was being made to steal its very important manufacturing secrets.

Few cases of industrial espionage are so well documented, except perhaps for such *cause celebre* as the already mentioned Cyanamid case, and in this instance the company itself made the facts known to colleagues in their own and in different industries, as an object lesson, pointing the need for vigilance. The case was outlined by Mr Phillip Mayo, (a qualified Barrister who joined British Titan in 1957 and was its Company Secretary from 1969), during a conference organised by Lloyd Institute of Management and held January 1974.

British Titan Products Limited is the U.K. manufacturing company of the British Titan Group, which has manufacturing companies in a number of countries throughout the world. British Titan,

Mr Mayo told his audience, is essentially a one-product Group; the product being Titanium Oxide, which is used as a pigment in the manufacture of paints, plastics, paper, printing ink and a number of other products in everyday use. Because it is essentially an industrial product, it is not particularly well-known. Nevertheless, the world market, which is a highly competitive one, is worth hundreds of millions of pounds a year.

Processes can rarely be patented, at any rate not fully protected. The know-how, in essence the secret of knowing what to do when, to what extent and so on, constitutes the most vital asset of such a company.

The Titanium Oxide industry was previously based upon a lengthy process known as "the sulphate process". It was replaced, just a few years before the spying operation commenced, by a new process known as the chloride process, whose process was neater and the capital cost lower. However, involving as it does very high temperatures and the use of highly corrosive materials at certain stages, it posed important and complex problems of plant layout and plant construction — and of plant operation.

In October 1970 the Works Manager at Titan's Grimsby works (which does not use the new process) was told that an employee of a London detective agency had hired a taxi and asked the driver to drive along the perimeter road outside the works so that she would be able to take some photographs. The factory is situated between a public road and the bank of the River Humber. It would be quite possible for photographs to be taken outside the factory wall — photographs, as it happens, which would have been quite useless for their intended purpose, since the plant was of the sulphate or chloride type, and certain parts of the equipment which would indicate this were quite unmistakable.

The hirer of the taxi was not satisfied with the information gathered thus far, and asked the taxi-driver if he knew anybody in the Company who would answer one or two questions about processes employed there.

The taxi-driver said he did know one or two, and having been given the questions his strange fare wanted answered, referred the matter to his employer on his return.

The taxi-driver's employer saw at once that something suspicious was afoot, and informed the Works Manager of British Titan.

Although the approach made by the industrial spy was the clumsiest imaginable, the questions showed clearly enough that somebody, somewhere, had been trying to wrest from them the secrets of the new process. The questions were:—

1. At what stage of development is BTP's process?
2. What are the details of the method of oxidising TiC14? (TiC14 is an intermediate material in the manufacture of Titanium Oxide).
3. Details of the process beyond the first stage are required.
4. Details of any processing problems experienced.
5. When will the final product be on the market?
6. What is TCE14? How is it made? (it was subsequently discovered that TCE14 was a misprint for TiC14).

It was a curious spy's shopping list. The questions revealed an odd mixture of knowledge and naivete. The last question in particular betrayed the amateur, somebody whose knowledge of the industry was sketchy but the earlier questions revealed some knowledge of the processes involved.

It was decided to lead her on in an attempt to discover who was behind it all. A meeting between the woman and the Works Administration Manager was mounted, with the Works Manager so placed that he could hear the conversation. These facts emerged:

1. The investigator worked in a London Detective Agency.
2. The detective agency had strong contacts in Germany.
3. The girl did not know the name of the client and would not discuss the name of the agency until some information had been passed over to her.
4. Money would be paid in cash for information.
5. She had tried other means of securing the information she sought. She had applied for a job with the company, and although offered a further interview had not taken it up. She boasted of being married to a senior police officer, and of being able to involve protectors capable of using strong-arm tactics where these proved necessary. She offered an initial payment of £150 for information, but the Administration Manager said he was not interested in pursuing the matter, but had meantime been given the name of the agency concerned.

Scotland Yard was informed, although Mr Mayo claimed "the police required a surprising amount of convincing that any crime could have been committed." It was eventually decided to proceed under Section 1 of the Prevention of Corruption Act, 1906. Both the head of the detective agency and his assistant were charged with an offence under the 1906 Act.

The prosecution was successful. At Lincoln Assizes in October, 1971 the two accused were found guilty, the head of the Agency being fined a total of £1,500 and the bungling investigator £100. Unfortunately, the principal culprit — the initiator of this piece of industrial espionage — kept well and successfully in the background, and although Titan Products believed that the original client was in Germany, all attempts, including those by Interpol, to identify and trace him were unsuccessful. It was known, however, that the head of the London detective agency, who has sent his assistant "into the field", had widespread contacts in Germany. Presumably he still has, since he now operates from an address in Cornwall, and is recommended in a circular issued by a German detective association. He also, to my certain knowledge, acted for a detective agency in Frankfurt.

Lest the phrase "detective agency" should be taken to imply any assumption of integrity on those who run it, I should make the point — briefly, just now, as I shall be reverting to it at greater length later on — that almost anyone can set up and run a detective agency, or describe himself as a security specialist or consultant. No licence is required, no minimum standard of training or integrity is insisted upon, and in consequence many undesirables find their way into this business, to the annoyance of their clients and the embarrassment of genuine enquiry and security agencies, most of whom maintain very strict standards, keep within the law in everything they do. Also employ only those whose training is adequate for their work, and whose personal and professional backgrounds bear the closest and most critical scrutiny. I have argued and worked for years to bring about an acceptable scheme for the registration of private detectives and enquiry agents — and, of course, security experts. It is still my hope that, for the benefit of the community in general and the industrial world in particular, this will be achieved.

In his paper to Lloyd Institute of Management, Mr Mayo gave some interesting points made by the Judge, Mr Justice Bristow:

1. "A company or individual must take reasonable steps to safeguard secret or confidential documentary information, otherwise there is no offence in law should a person either copy or photograph the documents." Although not relevant to the case of British Titan Products, this point is vital to companies; if proper care has not been taken of

plans, campaigns, designs, formulae and company policy
and planning, an accused might plead that there was no
offence to answer, since the company itself did not regard
the information as secret.

2.   "An employee of a company is under a legal obligation to
keep the secrets of his employers and commits an unlawful
act should he confide secret or confidential information to
an outside source." In this case money had been offered to
an employee to breach the confidentiality inherent in his
employment.

One aspect of the British Titan case is of especial interest, and
points a warning. Both Japan, and the Iron Curtain countries, were
technically backwards as regards this process. Indeed, prior to this
attempt at industrial espionage (an attempt to discover the secrets
of the chloride process), the company had been in negotiation with
the state authority of an Eastern European state for the sale of
know-how for the *sulphate* process for the construction of a large
factory in their country. At one point in the negotiations, the state
authority had requested that know-how for the *chloride* process be
supplied to them.

Naturally, this request was refused. British Titan were not yet
ready to licence chloride process know-how. Did that state suspect
that they might be buying out-of-date technology, and so make
overt efforts to wrest the secrets of the newer technology from the
British company? If so, they covered their tracks pretty well, since
even their intermediate agent in Germany kept his anonymity. This
must remain conjecture; but the coincidence of the industrial
espionage attempt following upon a refusal by the company to part
with information of the same secret process, is at least worth noting.

It is interesting to note that, two years later the same private
detective was fined £2,000 and given a two-year suspended jail
sentence for faking divorce evidence.

The methods employed by an American special agent, hired by
the United States Internal Revenue Service a few years ago come
well within the definition of industrial espionage.

The American income tax authorities had begun to suspect that
the Castle Bank and Trust of the Bahamas was being used as an
illegal tax haven. Under the code name of *Operation Tradewinds*,
an expensive operation was mounted with a view to discovering
what American citizens had cash and valuables salted away in safe
deposits, and where. It is a sidelight on the degree of secrecy with

which their supposedly "undercover" operations were conducted that, as Ted Harrison put it in his report to the *Sunday Times*, the whole affair "seemed to be degenerating into a keystone cops farce of empty safety deposit boxes and missing customers."

To break the Castle Bank's secrecy, the Inland Revenue Service hired Norman Jaspan, listed dramatically as Agent TW24. He went to the Bahamas, and, having established the necessary contacts there, obtained the names of some of the Castle Bank's depositors, the most prominent of whom, it was said later, was Richard Nixon.

Such piecemeal information, however, was unsatisfactory, the more so as *Operation Tradewinds* had proved thus far a protracted and very expensive undertaking. What the IRS was anxious to procure was a complete list of the Castle Bank's deposits and depositors. Jaspan hired a locksmith, a photographer, a lookout and a decoy — a pretty young girl called Sybil Kennedy.

The net results were later outlined in an Illinois court:

> "Jaspan managed to ingratiate himself with the manager of the Castle Bank, Michael Wolstencroft, and learned that Wolstencroft would be flying to Chicago via Miami to discuss the affairs of his clients. Jaspan arranged an assignation with Sybil Kennedy."

The rest of the action reads like a second-rate feature film. The attractive decoy succeeded in getting the bank manager to leave his briefcase containing the list of clients in her apartment. She then offered herself for his sexual pleasure, and, while thus diverted, IRS agents spirited the briefcase away, photographed its contents, and returned it to the spot from which it had been borrowed. As all this took time, there was ample time for dalliance.

From an espionage point of view — and all this, surely, was *industrial* espionage, since it was directed against a business house, and against the business men who were that Bank's clients — that could be considered a scoop. Yet it failed to satisfy the official appetite for surreptitious knowledge. The IRS arranged for Sybil Kennedy to visit Wolstencroft in his office, where she managed to get hold of a rotating-type file of information cards. For her part in the operation she was paid $1,000 while Jaspan received $8,000.

With this stolen information, the Government department then went to work, slapping in demands for tax on individuals whose returns did not mention the sums and property deposited with Castle Bank.

As a matter of record, the whole operation cost the U.S. Government $40,000,000. An Ohio court sharply rebuked the IRS for its tactics; in Illinois the IRS was asked to drop all evidence secured by illegal means, while Florida lawyers saw another way of repaying this official incursion into industrial espionage by charging the IRS with securing the services of a prostitute for financial gain!

In this instance, the Government agency initiated and condoned what they knew to be illegal acts, and the reaction of the average sensible citizen to the ensuing publicity might well be: why expect *me* to obey the laws which you violate so blatantly yourself? When State Departments actually practise crime, they encourage the spread of crime amongst those they govern, who merely emulate them. In this instance, the government officials concerned, and the departments they served, were called sternly to account. It is doubtful however if that was an isolated case; it just happened to be one which was discovered, exposed and so destined to hit the headlines.

The real security experts are those who, on the basis of genuine training in all aspects of security, whether in government service, or out of it, or both, often come across professional industrial spies in the course of their work. At least, they frequently encounter evidence of the professional's activities. Actual encounters with "Mister Big" are less frequent because, in the nature of his work, he works through intermediaries, front-men, hirelings and stooges.

A security expert who has encountered industrial spies, including some real professionals, is Mr R.B. ("Tim") Matthews, a former Major in British Intelligence who at one time served as security adviser to the Director of Military Intelligence in Cyprus and has commanded a counter-intelligence unit. He was one of the first to draw public attention to the growing menace of industrial espionage, and to organise, through his concern, Management Investigations Limited, a conference of counter-industrial espionage experts in London in the sixties. He has been very active in this field ever since, and has informed me of a few experiences which I consider worth re-telling.

He knows a happily unmarried couple living in luxury in a villa in Marbella, Spain, who amassed their fortune in four years by stealing haute couture designs from famous fashion houses in Paris. She was formerly a model working for one of the principal fashion houses; he a not very successful photographer. Working as a team they photographed *every single design* that was created over the four years and sold the pictures to three mass production clothing companies in the U.S.A., Hong Kong and Holland. They were never discovered. In fact, Mr Matthews recalls "although they live together in a delightful villa complete with swimming pool, they are not married. As this very beautiful young woman said 'We do not need to be — we have a sort of bond which keeps us together'."

Perhaps that instance is more a case of the opportunist seeing how treachery to her employer could be made to pay, and learning, by the process of doing, how to do this professionally. A case of the apprentice turning professional. Their field, however, was narrower than that of the true professional.

There are agencies, as well as individuals, which operate an industrial espionage service. They handle a variety of industrial espionage requirements. Tim Matthews cites two instances of quite different character, illustrating the streamlined efficiency with which this type of dangerous theft and piracy is pursued.

When investigating a loss of information by a company in Jersey in 1978 it was discovered eventually that a carpet cleaning contractor, working without supervision over the weekend, had removed two complete 4 drawer filing cabinets in his van and taken them to another office. A team of seven girls and two men with three photocopying machines, copied the entire contents in 23 hours, working in shifts. The cabinets were then taken back and replaced without arousing any suspicion.

The Managing Director of an international group engaged in the production of industrial electrical equipment compiled a heavy dossier about his main competitor. To do this he used the services of a "determined industrial espionage agency" who supplied him with extremely delicate information.

He left the dossier in his hotel room when he went out in the morning, and when he visited the competitor for a highly confidential lunch to discuss a take-over bid his own confidence was shattered. Conspicuously the dossier was placed on a side table opposite his chair.

The Marketing Director of an American-owned company visiting Mexico City on a business trip returned to Canada quite unaware that his entire visit had been recorded on film or tape by an agency which specialised in selling what they described as "interesting documentaries" to anyone who would buy them.

Two weeks after his return he received a telephone call from a complete stranger and was invited to listen to a compromising recording of his own bedroom activities in Mexico. He was told there were pictures too. The price tag was $50,000. He paid up over three months. When he received the final spools of film he was given a small printed slip which read:

1. Thank you for completing the transaction so promply.
2. It is certified that no other copies of the records exist.
3. Now that our capability has been proved you may wish to use our professional services yourself. All you need do is to insert the following ad in the International Edition of the New York Herald Tribune and we will contact you.

The advertisement referred to an apartment to rent in Paris.

Let me now go back to 1968, and to recount the details of a scene which has all the ingredients of a typical spy thriller. The culprit in this instance was certainly an industrial spy. He could equally have been any other sort of spy — in this case it is a distinction without a difference.

An official of the Rome branch of the American firm of Procter and Gamble was telephoned one day by a commercial traveller, Mr Renato Ratti. Neither knew each other. Mr Ratti came swiftly to the point. He could offer them soap and detergent secrets, the advance marketing and manufacturing plans of the giant concern Unilever, as far forward as 1975.

What he was offering was worth £750,000. The price he asked was £30,000.

The two companies conferred, and a trap was laid.

Ratti telephoned, as everything seemed set for a deal, and made the assignation: "I shall be in the Bar Pom Pom with all the documents. As a sign I shall drink coffee and then place the cup face downwards."

On November 24th 1968 Ratti visited the bar, ordered his coffee, drank it, and turned his cup upside down. He then looked around and, seeing a well-dressed man approaching in recognition, he rose to greet him with outstretched hand. He received instead a quick and cold reception — from police captain Giuseppe Vitali.

The same drama had happened once in reverse to the same firm. Instead of being offered a rival's secrets this time, their own were stolen and offered to a rival concern, Colgate-Palmolive.

John Louis Brand, a 30-years-old advertising executive, was found guilty at the Old Bailey of receiving confidential documents knowing them to have been stolen. He worked as an advertising executive, but not for the advertising company handling the account of Procter and Gamble; nor, indeed, were his own employers involved in the least degree with the illegalities with which Brand was charged.

In effect, Brand offered to sell for £3,000 detergent secrets worth £750,000. A fierce "detergent war" was on for mastery of this highly lucrative market, and an industrial spy might well have felt that here were easy pickings. In this instance, so far as these two companies were involved, they were quite wrong. The firm which had been offered the stolen property at once informed the police, and Brand and his accomplice were charged with the stealing of documents.

It is a sidelight on the rather crazy laws as they stand at present in Britain that, although the documents contained advertising and marketing secrets which would have been according to the prosecution "red-hot in the hands of a competitor", they were discharged on the charge of conspiring to injure Procter and Gamble and their agents, Young and Rubicam Ltd., by divulging the contents of confidential documents.

Judge Aarvold, in sentencing Brand to 13 months imprisonment, commented: "Here you are so lowering your standard as to receive stolen property and to use that property to enrich yourself by a sum of no less than £3,000. You yourself called it a dirty business and I regret to find that description an accurate one."

Once, twice . . . and then, for the third time, Procter and Gamble found themselves involved unwittingly in another industrial spying attempt. Colgate-Palmolive were approached by a junior executive employed by Procter and Gamble, who offered details of his employers' sales and promotion campaign for a new toothpaste, for $20,000. The climax was like a scene from a third-rate feature film. "Mr Crest" (using the name of the proposed new toothpaste) went by arrangement to one toilet cubicle at Kennedy Airport; "Mr Colgate", the presumed purchaser was to be in the adjoining cubicle. There was, as is usual enough in public toilets, a space underneath the partitions. Mr Crest asked Mr Colgate to take off his trousers with the $20,000 in the pocket and pass them under the partition; this being done, Mr Crest pocketed the money, put the plans into the trouser pockets, and passed the trousers back again. He then fled, as the *Sunday Times* put it, graphically, "straight into the arms of the waiting G-men."

In this ubiquitous game of industrial espionage, there are broadly three types of operatives:

The professional;

The opportunist;

The vindictive employee.

All, at different times, have effected, or sought to effect, considerable damage. These categories are not identical either in their motives or their methods.

Professionals are people hired to do a specific job. I will give a purely hypothetical brief: ". . . Cameras Ltd is supposed to have developed a 110 model which combines instant photography, motorised wind-on, wide-angled and telescopic facilities, and light-sensitive control of shutter speed, aperture and distance. What are its main features? To what degree is there computerisation of the works? What sort of lens has it — or lenses? What are the new features of its motor? What does it cost to make? What are the numbers of its various patents? Is a new factory planned, or is all the production of the new camera in one place? What are the names of the managers of the respective departments? What sort of people are they — where do they live? When will the new camera be put on the market. Who are the advertising agents? How much has been allocated for the launching of the new camera? Who does their public relations? What does the camera cost to make, and at what price is it proposed to sell it? How many cameras is it proposed to make in the ensuing year? Are there plans to export it, and, if so, to which countries?" And so on.

Hypothetical though it is, there is nothing unusual or unlikely in this imaginary briefing. There are plenty of individual spies and companies operating as industrial spies, who would accept and act upon it. Perhaps some of the information would be gained by enquiries with sub-contractors. Some facts might emerge by a spy posing as a freelance journalist, and going to interview the company on the basis of what he claims may merely be a rumour. There may be employees of the camera company, their advertising agents, or their public relations representatives, who could be bribed and used.

However, a professional industrial spy is not, by inference, a full-time spy. His usefulness would be severely limited if he were; how would he account for his style of living, his need to travel, to entertain, to ask questions and conduct investigations? A prosperous individual with no obvious background of productive activity would automatically attract suspicion. No, industrial spying is seldom a person's sole activity; it is an ancillary part of his occupation.

The professional has a professional approach to his job, as a Fleet

Street journalist I know soon discovered. Investigating the subject of industrial espionage, he went through the yellow pages and contacted at random various enquiry agencies. He had thought up some information he would (if he represented an unscrupulous company) like to acquire about a rival company, and asked several concerns to take the job on. Most refused, but one bit. The journalist outlined his requirements, which were (at face value) quite obviously an attempt to steal the secrets of a company. The industrial spy listened attentively and then said "Yes, I'll do it."

"Fine" said the journalist, "when do we get airborne?"

"When we've settled one point," the spy replied, "what you're asking me to do is not an honourable thing, so please do not expect to receive from me an honourable account. Tell me, then, how much are you going to benefit from the information you're asking me to produce? How much would it save you in research costs?"

"About a hundred thousand pounds".

"Fine. Then my fee will be £10,000."

That is what I call a professional, as distinct from an opportunist. The advertising executive John Brand who saw that the plans of his employers had a potential sale as stolen property was, if you like to put it that way, an imaginative, ad hoc thief. It was a mean act, proceeded with in cunning, but he was not making a profession of it, nor was he doing it in a professional manner, in the sense that he had not considered, logically, what such a transaction demanded in strategy and psychology. He walked easily into a trap.

The professional touch in an industrial espionage operation was revealed by Lord Chalfont, writing in the *Financial Weekly* of February 16, 1979:

> Only a few years ago an employee of a large British office equipment company was arrested outside a London underground station in the act of handing over confidential documents to a "rival organisation" — the rival organisation in this case being the police, who had been called after the company to whom the secrets had been offered had informed the original owners.
>
> What was most bizarre about the whole operation was that it was carried out with all the trappings of a second-rate spy thriller — drops, cutouts and code-names, and even, at the end, the crucial rendezvous in which the principal spy was to be identified by a red carnation in his buttonhole and a copy of a well-known financial newspaper under his left arm.

Sir Richard Powell, has said, of those attracted to industrial espionage:

What kind of people are trained for industrial espionage? Ex-policemen, housewives and former army intelligence men all make good recruits. But most spying is done by brilliant technical men anxious to get on.

He adds: "No industrial company, obviously will openly confess to employing spies. But they are ready to talk — off the record — of the terrible things their competitors do . . ."

Sir Richard was stating, in his good-humoured way, what is obvious from the number of industrial spies operating and the scale of industrial espionage — that the mere fact that some agencies distribute circulars inviting individuals and companies to hire them to secure information about rivals shows that legal safeguards against such activities are of little use. Only positive and strategic thought for the protection of a firm's secrets is likely to protect them against this dangerous form of theft. Introducing defensive methods *after* the damage has been done is like locking the door after the horse has bolted; the damage is often irretrievable.

One firm, G. and F. Mihm (UK), described as a "civil intelligence agency" and operating from an address in Kensington, London, with headquarters in Kassel, Western Germany, offered in a circular letter dated 4th October 1971 to collect information about a firm's rivals:

"To give an edge to knowledge as a managerial instrument, it must (a) embrace all aspects of the market at home and abroad, and all aspects of competitive activity, including financial structure and current monetary situation, and (b) it must be organised, not haphazard."

The organisation, it was claimed, had for nearly 20 years "provided civil and industrial intelligence to European Industry, *using professional investigation techniques* (my italics) checking, cross-checking and cataloging information and presenting it in a form most suitable to the client."

Then there is the RICA (Research into competitive activity) Service which smacks very much of industrial espionage as I understand the term. It advertises its service as embracing (a) companies in opposition; (b) Products in opposition; (c) Promotional activity in opposition. It undertook to report on "the financial structure of competitors, their liquidity and cash-flow, their assets, turnover, credit-worthiness, their managerial and executive personalities, their connections, their special expertise, their individual achievements, etc. We report on organisational structure, research and development activities, their purchasing and production strengths and weaknesses, distribution problems and their administration . . . "

You can hardly get more comprehensive than that. I will not presume to speculate how this concern goes about its work, or with what success, but from their own claims it would seem that there is little or nothing about a rival which they feel they cannot discover, and much of that which they undertake to discover would be unlikely to be in the public domain.

One of the most remarkable industrial spies, in my view, is Robert Sancier Aries, aged about 60, who claims to have been born French, and who became a naturalised United States citizen in 1950. During his years in America he obtained an M.A. degree from Minnesota, a science degree from Yale and two advanced degrees in chemical engineering from the Brooklyn Polytechnic Institute. He traded as a "consultant" to a number of large American Corporations and took out more than 40 U.S. patents.

In 1959 an employee of Merck and Company stole some cultures being developed by his company and some data concerning secret manufacturing processes. Naturally, Merck and Company were gravely concerned that the benefits of developments which had cost them years of labour and millions of dollars would go without effort or expense to their rivals; their security officers and staff soon established that valuable information had been passed to various companies controlled by Aries and his business associates.

Merck, making no bones about it, alleged industrial espionage, and filed a suit for 7.8 million dollars, filing also two criminal indictments in New Jersey and Connecticut claiming that Dr Aries hired a Merck employee to give him data of a new anticoccidiosis drug for poultry called Amprolium. This data he was alleged to have stolen, falsely patenting it under the name of "Mepyrium".

Rohm, & Haas Company and the Sprague Electric Company also brought suits against Dr Aries. On 27 November, 1964 the Federal Court in Hartford, Connecticut made an order of 21 million dollars against the doctor, and injunctions forbidding Dr Aries or his associates from using the stolen information were also obtained.

By this time, however, Aries had left America and was living in Switzerland. Now the complexities of International Law, the complications of the United States laws, and the numerous variations in the different States laws made it virtually impossible to compensate even slightly for the tremendous harm which had been done to these companies by the misappropriation and misuse of their most priceless asset — the secret processes, so expensively developed, on which they depended for their existence. Neither Aries nor his associates had any worthwhile assets. The flight of Aries to Europe made confusion more confounded; the original charges against Aries in the Federal Court at Hartford had indicted him for *transporting* a stolen product. This not being a crime in Switzerland, he could not be extradited. This is strange, seeing that industrial espionage itself in Switzerland is a crime.

Naturally, lawyers acting for the aggrieved companies searched desperately for some formula by which the judgements made in the U.S.A. could be implemented. Finding that the Essex County Court had also indicted Aries under New Jersey Penal Law for the *receipt* of a stolen product, a crime recognised as such by Swiss law, and justifying an application for his extradition, procedures to this end were set in motion. Dr Aries, whose training makes him, if I may say so, a connoisseur of information, was aware of these moves being made against him, and went to France, where he claimed dual nationality.

Prior to his departure, lawyers acting for Merck and for Sprague Electric found a section in the Swiss Penal Code under which Aries could be taken to law; it defined 'unfair competition' as 'any abuse in the field of economic competition arising as a, result of fraud or of other acts contrary to the rules of good faith!' Civil Actions were instituted on these grounds, and in October 1961 he was arrested by the Swiss Police. After only four days of preventive detention he was released on $46,500 bail, and fled immediately to his apartment in Paris.

The United States sought to have Aries extradited to the U.S.A., but, because of his dual nationality, this request was withdrawn on the assumption that the French would try him; under French Criminal Law if a French citizen commits a crime in another country of a kind which is also a crime in France, he can be tried in France for that extra-territorial offence. In fact no prosecution in France was instituted.

However, legal procedures continued to be pursued in Switzerland, as a result of which, in 1966, a Geneva court found Dr Aries guilty on seven charges of unfair competition against Merck and Sprague. He was also convicted on three charges of swindling the famous Swiss firm of Hoffman La Roche by selling them the Merck culture for 51,000 dollars on the pretext that it was his own. He was sentenced in his absence to two and a half years in prison, ten years exile from Switzerland and ordered to pay 51,000 dollars in damages to La Roche, plus the court costs.

At the Geneva hearing it was stated that he had sold his stolen information to many other companies.

While all this was going on, Aries filed patent applications in 40 countries in respect of information obtained in America and elsewhere; in most countries proof of being the inventor is not required as a condition of granting a patent.

Nobody could dispute the competence of Dr Robert S. Aries to write or edit a work on industrial espionage, and this, indeed, he claims to have done. In 1976 he was advertising in *Fortune* magazine, through Aries International of Paris, an Industrial Espionage Encyclopaedia. Ostensibly offered for defensive purposes, its information could equally be used, judging by the statement of the encyclopaedia's contents, for *offensive* purposes — for conducting industrial espionage.

Unfortunately, I have never seen the work, or met anybody else who has. The price may be a factor here — the encyclopaedia was offered at a price of £7,400.00 and despite the interest of the subject and the manifest competence of the author to handle it, it is a lot to pay for factual anthology. It claimed to offer in its appendices such topics as:

Electronic devices which work and which do not work;
Spy gear and practices which are only in story books;
The real problem of changing employment;
Company personnel and its temptations;
How to fabricate fake memos for competitors' consumption;
How to make your competitors work in the wrong direction;
How to handle investigations;
Swiss and other "secret" bank accounts;
Facts on microphones, cleaning women, industrial spies, and loyal and disloyal employees.

Whether the advertised contents of this expensive encyclopaedia led to many sales, I do not know. I think it likely, however, that it would induce many people interested in industrial espionage — whether to counteract such espionage or engage in it — to get in touch with Dr Aries. One can only speculate on what might have transpired after that.

The address given for Aries International of Paris is in a fashionable residential thoroughfare off the Avenue Foch in the

16th Arrondissement. It is a block of flats giving no indication whatever of any business being conducted there. Some diplomats interested in following up the advertisement would, however, not have far to go, for there are several embassies in the same street.

Attempting to get information on tenders submitted by rival firms is very common indeed. Sometimes overtures are made to employees, either directly or indirectly, with promises of specific payment, gifts or favours if the required information is forthcoming. The disloyal employee who yields to such blandishments does so from a variety of motives. They may be jealous of the boss because he has shown favour to another employee or assistant — promoting them (in the view of the aggrieved) when they themselves were deserving of preference. There may be sexual jealousy; a girl may have been courted, or seduced and subsequently discarded. At least, this is the way some women might see it; more realistic, or less charitable, onlookers might merely conclude that the liaison was ill-conceived, or simply petered out. Or the employee is simply acquisitive beyond his ability to earn sufficient to buy all the things he thinks he needs. Worse still, he may be in debt, for gambling, over-spending or, if a married man, maintaining a mistress in a way that strains his financial resources to the limit.

Jealousy in an office, from somebody handling sensitive or secret information, is an obvious warning sign. It does not imply disloyalty, and should not be so construed; but it can, at least, be noted as a predisposing factor.

Such employees can and do take the initiative themselves in obtaining and selling their firm's secrets. Equally, and by chance, they may succumb to an initiative of an outsider, an amateur or professional industrial spy. Many such approaches are made by people who do not acknowledge that what they are doing is industrial spying at all. Consider this piece of dialogue during a case in which a man was accused of bribing councillors to find housebuilding work for a Poulson company in the seventies.

In the corruption trial at Leeds Crown Court a journalist was being cross-examined about his public relations work on behalf of Open Systems Building (OSB), a Poulson company, and his relationship with another of the accused, Tom Roebuck, a member of the former Mexborough Urban Council.

Mr Peter Taylor, Q.C., for the Crown, asked the journalist:

"You had an agent on that Council who was spying for you?"

"I do not regard it as that."

"Here is a man showing you comparative prices from other tenders?"

"Yes."

"You did not think there was anything wrong in that?"

"No, I did not, because there is industrial espionage where firms try to find out what their competitors are doing."

"Is espionage how you regarded it?"

"No. I was only trying to get houses for OSB."

It was stated that the journalist's council contact was "a mine of information" who supplied a list of local authorities, together with the names of members. Counsel queried: "Mr Roebuck had not only given you the names but in fact lent his own linkage with these people. You were writing on the personal recommendation of someone they knew?" The journalist answered "Because Mr Roebuck was apparently a great figure."

Where an assistant or a secretary of a Chairman, Managing Director or executive of comparable status becomes the mistress of somebody equally important in a rival company, there is an obvious possibility of confidential information being passed on. However despite the misgivings inevitably aroused in circumstances like these, some allowance has to be made for the fact that such relationships do occur for no other reason than mutual attraction. A case in point is of Tiffany ballrooms case in July, 1979. There an industrial tribunal ruled that the possibility of a woman giving away office secrets in "pillow talk" with her lover was an insufficient reason for her dismissal.

Giving the decision, the chairman of the tribunal at Birmingham, Mr Gerald Foster, said that the question was one of degree — in particular the degree of responsibility held by the woman in her job and also the degree of discretion, intelligence, loyalty and service which she had.

Mrs Nora Taylor of Newcastle-under-Lyme (Staffordshire), won a claim that she was unfairly dismissed by Mecca Ltd from her job as chief cashier in one of Mecca's Tiffany ballrooms in the Stoke-on-Trent area. She was dismissed 12 months after she started to live with Mr Ernest Shaw, formerly the manager at Tiffany's, who was, at that time, managing a rival dance hall, named Romeo and Juliet, owned by E.M.I.

Mecca claimed she had left by mutual agreement. She had been its employee for about 15 years. It was stated on her behalf that there was no proof that she had passed over information to Mr Shaw, but that "it would seem that a battle akin to the Battle of the Somme was going on in Hanley, Stoke."

For Mecca it was said that it could prove embarrassing if knowledge of till receipts and future promotions were passed over. He added "It would be very difficult to get concrete evidence of what was said in pillow talk. There could not be a tape-recording or an investigation."

The *Reading Evening Post* of 17 June 1977 published an interesting article by Linton Mitchell in which he quoted at length the experiences and views of a security consultant, Roy Winckleman. He gave it as his view that there is no mould for the successful industrial spy, but that he does have certain characteristics, and "more than one underpaid night watchman or security guard has come across him, operating bold as brass in the middle of the night, and let him continue his business prior to making his escape, in exchange for money."

Said Mr Winckleman:

> "You are talking about a very highly educated expert in electronics and security. This man has a university degree. He has worked for — or at least been trained by — a government agency. He is polite, well-dressed, totally articulate and probably carrying the equivalent of £2000 in cash. If some poor old night watchman, who is lucky to pick up £60 a week before the tax stumbles across him, then what happens? The night watchman is offered, probably, more money than he has ever seen at any one time in his life. It's a big temptation, isn't it?"

It is. There have been many instances of people employed in security, or as night watchmen, who either had not sufficient strength of character to resist corruption, or had already a background of dishonesty or even serious crime. Firstly, security ought not to be an afterthought in company organisation, a mere extra for which anything will do; it is a fundamental service which should be properly paid and attract the best people. Secondly, there should be adequate vetting of such staff before they are entrusted with their responsibilities.

CHAPTER 4

Stealing Secrets: Methods

If a secret is of any value, it is going to be worth somebody's while to steal it.

If a company, a government or an individual possesses information on which their power or wealth is based, it is virtually a certainty that somebody, sometime, will attempt to steal it.

Should the information concern some *fundamental* human need, or be important in the field of power and sovereignty (aerospace projects, for example) there is an *absolute* certainty that attempts will be made to steal it.

These are, or should be, the fundamental assumptions underlying all security and, in particular, industrial espionage.

There are times when the methods employed in industrial espionage are barely distinguishable from those commonly used in the 'ordinary' world of espionage. A great deal of technical apparatus, which I shall describe in due course, may be used for spying, counter-espionage, industrial espionage or counter-industrial espionage. The same goes for methods.

Of very ancient origin, and a technique commonly used today in the theft of industrial secrets, is the 'sleeper'.

In the dark world of espionage 'sleepers' who, needless to say, do not sleep in the figurative sense but are very wide awake, are planted in the rival organisation or territory, where they carry on with their declared profession while awaiting a call to action by their secret masters, or, having worked their way up by good work and acceptable behaviour, are trusted increasingly and so have access to secret or classified information.

The most obvious example of this is the case of Guy Burgess, the notorious British double agent. Well connected in the press, in politics and in governmental circles, he acted as courier between Britain's Prime Minister and Mussolini and, after working in the peripheral services of British intelligence, was offered a staff job in a government department set up in 1938 to counter enemy propoganda and subversion.

Burgess, who came to do top intelligence work for the Secret Service and the Foreign Office, was recruited as a Soviet Agent while still at Cambridge University. Although he visited Russia in 1934, he claimed to be disillusioned with what he saw, and came to be trusted increasingly by the establishment. The establishment knows now that it made a terrible and irretrievable mistake. Burgess was a sleeper. He just waited, patiently, cynically, keeping the secret of his real backers well to himself.

A super-sleeper was Harold Adrian Russell Philby, who worked underground as a Soviet agent for 30 years, waiting, watching and occasionally reporting. He had been a Communist at Cambridge University and in 1934 married an Austrian Communist. Thereafter he dissembled, in brilliant fashion, his true affiliations; he joined the pro-Nazi Anglo-German Fellowship, indifferent to the condemnation this would, inevitably, attract to him. When he reported the Spanish Civil War as a journalist he wrote pro-Nationalist articles for *The Times*.

The object, of course, was to be what Communists would call a 'reactionary', so that he would be observed to be at loggerheads with Communists, while his seeming advocacy of right-wing and Fascist causes would make it seem impossible that he had any sympathy with far less be in league with, Soviet Russia.

With the outbreak of war, and because of his widespread connections and journalistic standing, Philby was recruited into British Intelligence. By 1945 he was head of all British activities against Soviet espionage. When a Soviet diplomat called on the British Embassy in Instanbul to reveal the identity of a high-ranking British traitor in British counter-intelligence, Philby flew out personally to interrogate him. The would-be Russian defector, Volkov, then disappeared!

Another 'sleeper' in the world of (State) espionage was the 'Canadian', Gordon Arnold Lonsdale, an identity adopted by the Russian spy Molody. The real Lonsdale was born in Cobald, Ontario on August 27, 1927. His father was a Canadian who had married a Finn. His parents separated and Lonsdale, at the age of eight, went to Finland with his mother. The Soviets fancied the missing Lonsdale as a cover for their sleeper because they knew that records in the Haileybury area of Ontario had been destroyed by a forest fire. Thus, in 1954, the Soviet spy, using another innocuous name, travelled to Vancouver and began to collect documents in the name of Lonsdale.

Lonsdale the sleeper, having established a completely new identity (a birth certificate in the name of Gordon Arnold Lonsdale) obtained a Canadian passport, crossed the border into the U.S.A., contacted the Soviet spy Rudolf Abel, and sailed off from New York to Britain where he enrolled as a student of Chinese at London University School of Oriental and African studies.

In 1956 'Lonsdale' went into the vending and amusement machine business as a cover, becoming export director for the firm. This enabled him to make frequent trips abroad, ostensibly to Canada, but in fact to Europe and Moscow. His whereabouts were covered by postcards, previously written to friends in England, posted by others in the spy network from Canada.

This was the origin of what became known as the Portland Spy Ring, which set out to wrest the secrets of the Portland Underwater Research Station in Great Britain, and resulted in Lonsdale's eventual arrest and a prison sentence of 25 years. In fact he never served the sentence, being swapped for a British secret service man, Greville Wynne.

The sleeper had done his deadly job well, but made a mistake in his cover. The doctor who had attended the birth of the real Lonsdale, when tracked down by intelligence agents, revealed that he had circumcised the baby. Molody was not circumcised. His cover was finally and truly blown.

The case of Lonsdale was an example of the patience with which an enemy will plant a man and wait for their plan to mature. So, too, is the case of George Blake, who was snatched from Wormwood Scrubs prison after receiving a 42 years prison sentence for betraying secrets to the Russians, and who found refuge, and comfort and honour, in Moscow.

Blake, the son of an Egyptian married to a Dutchwoman, had joined the Dutch Resistance Movement during the occupation of Holland by the Germans in World War II. He escaped to Britain, joined the Royal Navy as an ordinary seaman, rose to officer's rank and, because of his knowledge of languages, was later employed on intelligence work. After the war he became a secret service agent in Germany. In 1948 he was appointed a vice-consul in Korea. He was interned by the North Koreans, subjected to brain-washing during three years of captivity, and on his release when the Korean War ended in 1953, rejoined the British Secret Service and was sent to Berlin to infiltrate the Soviet spy network and to pose as a double agent.

There is no doubt that Blake did irreparable harm in his new role of sleeper. He had been prepared for such a role for three years, and now, systematically betrayed agent after agent. His masters, once they had trained him, were content to wait and see. It was precisely because of the enormous success of the Soviet operation that the KGB went to such trouble to rescue him from a British prison. Whether it was particularly intelligent of the British authorities to have put Blake in the same prison as Molody — thus bringing two Russian spies together — is something we shall never know, as neither party had admitted having had contact with the other. The sleeper cases quoted have been of those implanted for conventional espionage where individuals are recruited at university stage. It follows that the same proceedure might and could be adopted by foreign governments for industrial espionage.

A classic — and ancient — case of industrial espionage is described by William F. Leggett in *The Story of Silk* (New York: J.J. Little and Ives Company, 1949). For three thousand years the Chinese had kept secret how silk was made. The secret was a source of wealth and power. The Roman Emperor Justinian (A.D. 529 to 565), finding that his subjects were importing raw silk from the Far East at enormous cost, the garments being made up in his capital, Constantinople, decided to steal the secret from the Chinese so that both silk thread and woven silk could be produced in his own country.

He sent two emissaries to China, who lived there as monks, working in the silk industry for two years until they had mastered the art of raising silk worms, growing the mulberry bushes on which they fed, and preparing and weaving the silk fibres. Jusinian was astounded to learn that the secret of this wonderful fabric was a worm! The eggs were smuggled out to Constantinople in a bamboo stick, the eggs were hatched out, and in the ensuing 600 years Constantinople was one of the great silk markets for the Middle East and Europe. The secrets which Justinian stole with his sleepers brought untold wealth to his country and untold loss to China.

Late in the fifteenth century there was similar theft of valuable trade secrets by Western traders from the Far East. The civilisations of the East being far older than those of the West, it necessarily follows that they possessed many secrets of production, accumulated over thousands of years of coming to terms with their environment, and both observing and discovering uses for their resources.

Chinese porcelain is a case in point. The high prices received for porcelain imported from the Far East into Europe persuaded traders and entrepreneurs that a fortune awaited anyone who could wrest from the East the actual processes of porcelain making. There was so much to know; what ingredients were used in the original mix, where those ingredients came from, in what proportion they were used, and indeed, in what order, for they were not necessarily put together and mixed in one go. So many things came into it — the fashioning of the shapes, the constituents of the colours used, or the colour mixes; how colours were supplied, and at which states, and, of course, the processes of firing.

It fell to Father d'Entrecolles, a French Jesuit who went to China on a mission of conversion, to observe and record the secrets of porcelain manufacture in a series of long letters commencing in September 1712 and continuing, with a prolificacy of detail, for ten years. He penetrated the royal kilns of Chinh-te-Chen and spied out every detail of the making of the fabulous porcelain envied by every ruler and rich merchant in Europe. He combined piety with piracy in equal proportions.

In due course a French scientist, Rene Antoine Ferchault de Reaumur, was advised of the valuable and detailed contents of the Jesuitical letters, and requested him to despatch, as soon and as secretly as possible, some of the raw materials of porcelain. This the French priest did (not without risk, as any discovery of his complicity would have brought him condign and terrifying punishments) and, as a result, France's porcelain industry — the now world-famous Sèvres factory — took root.

Father d'Entrecolles may fairly be termed a 'sleeper' as his avowed function — to save Chinese souls — caused him to be received and harboured with the trust which he so cynically betrayed.

Twice has the British Secret Service used 'sleepers' to acquire valuable industrial concessions for Britain. The two most historic cases that come to mind are the founding of British Petroleum (BP) after oil concessions in Persia were acquired by means of a trick, and the repetition of that trick in very similar circumstances in respect of oil concessions in Iraq.

There are many accounts of the Persian oil affair, although a key source is in Robin Bruce-Lockhart's *Ace of Spies*, the story of Sidney Reilly, one of the most extraordinary and resourceful secret agents of modern times.

William Knox D'Arcy, an Australian adventurer with a strong romantic bent, travelled to Persia at the end of last century and was given permission by the Shah of Persia, Nasser-el-Din, to explore his country.

D'Arcy combined an interest in religions with acute business perspicuity although, strange to say, his interest in the former proved, eventually, stronger than his interest in the latter. D'Arcy knew that Iran had long been the home of fire-worshippers and that in some temples sacred fire had been kept burning for centuries. Some were temples of Zorcaster who, according to Parsee tradition, lived between 660 and 583 but who official histories list as living between 628-551 B.C. D'Arcy reasoned to himself: if the temples of the holy Persian prophet were marked by a perpetual fire, *where did the fire come from*? If the fire were not fed with fuel, then the fuel must be artesian; it must come from an underground oil supply.

For years D'Arcy, pursuing his dream of great riches from a yet-to-be-discovered oil supply, roamed around Persia, boring at insufficient depth and in crude and ineffectual ways. The City of London regarded him with cold suspicion — to them he was a crank always wandering around in far away places and coming back with nothing.

Then a new Shah ascended the peacock throne of Persia, and D'Arcy found himself in favour, as a skilled engineer and one who had explored Persia thoroughly. He built Persia's railways, and in a fit of gratitude the Shah gave him a total concession for a period of sixty years, to prospect, drill and extract oil in Persia. D'Arcy now possessed a sixty-year monopoly on one of the richest oil supplies in the world.

It was not an outright gift from the Shah, of course. The Shah was to receive a 10% royalty on oil output and £5000 in cash — a substantial sum then, equivalent to a modern £200,000.

The news got around, and businessmen and governments of every description came chasing after D'Arcy to do a deal with him. But D'Arcy had fallen in love with Persia, a country which had claimed a large slice of his life, and whose mystical religions appealed to him so strongly. An older man, the intellectual and spiritual aspects of his life's quest overshadowed financial ambitions. To all who wooed him for his precious concession his answer was a firm "NO!"

To shake off his pursuers, D'Arcy decided to visit America. On the boat he became friendly with a missionary from Africa, whose stories of hardship and spiritual satisfaction in trying to spread the word evoked in the heart of the romantic D'Arcy an immediate response. When D'Arcy spoke of the conflict sparked off by his document from the Shah, and of his determination not to permit its use except for a purpose he considered good, the missionary from Africa put, guardedly, an interesting proposition. The Shah had set his face against Christian missionaries, yet, as Christ had enjoined, there was an obligation upon all sincere and committed Christians to go abroad and spread the Gospel. Now, were he to possess D'Arcy's document, he would, as the missionary from Africa, be at liberty to take others in at will, with the Shah's permission and so in due course that heathen country could be converted by these missionaries. If you like, it was conceived, as a sort of religious Trojan Horse.

D'Arcy bit at the bait, seeing the proposition as a worthy use of his concession and also as a release from the fierce competition with which he was beset on all sides. He handed over his concession — and Sidney Reilly, one of the most brilliant and resourceful spies ever to work for the British Secret Service, secured thereby an historic coup. Throughout that sea voyage Reilly, in a dreamy, clerical way, had played the sleeper, though but for a brief while. His role, admittedly, was different to that of the spy put into an organisation for a long while, to await activation as occasion might demand, but there is one strongly valid point of comparison — it was certainly industrial espionage with a vengeance!

Strangely, it was a missionary, the Reverend Harwood who, in the course of years of evangelising in Iraq — not, even then, very promising territory for such activities — had managed to get the good will of Emirs and to convert many thousands to the Christian faith. Most of the time he was working amongst nomadic people, and his travels took him all over the country, including many long and dangerous journeys through the desert.

Like D'Arcy, he saw the value of oil, and obtained many concessions in the course of his wanderings. His amiable disposition, his physical courage (always admired by Arabs) and his fluent spoken Arabic smoothed his way. As he reached the age of eighty, he needed a younger man to help in his work. He found such a one, and, when he died, left him his concessions. But here again, according to historians of the growth of the oil industry, British

Intelligence had played a part. In this case, the sleeper infiltrated into the missionary's small entourage and had to wait a long time before his plan could become effective.

In modern times, sleepers are thoroughly trained in the qualifications they will need, and 'planted' in a rival organisation, there to work, wait and observe, and to work their way up into positions of trust and responsibility until more and more confidential matters are available to them, or their source know. With the growth in size and scope of indigenous companies, and the growth of huge and rival international consortiums, the stakes are larger, the plans for informational piracy more ambitious and more heavily financed, and the methods pursued more sophisticated.

If you were looking for a 'sleeper' within your own organisation, what first signs would you look for?

Firstly, the sleeper would be somebody whose job kept him informed of policies, plans, formulae, production methods or the details of quotations received or submitted.

Secondly, the real sleeper is unlikely to be in any of the obvious senses, conspicuous; over-dressing, over-entertaining, exceeding one's known income in obvious ways such as possessing jewellery, expensive cars or taking costly holidays are not likely to be signs of a sleeper, although they would certainly arouse suspicion. After all, if a man chooses to do without smoking and spends hundreds of pounds on a night at the Ritz instead, nobody is to deny him. There can be innocent explanations for apparent over-spending — a win at gambling, a bequest, a profitable sale of some asset, such as a home, which has appreciated in value. A sleeper new to his conspiratorial job *might* attract attention in such ways — but it is unlikely.

A sleeper may, however, show interest in aspects of management, methods and plans which are extraneous to his own field of interest in the company (or organisation) and which do not bear explanation. It is no bad thing for an employee on any level to want to be informed about his employers; but information which would not normally come his way, or which is specifically withheld from all but a few selected staff or directors, is another matter. The more so if the suspected sleeper reverts to the subject, having once failed to get an answer to a question ("have they got the contract with —— yet?" — "Why are we opening up in Angola? I thought we were already exporting to them there").

A sleeper may be first at work and last away, or have an unexplained or inordinate passion for overtime. Most people, of course, like to be able to earn a little overtime money, while there still exist some conscientious workpeople and executives who do not like to leave a job half done merely because it is officially the end of their working day, and so prefer to stay after hours. Where, however, this staying on in the office or workshop alone falls into a consistent pattern, the question may well be asked (of oneself, not of the person under surveillance!) why that employee likes to be alone, and so unobserved, so much and so often. As for consistently taking work home, a practice very common today, not excepting the Civil Service, it is, from any security point of view, deplorable. There is always the possibility — even if the act of taking documents home is well-intentioned or perfectly innocent — of the case being lost or stolen — stolen in transit or from the place to which it is taken. In any case, documents taken away from the premises can easily be photocopied. Whole files of companies have been copied in this way.

There is no particular kind of person likely to be a sleeper. They may be young or old, poor or prosperous, intelligent or a bit dim. They will all be either corruptible or caught up in some messianic cause or other, some cause which seems to justify their actions to themselves.

Since sleepers are unlikely to be detected, it is of far greater importance to protect secrets at source, to limit rigidly and under proper controls the extent to which such secrets are allowed to circulate, and to keep effective and constant records of when, and to whom, files and documents are made available. Obviously the files and documents should all be given tamper-proof storage. The physical and planning aspects of protecting important data will be discussed later.

One characteristic common to sleepers — of working late after hours, or working during their holiday periods because they "can't leave the work" — has led many American concerns to make it mandatory for every member of the staff to take his or her full entitlement of holiday every year. And the habit of staying on at the office or works when others have gone home, on the pretext (sometimes genuine) of "wanting to catch up with things" is also increasingly discouraged. This, too, has been a frequent ruse of industrial spies.

*   *   *

It will be obvious to the reader that such cases of industrial espionage as receive publicity, do so merely because they have been uncovered, whether followed by legal action or not; it will be equally obvious that such cases represent the merest tip of the iceberg. In the very nature of their chosen calling, real industrial spies seek to avoid detection. The extent and damage of industrial espionage, measured against those whose designs have been uncovered and frustrated, prove that the majority of industrial spies cover their tracks very effectively indeed.

The reminder is essential because of the complacency which is so usual in a large and prosperous business. Commercial success begets a kind of cosy confidence. There is nothing wrong in confidence, a natural sequel to enterprise rewarded; but over-confidence easily becomes complacency, particularly where secur-ity matters are concerned. The executive reads that so-and-so has had his industrial secrets stolen. Foolish man! What is to be expected of such an incompetent rival, etc. etc. Now that could never happen to *him*. He is too observant, too discriminating in his choice of staff, too chary of discussing his business with anyone who is not a close and trusted colleague . . .

It is precisely this kind of cosy thinking which has made many industrial spying coups possible. The industrial spy is almost as common as the burglar — he is a sort of burglar, anyway, out to steal valuable secrets. He may even use some of the devices employed by the professional burglar. The assumption of personal invulnerabil-ity, and an under-estimation of the cunning and technical resources of the secrets thief are the two prime factors making such offences possible.

Having surveyed in following chapters in a general way the spy's aids to eavesdropping and surveillance, I must make the point that his potential armoury of gadgets and apparatus does not end with bugs, transmitters, tape-recorders, telescopes, binoculars, wire-tappers, cameras and the rest. The methods he may employ may demand supporting gadgetry of other kinds.

For example, disguises. The industrial spy, if he is tailing somebody to discover who his clients or associates are, will need to draw upon an extensive wardrobe. He may want to mix with city gents and be lost in a sea of black suits and white shirts. He may need to merge into a hippie background with scuffed shoes and dirty jeans. To gain illicit entry to factories, workshops or offices he may need the same sort of uniform, overalls or other clothing which would disarm suspicion.

There are, of course, many people in the underworld who specialise in makeup and disguises, but the true industrial spy is more likely to "go it alone" and do the job himself — but not without sound information. A variety of tinted spectacles and sun-glasses is one obvious item. Quite realistic wigs, toupees, moustaches, sideburns and beards are easily obtained, although expensive.

The infiltrating spy finds the guise of a refuse collector very useful. For the pose to be successful, he must ape the appearance of the kind of refuse collector commonly seen — no use turning up in, say Wimbledon in the bright blue overalls common to refuse collectors in the Royal Borough of Kensington! The industrial spy uses any uniform that serves his immediate purpose — whether of policeman, chauffeur, delivery man, gasman, electricity worker, post office engineer, health visitor, local council official or an official of any government ministry. Many industrial spies own their own stock-in-trade and would not care to risk hiring an appropriate uniform from, say, a theatrical costumier.

Illegal access to sources of industrial information, such as plans, designs, work layouts (and indeed, where portable, prototype models in themselves) may involve actual burglary — and, of course, may be the case where bugs, transmitters and similar apparatus is planted. In the U.S.A. and other countries there are, freely available, books listing the know-how of criminal behaviour with the utmost technical detail. One such book, which in the interests of law and order I prefer not to name, presupposes few scruples on the part of some of its readers. Listing the many types of surveillance, and coming to how to tail somebody on foot (which has frequently to be done) it says "Should the bus leave before you are able to board, grab a cab, *steal a car*, or some such, and follow the bus until he (i.e. the person being tailed) departs."

This particular book, of great usefulness to every kind of criminal, anarchist, terrorist or crackpot, gives detailed instructions for obtaining, or making, the tools necessary for picking locks, formulae for making explosives!

There are broadly four approaches most commonly used in industrial espionage — (a) mock interviews; (b) Subversive staff; (c) infiltration and (d) aggressive market research.

Mock interviews are really a confidence trick played on the employees of a rival company, in order to extract from somebody who thinks himself a prospective employee of the interviewing company, valuable information about a rival company. No doubt, but is he vulnerable? To what extent would he be likely to talk if he were approached about being given a new and better job by another company? So the ground is reconnoitred. The Voters List is examined to discover where he lives and the names of his neighbours. It being a fair bet that he banks with a local branch of the Big Four, a bogus credit agency call to the four branches will quickly establish where he has an account, while the feelers thus thrown out are untraceable: "The Something Credit Agency here. A small query — we didn't think it worth while taking up your time and ours in correspondence — but we've been asked to authorise a credit of £10,000 for Mr So-and-So. On our information he appears to be perfectly satisfactory and his request a viable one, but we felt we should ring you to confirm." Thus one of the four banks will probably acknowledge having such a customer, perhaps after unsuccessful approaches to other banks, and information may change hands. Details of his bank account may be covertly and perhaps illegally obtained by which it can be seen if he is always in the red and therefore a likely target.

Alternatively, a call to a Credit Bureau may produce a clue as to the man's credit worthiness. If he is in debt or difficulties, so much the better. Perhaps he gambles. Possibly his home mortgage and other expenses are too much for him. He may have recently married, perhaps started a family. He has extravagent tastes in clothing and entertainment. He is ambitious, efficient . . . and vulnerable.

Perhaps the company unearths such information by its own efforts, or use an industrial spy to procure it. Once possessing this necessary background, the rest is simple. They bug their victim's office so that every word spoken in their interviews with their victim goes on record. They draw up a list of points on which information is required, on a sheet of paper which rests inside the open drawer of their desk, perhaps on top, at any rate, visible to their caller. They write to him at his private address, confidentially, to the effect that an important vacancy is likely to occur shortly in their organisation. All this to judge his reactions.

Let us consider mock interviews first. Where industrial espionage is concerned, as distinct from an attempt to get a little, quick money on the side, there is always prior planning. Although apparatus and gadgets have often to be employed by the ideas and information thief, no intelligent man is going to bother with them if he can achieve his purposes by means which are either simpler in execution, or avoid the risks and physical difficulties of 'planting' bugs, transmitters and so on, on other people's premises.

The first requirement is sound information. The second, sound strategy.

A rival company is making a similar piece of apparatus to yours, and competing in the same fields for customers. Are they under-cutting you on quotations? Have they evolved some detail of production which gives them speedier and/or better quality of production? Are they planning to launch some new model, whose prototype you suspect exists, but whose existence has never been revealed? You have noticed a certain coolness on the part of your most important and profitable customer — what can it mean? That a rival company are courting your customer with promises of cheaper rates, speedier deliveries, better service or improved designs?

Well, how do you find an informant in that company?

You opt for what industrial spies sometimes call "the mock interview" — an interview arranged, ostensibly, with the object of offering a man a better job than he already has with his own company. But *who* will you interview? It has to be someone sufficiently senior to be well informed. You turn first to the most obvious source of information — the trade or specialised press. You read that a young man has recently been promoted to Sales Manager. He is only 26. Naturally, he will know what his employer's present and projected range of goods is; he will know who does what in his Company; in short, he will have much useful information. So you write to him to say that an important vacancy exists in your Company, and that someone has put forward his name as a man who might be interested in applying for the post. There are, you explain, several applicants, but he is on a short list of suitable potential employees, and, if he is interested, will he telephone for an appointment?

So an interview is mounted. You start by outlining your firm's activities in glowing colours (increasing business, high quality products and services, happy, well-paid staff, good prospects, etc., etc.) and then ask the usual, normal questions about his present prospects, his salary and what degree of improvement in both may induce him to change his employers. Gradually you draw him on his company's activities, moving carefully from requests for information already in the public domain to questions more probing and private: the size of that company's staff, their principal customers, their sources of materials and services, their marketing plans, their work sequences and production plans. A friendly atmosphere is maintained, but the atmosphere is kept sufficiently formal and dignified to maintain the fiction that an important company with something worthwhile to offer as a job, is carefully vetting applicants for so important a post. Once you have squeezed from him information like a lemon, you tell him that a decision will be made within a stated period, and that he will be advised of the result.

Most people at some time in their lives are interviewed for jobs in which they hope to better themselves, and unless the man is especially sharp, he will not realise that he has been cruelly hoodwinked. Everything he has said has been tape-recorded and transcribed.

There may be unexpected and welcome by-products of the interview. The young man may, supposedly in confidence, have expressed dislike of some senior executive, commenting, perhaps on his excessive expenses, his dubious moral life, or the fact that he is in disfavour with the board, and likely to be pushed out of the company. If such a man is in receipt of board secrets, and familiar with the structure and policy of the company, he, too, can either be suborned by being offered a job more profitable than his present one, or even find himself being blackmailed into the disclosure of information. In such a case the company is unlikely to show its hand direct, but to deal with the victim through an intermediary, probably a professional industrial spy or one of the spy's associates. Thus, subversive staff can be recruited and controlled as a secondary step to the mock interviews.

As in ordinary espionage, with which there are certain parallels in procedure and technique on occasions, the stooge will probably find himself treated — after the 'honeymoon' period of sweet words and sweeter money — to decidedly more arbitrary treatment. As one detailed handbook on how to be a social nuisance puts it (*apropos* industrial spying): The spy is at work:

> You can either flash some phoney identification badge or just imply you've been hired to do an investigation. What sort of investigation? My first choices are 'The Management wants to know what certain employees are up to and wants your help' or the 'I've been hired by a company which is thinking of buying this company and wants a friend on the inside'. In either approach, you must convince the guy he is an 'investigative consultant', or even assistant detective.

> The first thing is to put him on a "retainer". Lay a couple of hundred on the buy and ask some idiotic questions about what he has noticed, or how to boost output, or who's doing his job (properly) and who is not. Get the guy thinking the management (or new management) is putting a lot of faith in his opinion, get his ego as large as possible.

That's the honeymoon period, as one may fairly describe the initial efforts of an industrial spy to suborn a likely informant. But, since fear is often a more effective control than bland inducements, the tone of the relationship soon changes. An industrial spy is out to get results, and is not concerned with the individuals who enable him to do this, or the methods by which his profitable ends may be achieved. He is concerned with getting results as quickly as possible, by whatever means, and collecting his rewards. As in war, it is the result that matters and not the casualties that lead to victory. So the crunch comes:

> After a few weeks of listening faithfully to his "reports" you change his "retainer" over to a check . . . after he cashes a couple of your checks you lay it a bit heavier . . . he is to steal, get, photograph, or just help you to get into the plant/office alone some evening. Once you're inside of course, your friend is promptly told to get lost, or to "guard" the door. If he baulks at any point you lay out a double payment and remind him of the checks he has cashed. *A few prudent words here about what his employers would do if they saw the checks or the fact that you are both going to jail if necessary will destroy most morals faster than you can say Shazam.*

One ploy, and especially if your victim works in a highly specialised calling which has its own trade newspaper or periodical, is to advertise a vacancy whose requirements fit the victim absolutely. Thus, if the man you want to turn informant is in a senior position, but not particularly young, the advertisement can include such phrases as "maturity of experience and judgement more important than age" and, if the intended victim is known to have a penchant for night clubs or the social life, "the work involves participation in interesting social life and would appeal to man with sophisticated tastes . . ."

The point of such an advertisement is to get the intended victim ringing for an appointment once the advertisement has caught his eye. It makes an even better opening than an approach to him.

To the susceptible business man, the experienced call girl who works either for or in conjunction with an industrial spy, makes an easy bait. Her car can break down on the road he is known to use; conveniently, they find themselves bumping into each other in a club, pub or hotel. Once the man has carried his involvement as far as the bedroom, he can expect bullying correspondence or visits from real or alleged husbands or lovers of the decoy. Both in actual or industrial espionage, it is amazing how this hackneyed device works. Yet cases are constantly being reported in which it has.

The business of infiltration (gaining access to plant, offices and premises for the purpose of observation and the theft of information, in whatever form) is by no means as difficult as some might imagine. Access to premises whose security is supposedly strict is often laughably easy. The *bona fides* of industrial spies or their agents, dressed as refuse collectors, telephone engineers, office cleaners, window cleaners and so on, are seldom checked. It is not difficult to dress up like a workman, carry a well-battered bucket and leathercloth, and find your way into some inner sanctum. Telephones seldom go right for long, so almost anybody who looks the part and carries some obvious electronic gear can come in response to an alleged telephone fault.

But the phoney office cleaner is perhaps the most-favoured infiltrator. In one huge factory a pair of them went round with a bin collecting all the waste in sight. On another occasion a large wicker basket on wheels was pushed around, large as life, with the letters "for shredding" on it. Needless to say, the unwanted documents never reached the shredder!

The carelessness of quite responsible (by which I mean, seemingly responsible) organisations such as banks and insurance companies often passes belief, proving how even an amateur industrial spy can sometimes have an easy bonanza. For example, passing some refuse bins in the City of London, bins so crammed with abandoned files that they were spilling over on to the pavement, I picked one up, as a matter of idle curiosity. It contained all the documents pertaining to an insurance policy for theft. The insured party's name and address were there. So was the sum insured — an indication of the value of the property so protected. The correspondence inside the file included a list of six addresses at which securities were held. All this information was confidential to the insurer and the insured, yet, as with the other scores of files thrown out for the dustman to collect, it could be collected by anybody who bothered to pick it up. It would, indeed, have constituted no offence had the whole load of files been taken away by anybody; the property was abandoned. I accept that this opinion can be argued at law.

Once inside premises, the industrial spy finds everything far easier than many might suppose. The waste-paper baskets will be crammed with discarded notes, faulty carbon copies, photocopied material, sometimes even discarded shorthand books. Used carbon ribbons provide easy reading of the letters which were typed through them; each letter leaves a clear transparent imprint. Writing pads can be read, even when a sheet on which the note was written has been detached and taken away. The tiny ball-bearing of somebody's ballpoint pen, or the hardened graphite of a lead pencil, or the pressure of a fountain pen's gold nib, leave an incised record of the writing on the blank sheet below. There are many methods of reading this "invisible" writing. The most elementary, and perhaps the cheapest and most effective, is to *lightly* rub the lead of a 6B pencil (not point at right angles to the paper, but keeping the lead as near horizontal to the paper as possible) over the paper's surface. The lead will miss the shallow crevices left by the writing, which then becomes clearly visible. There is also sophisticated equipment available which does this.

Few filing cabinets pose any problem to an industrial spy. They usually have the cheapest locks, easily picked. Tape recordings, photocopies, correspondence, designs, contracts, staff records — all offer a rich harvest, and are usually very insecurely protected. Indeed, in my long experience of checking premises for security weaknesses I have quite often found that doors to vital departments are unlocked, that files are not closed, and desks in particular left with all their drawers unlocked.

Once he has gained access, by whatever means, the experienced industrial spy knows what it is he seeks, and homes in on his material. But even if the territory and layout are strange to him, the sources I have mentioned, which are by no means all, will, probably, not only give him what he seeks but much else besides.

Finally, what is called, euphemistically, "aggressive market research". It means, in simple language, finding out all you can of your competitors' plans, methods, production schedules, sales techniques, markets, resources, staff, salary scales, designs, work schedules, production sequences, sources of raw materials and spare parts, formulae and future development plans.

Much of this can be culled from printed sources. It is a mistake, however, to suppose that any minor clerk can do it. What is spotted, and noted, depends upon the alertness of the individual reader and his knowledge of his firm's requirements. In short, it needs both know-how and imagination.

Advertisements for personnel may indicate the enlargement of one or more departments in the rival firm. Advertisements of a highly specialised character may, properly analysed, be of great significance. An advertisement for a personnel manager may indicate the extent of the work force he will be expected to manage — and the figure may be higher than was commonly supposed.

Market research, however, as Louis Moreau, the self-confessed industrial spy, and author of *So you want to be an industrial spy?* so amiably points out, is an ideal cover for industrial espionage. Market researchers habitually devise Questionnaires containing very many questions. It is the analyses of such questions which may give them a line on their competitor. Suppose that one breakfast food manufacturer is spying on another; suppose, on the pretext of studying the nation's breakfast preferences, the question were posed; "Do you eat a proprietory breakfast food — if so, which?" That looks straightforward enough. But if the survey should be nationwide, and an unusual incidence of consumption of the rival breakfast food is noted in a particular town or county, this could presage some breakthrough in industrial intelligence. The industrial spy would immediately ask himself — *why?* Why that area?

Purchase of the same product in the "exceptional" area and the "normal" area might supply the answer. Is there a difference in the packaging? Is some new sales approach being used, as a pilot scheme, in the unusually successful area? Is there some ingredient in the food offered in the area where sales are strongest, which is not to be found in the areas where sales are lower? Perhaps a laboratory analysis of different packets of the food might show that those which sold most were being tried out in the high-sales area without advertising to reveal the fact that some alteration had been made in the formula. (Note: Although this instance is a hypothetical one, I can assure the reader that it is not unduly fanciful; long ago, for example, one famous manufacturer of brass polish sold, under identical labels, two different formulae. The mixture sold in the North of England demanded more elbow-grease than that sold in the South. The manufacturers knew that Northerners liked to put plenty of elbow-grease into the operation, and got less satisfaction if the shining result was produced too early. More recently, a famous brandy company put expensive cognac brandy into ordinary bottles without revealing that the contents were of unusual quality. The sales rocketed and, once at a healthy level, the exceptional quality was dropped and the ordinary quality bottled instead).

It will be seen that industrial espionage is conducted very easily — though expensively — under the umbrella of a market research firm.

Business Intelligence Units, which have become, increasingly, a department of large industrial complexes, use methods which often come near to outright spying. Such units frequently comprise an intelligence director, statisticians, analysts, archivist (for listing sources of data) and, very probably, a computer expert as well. Writing of industrial spies as long as two decades ago, Richard Gelman wrote in *Cosmopolitan* magazine: "In business it's not only ethical to steal secrets, it's obligatory. If you're planning to stay in business, that is."

Somethimes, of course, market research is made a mere excuse for access to a business organisation, an excuse to speak to employees. Questions such as "Where do you go for your annual holiday" or "what cigarettes do you smoke?" may be wholly irrelevant to the true nature of the operation; they may be a mere opening ploy by which to strike up a personal relationship with employees, who may be approached on a later occasion and pumped for inside information about their company.

When the Harvard Graduate School of Business Administration did a survey on industrial espionage, they discovered that, in a survey of 200 companies, some 27 percent reported that spying or other types of under-cover information collecting had recently been discovered in their industry. Executives asked as to the extent of industrial spying in their industry showed that nearly six percent had noticed specific instances of it. A much higher percentage (17.5%) had evidence of spying against *their* companies. The disparity between these proportions may be explained by the fact that most people are readier to expose spying by others and are considerably more reticent when it comes to admitting that they do any spying themselves!

In the same survey, 77% of executives questioned believed that there had been a sharp decline in ethical standards.

These are some of the approaches used, and some of the devices available to users. There remains for our examination, however, a most important, and ever-widening field of industrial espionage which, because of its technical complexity, makes it the biggest menace of all — computer espionage. Since computers store information of every imaginable subject, they offer a rich source of plunder to the technically-minded industrial spy.

CHAPTER 5

Bugs and Electronics

There was a time when a 'bug' meant an insect of some kind.

Nowadays, one thinks immediately of bureaucracy's secret armoury of electronic gadgets by which it can spy upon its own citizens, or those of other countries, or by which it can control its populace to greater or lesser degree.

This same armoury is at the disposal of legions of private investigators, criminals, crackpots, anarchists, the police and armed services of every country in the world — indeed, to anyone with the money to buy them, the knowledge of where to obtain them, and the technical know-how (in some cases negligible) necessary to operate them.

The range of hidden microphones, miniature radio transmitters, microscopic walkie-talkies, tape recorders, still or moving cameras and telephone bugs is now enormous. And in the ever-growing world of industrial espionage they are in increasing use. It would be correct to say that their use is out of hand.

Those concerned with security should neither exaggerate nor underestimate the range and uses of the tools of what is called, euphemistically, "electronic surveillance." It sounds so harmless. As a protection against terrorists, criminals and the requirements of protection of life and property, such apparatus and gadgetry have an obvious and legitimate purpose. Their repressive use against citizens in many countries in the world today and their very considerable use in the twin worlds of espionage and industrial espionage make it necessary to explain some of the categories of spying aids.

The legal and moral problems implied in the wholesale production, availability and use of instruments and apparatus used for surveillance and eavesdropping will be reviewed later. For the moment I am discussing the nature of such things, and the uses to which they have been, are and may be put.

Let us start with 'bugs'. I mean by this, eavesdropping devices which pick up noises and conversations electronically and surreptitiously, recording them on the spot, or perhaps siphoning the sound to some distant recording point, or transmitting the picked-up sounds by radio, to be received on a VHF receiver and, perhaps, recorded at that point as well.

I have myself conducted hundreds of sweeps to locate such bugs in boardrooms, offices, factory premises, hotels and private homes, by a procedure which I will describe later. I was recently called into an engineering company where a leakage of information was suspected within the company, for on a wage negotiation with a member of the union it was clear that certain of the company's confidential plans were known.

A search was made, and a bug, or radio transmitter, was found in the Managing Director's office. Investigation continued and a shop steward admitted planting the bug. His resignation was accepted and no further action was taken by the engineering company.

In that case a union official was spying on his employers. On one occasion it was Transport House, headquarters of the Labour Party in London. Mr Ralph Matthews, a director of Management Investigation Services, was carrying out a routine surveillance of a building nearby when he heard on his radio conversations clearly emanating from Transport House. These broadcasts continued for a considerable period in the early seventies, and although Transport House were informed, a surprisingly casual and unrealistic attitude was taken. Later Mr Matthews was walking to his car in Smith Square when he passed a van with three aerials on the roof. One of them he knew to be a small directional aerial. As he walked past he peeped inside and to his surprise saw a man sitting in the back, looking at him. The man signalled to the driver and they drove off, just brushing a car, which is the reaction of somebody doing something at which he does not wish to be caught. Mr Matthews gave chase in his car, but lost it.

At this time there had been a leak of a speech by Mr (Now Sir) Harold Wilson.

Months later Matthews saw another man was standing outside Transport House with an earpiece which was quite clearly part of a bugging device — i.e. of a type well known to be used to receive the short-wave transmissions of a bug.

Recently the Syrian Ambassador to Belgium, Mr Adib Daoudy, after a sweep of the embassy premises in search of bugs, was informed that hollowed-out wooden plants had been found containing hidden microphones. In this instance the search was made after neighbours had seen a light in the Embassy at night, when, as they knew, the building was normally deserted, and called the police.

A few years ago a radio ham, Mr William Borland, of Bromley, Kent, picked up a rather curious broadcast. He heard a voice saying "Get off the bed Bess . . . Daddy's going out now . . . be a good girl while I'm away." Knowing that no radio amateur would carry on such a weird conversation over the air, he used his radio receiver as a direction finder and narrowed the search to a hotel half a mile away. He then spoke to the proprietor:

"Do you know anyone who has a dog called Bess?"

"Yes," said the hotel proprietor, "I have — a Dalmatian."

"Well," said the radio ham, "you're being bugged."

In his bedroom, fixed to the wall behind his bed, was a tiny transmitter. The police were called. They watched and waited, and eventually pounced on a private detective, who had bugged the bedroom on behalf of a client in an attempt to secure evidence. There was none. Nearby was found a van, with a radio tuned in to the bug's wavelength, and a tape recorder recording everything said in the bedroom.

In Italy there has been an epidemic of bugging, some of it carried out by police who were formerly in public service. One chief commissioner of police was arrested on orders of a judge because he was found to be bugging the premises of political and business personalities.

It was the bugging of the Democratic Party's headquarters in Washington — after a break in to enable the bugs to be planted — that sparked off the Watergate Scandal and caused the ruin and disgrace of Ex-President Nixon. This case has been ventilated to such a degree that I need only say that bugging is so general in America that it would be unrealistic to suppose that — politically speaking — it is the monopoly of any one party or sectional interest. Its interest in this context is merely that it is a classic case of bugging as a means of stealing information, of the sort that is habitually used for the stealing of industrial secrets. The man who planted the bug in the hotel bedroom, and who eventually figured in a trial at the Old Bailey, told a reporter at the time: "Bugging is going on all the time. Everyone is doing it, and quite openly. I can't see anyone stopping it . . . when I was planting a bug I would gain entrance to the premises on any pretext, by saying I was a surveyor or a telephone engineer. Then I'd plant it and leave. After that it was simple . . ."

One of the oldest and most widely used of all system of eavesdropping is the *Microphone System.*

In simple terms, this means the placing of a microphone somewhere in a building, in any place where it can do its job of picking up whatever information is sought.

It may be simply a microphone, with wires (concealed, of course) leading to a recording or listening point. Nowadays, because of the rapid development of micro-electronics, the most sophisticated apparatus can be made smaller and smaller, becoming easier to carry and simpler to hide from view. For this reason, although permanent microphone systems are 'built in' to such buildings as hotels in Iron Curtain countries, allowing all conversation to be monitored at a central point, the spy, and the industrial spy, will mostly prefer the true bug, or microphone-transmitter. My description describes its function; it hears, it transmits. According to the cost and construction of the apparatus, it may transmit over a very limited radius, say 200 metres, or over a far longer distance, from 1000 metres upwards.

The older microphone system has features which make it more secure (for the eavesdropper, not the target!) than the transmitter. If the sound goes direct to the listening point *by wire* there is no transmission to be picked up on a particular frequency, as happened in the case of the radio ham who, accidentally, found himself listening to sounds being broadcast by a hidden transmitter from a bugged hotel bedroom. The wired sound can be directed straight into a tape recorder for permanent record, and may be monitored by either loudspeaker or headphones.

Where a microphone system is a permanent installation, it may literally be anywhere — in an electric switch, in a tiny hole bored into a skirting or wall, in a ventilating shaft.

There are various types of microphones. None of them is limited in use. Each can be linked or adapted to any other surveillance system, such as bugs and so on.

The earliest microphone, invented by Alexander Graham Bell in 1876 was a carbon microphone, which, with little variation, has been almost generally used through the telephone systems of the world, and is still very widely used today. It is featured in the mouthpiece, and owes its popularity to its ruggedness and ability to stand up to strain and to changes in humidity and temperature.

The carbon mike must be activated by a low-voltage electrical supply, to which it is connected by terminals at the end of wires. The mild current flows down one wire, through the microphone and back to the eavesdropper. While the electrical impulse performs this round-Robin journey, modulations of the current are caused by the sounds picked up by the microphone.

The carbon microphone is larger and clumsier, however, than the *Magnetic Microphone*. Its principle is simple. A magnet, placed near a coil of wire, will cause an electrical current to flow through it. The magnetic microphone can convert sounds into electrical signals by vibrating a coil of wires. The advantage of the magnetic mike in eavesdropping is that it can be very small (as small as the cap of a collar stud, even smaller than that if necessary) and requires no other power to operate it.

Of course, if the magnetic microphone is allied to a transmitter, the transmitter must have power, perhaps (and more usually) from a small battery, to broadcast the sounds that are being picked up. These magnetic or dynamic microphones, because they can be so small, can be incorporated into a wide range of innocent-looking objects such as cuff links, tie pins, spectacles, ashtrays and so on. They are the heart, if that is the right word, of the modern bug.

Superior, for the purposes of eavesdropping, is the *Electret Microphone*. This does require, because it is non-magnetic, low-voltage power which activates a built-in amplifier. Thus it has the sensitivity and smallness of the magnetic microphone, but because of its power source and built-in amplifier, emits a stronger signal. Spies prefer this microphone because it is more difficult (though not impossible) to detect and more resistant to electronic neutralisation — i.e. will evade and stand up better to systems of jamming, or other counter-measures.

Low Level Sound Microphones have been specially sensitised to pick up very small volumes of sound, such as a whisper from a far corner of a room. For fairly obvious reasons, they are favourite with the professional industrial spy; it is unlikely that anyone but a professional would know they existed, even less where to procure them.

Finally, there are *Contact, Spike and Pneumatic Microphones* which in given circumstances are used by spies, industrial or otherwise.

Spike mikes are microphones with a difference. They do not pick up sounds from the air, but respond to the vibrations of the surface to which they are attached. They contain a crystal which, when slightly compressed, will produce an electrical signal. Thus, if a probe is placed against a vibrating surface, there will be corresponding — though faint — signals, which are translated into sound by the terminal apparatus. If the original sounds causing the vibration happen to be speech, then the end result will be the speech that is being made.

Though often used for illegal purposes, there are disadvantages and limitations involved in their use. The spike mike has two parts — a probe which drills a hole in the wall, and the spike mike which fits that cavity and impinges against a hole. But breeze blocks and most brickwork are awkward media in which to install it and, needless to say, since the idea is to hear what is being said the other side of the wall, it does not help to drill too clumsily or vigorously and leave tell-tale plaster, broken paint chips, sawdust or brick dust on the other side!

Less frequently used, but much favoured by professional spies (in which I include, as I invariably intend to do, *industrial* spies, the kind with which we are primarily concerned) are *cavity microphones*. Again, their purpose is to eavesdrop on an adjoining room. The cavity helps a conventional microphone by responding to surface vibrations. Only an expert would be likely to acquire, or be competent to install and use, such a microphone.

To come back to 'bugs' — the concealed microphone-cum-radio transmitter, in 1973. *The Times* of London estimated the turnover of the bugging industry in Britain to be 'above a million pounds a year' and although, in the nature of things, that could be little more than a guess, it is totally out of date now. My own estimate would be vastly above that figure — certainly more than £5 million a year.

I have for a number of years campaigned to make the sale of such bugs illegal and punishable as a criminal offence. They are clearly an intrusion into privacy to a degree which is intolerable in a democracy, and places in the hands of enemies of democracy a lethal weapon of blackmail and intimidation. Bugs could be described as one of the mainstays of the industrial spy. Many other devices are available to him, and many non-technical means of stealing vital information are open to him. But micro-transmitters, or bugs, are now so small, so effective and so ubiquitous that, unless the entire population gets into the habit of carrying bug-detectors with them everywhere they go (including bed) nobody's privacy can be secure, and nobody's secrets, industrial or otherwise, secure from theft.

Since bug-detectors are expensive and need expert knowledge to use, it is obvious that only in legislation, enforced with all the rigour of the law to discourage the offence and to punish it when discovered, can a remedy be found.

In Britain microbugs are regularly advertised and the fact that these advertisements appear constantly is sufficient indication that regular and profitable sales must result. Nobody *continues* to advertise a product if it does not sell in the first place. It is quite true that the Wireless and Telegraphy Act of 1949 prohibits the use of a radio transmitter without a licence; but who is to implement such an act if the means of breaking the law are so freely available?

On 8th August 1980 Mr Kenneth Warren, Conservative M.P. for Hastings, asked the Secretary of State for the Home Department for an estimate of the number of low power, including walkie-talkie, transmitters now operating illegally in the United Kingdom. Mr Timothy Raison, M.P. replied:

> We have no information on which such an estimate could reliably be based. As my Hon. Friend indicated on 15th April in reply to a question by the Hon. Member for Coventry, South-West (Mr Butcher) during the first quarter of this year some 8,800 illicit citizens' band stations were heard by officials of the Post Office Interference Service in the course of their duties.

The number of illicit stations heard 'in the course of their duties' would, I submit, be no guide to the numbers in use. It is a technical impossibility to comb the air for every illicit citizens' band radio for the good reason that they do not all operate at once, nor necessarily to any predictable time routine. Many stations are detected but are off the air before they can be located. Imagine monitoring an area such as London, with its seven million citizens — more than the population of Australia!

Without resorting to guesswork, or speculating as to the proportion of illegal broadcasts which it is possible to detect with the limited staff and equipment employed by the Post Office for this purpose, my own estimate of illicit broadcasts being made at a given time would be not less than 40,000. Even the spokesman for the Home Office had to confess that there was no basis on which he could proffer an estimate.

Exchange and Mart of the 4th February 1982 contained thirteen advertisements originating from 10 companies, firms or individuals, advertising bugging equipment Admittedly the magazine warns its readers (it had a general readership) that it is an offence to use transmitting equipment without a Home Office licence, but it is difficult to imagine any ordinary person buying such a device if they had no intention of using it.

Some of the devices offered to the British public include:

> A miniature VHF/FM transmitter for use in "security, surveillance, alarms, entertainment", operating on an ordinary PP3 battery. The device has a range of 500 yards and sells at £16.95. A "mini micron" with the more limited range of 50 yards is cheaper at £12.95.
>
> A Micro Transmitter described as "a marvel of miniaturisation" measuring only 1½″ × 1¼″ × ¾″ with a hypersensitive shirt-button type microphone picks up and transmits up to 500 yards, any sounds made in a room. It operates on the easily procurable 6 volt battery type 537. It is totally self-contained with no external connections. Adhesive pads enable it to be fitted "in any discreet place" (i.e. out of sight!) It comes with self-adhesive pads (for sticking it in some "discreet place".)

A "postage size" FM transmitter is offered for £25 by an advertiser who deals in mail order only.

A miniature listening device with sophisticated circuitry and having a range of 1¾ miles is offered by one advertiser for the extraordinarily low price of £9.50.

Another transmitter is guaranteed to "pick up whispers with crystal clarity," with no explanation (none being necessary) of what sort of person would have any interest in picking up whispers with crystal clarity and picking them up on a radio receiver up to a mile away.

More surprising still is the offer, through the columns of the *Exchange & Mart* of a "unique drop-in telephone microphone capsule" "Which replaces standard capsule in telephone handset." This is quite one of the most mischievous bugging devices in existence, the use of which, in the United Kingdom certainly, is illegal.

The "drop-in" telephone bug replaces the existing microphone in the telephone handset, fitting snugly into place and enabling the phone to be used in the normal way, while acting also as a micro-transmitter of everything said on the telephone and in the room or office. Since it duplicates perfectly the natural indigenous part of the telephone, it is not likely to be detected by anyone not initially suspicious, and, unlike 'planted' micro transmitters which run on batteries, the drop-in draws its power from the telephone itself, while the existing wiring acts as an antennae.

Freely available from a firm in Tottenham, London, is the "Tele Ear" (Infinitely Transmitter) Type TE1B, "for transmissions via the public telephone system."

Such telephone bugs have been easily available in the U.S.A. since the sixties, and have only recently been more widely sold (and, presumably, more widely used!) in Europe in general and Britain in particular. The differences in the respective telephone systems of the U.S.A. and the U.K. have meant that such bugs bought from or in the U.S.A. could not easily be adapted to use in Britain. And they cost between £400 and £1500.

Details of the infinity transmitter offered in the U.K. by this particular supplier offer facilities which would make an industrial spy's mouth water, e.g.:—

> No batteries required
> Supersensitive Electret microphone
> Easy to install — just connect 2 wires
> Self-answering facility
> Does not radiate radio signals
> No attention required once installed
> Smaller than a packet of cigarettes
> Does not affect normal operation of phone
> Virtually undetectable by P.O. line check
> Cuts off automatically if the phone is picked up while it is in operation.

The device, when fitted to a target phone, permits the monitoring of any sounds in its immediate area, from a telephone call made *from anywhere in the world* provided it is on the SDT system. If an industrial spy chose to plant one of these in the phone of a managing director, foreman, works manager, embassy or anywhere else, he could thereafter telephone from anywhere else on earth — from Tibet, Hong Kong, Novosibirsk or Birmingham. A simple induction coil, held against the telephone used by the eavesdropper could "siphon" the stolen sound into a tape recorder. The firm offered two types of these bugs. In the first mode the target phone can be called — as already stated— from any other phone. When the call is answered, the eavesdropper waits until the receiver is replaced after saying "sorry, wrong number" or making some other excuse, and then whistles into the phone. The device acts on a tone frequency which causes the bug to switch on, picking up noises and conversations for as long as the eavesdropper chooses to listen. There is another model which operates as soon as the call is received, often without the phone bell ringing at all. Ostensibly, it is sold to enable you "to monitor your home or your business premises."

However, while the facts of bugging devices are alarming enough, sensational or grossly inaccurate accounts of their possibilities tend to lessen the impact of genuine warnings, by making everyone doubt the claims made about bugs.

One example of this is a reference by Robert Farr in *The Electronic Criminals* (McGraw Hill Book Company) on page 97 of which he refers to the harmonica bug in a completely wrong concept. He claims "this is a device which you can hook up to your own telephone. Then you can dial any number, regardless of distance. An electronic tone oscillator deactivates the rigger of the distant telephone and opens up the microphone. This allows you to hear any sound within earshot of that telephone . . ."

Farr goes on to say that he once hooked up an infinity transmitter to a telephone in London and dialled a number in Los Angeles which had a direct line to the desk, claiming that he "heard his voice" as he gave dictation to his secretary as loud and clear as if he were in the next room. This is a mis-statement. I am thankful that it *is* for it would be a dreadful situation if the claim were true.

The sales literature of one firm (which is in no way breaking the law, or attempting to break the law, since under present law such gadgetry may be legally offered for sale) carries a solemn warning note:

> WARNING NOTE: The Post Office does not approve of the connection of unauthorised devices to their 'phone lines. The TE1B is intended to be used as a means of providing remote security monitoring of your own premises. To fit it into another's phone without their consent or for the purpose of bugging would almost certainly constitute a criminal offence and render you liable to prosecution.

In other words, "on your own head be it". The price of this particular piece of specialised merchandise is £159.00, not the sort of price most people would be willing to pay for something they did not intend to use.

The same firm also offers a miniature transmitter which can be sited, not merely into the receiver of a telephone, but at some convenient point along the line, such as a junction box; it can even be fitted on a telegraph pole or external junction box, since it is weatherproof. Once installed, this model, the TM3, needs no batteries or further attention. Whenever the telephone is used both sides of the conversation will be transmitted on a frequency of 114 mHz (Megahertz) where it can be picked up on a VHF Air Band radio.

In the U.S.A., telephone eavesdropping has reached such a scale that "most public officials and businessmen in America today are afraid to use the telephone except for the most casual conversations" (Govenor Grant Sawyer of Nevada in 1962, after 22 FBI bugs were found secreted in casinos in Las Vegas.)

When the *Washington Post* conducted a survey of the extent of eavesdropping in February, 1971, it was discovered that "about a quarter of the senators, congressmen, lawyers, businessmen and journalists" suspected or believed that their homes and/or offices were bugged.

Machine Design published a case history of how a bug was used to wrest important industrial secrets from a rival:

> The information leak was noticed almost as soon as it started. Somehow, the engineering secrets of the large West Coast company were getting to a competitor. Thinking it must be an internal leak, this company launched an investigation of personnel.
>
> After a year, with negative results and the leak still unplugged, the personnel director began to campaign for a professional countermeasure sweep. It took six more months before management agreed to the operation.
>
> The sweep was carried out and found a bug was being used to bypass the hook switch on the telephone in the key executive's private office. This microphone, which drew its power from the circuit, had been continuously picking up all conversations in the office and transmitting them out of the building over the phone lines. The eavesdropper was never caught, but the leak was finally plugged after 18 months and losses totalling $1,000,000,000.00 — (a billion dollars).

This is not only a classic example of the effective deployment of a bug, but an instance of how matters had been left to drift, because of the *assumption* that the leakage must have been an insider. A security professional could paraphrase a well-known motto — "A sweep in time saves nine."

A variation of the "infinity transmitter", sometimes known as the "harmonica bug" because it is activated by a caller blowing a whistle or a note on a harmonica (some now made respond to several different notes) is known as a "listen back" or "keep alive". These do not require a note of a given frequency to be transmitted over the telephone line to the target telephone by the eavesdropper, but once installed in the target telephone, hold the line open between the target telephone and the eavesdropper's listening post — i.e. his telephone, or whatever telephone he elects to be using. In other words, although the handset is resting properly on its cradle, and in the ordinary way the line should be closed, the line remains open between both telephones, the target phone's microphone picking up and transmitting along the ordinary telephone line all the sounds within the target's phone area.

The listener, of course, may amplify the sounds he receives, if he so wishes. Thus, a whisper in the corner of even the largest office, transmitted over the telephone, can be amplified to full pitch.

Such is the speed with which the world of electronics develops new or more sophisticated techniques that, in a certain sense, everything electronic is out-dated the moment it comes from the workshop or assembly line.

I am not saying that the devices will not do — and continue to do — what it claimed for them. But in the field of development, where countless millions are at stake, there is continual research for new and better methods.

Suppliers of such equipment are active throughout the world. The source of supply is Pan Universe International Ltd., of Tel Aviv, Israel, whose W24H bug guarantees "unlimited range electronic monitoring". "Wherever a telephone exists, the device will "listen-in", from any other place equipped with a telephone, on the sounds in that area — *there is no distance limit*. It operates under all conditions, is smaller than a matchbox, and turns an ordinary telephone into a highly powered and sensitive microphone. The device is manufactured in a single casting and is therefore hermetically sealed and not affected by temperature or humidity." The suppliers claim, with perfect truth, I am sure, that their device is "now much used by Intelligence Agencies, Government Departments and Police forces in various parts of the world."

This model is sensitive enough to pick up sounds in adjoining rooms, up to a radius of 50 metres. Installation takes seconds, and can be done even by an unquallified technician. It is claimed that it can be installed for lifetime use, requires no batteries (since it draws its power from the telephone line) and cannot be detected by any means. Its operation is simple, once it is installed. When you wish to listen in, you dial from any telephone, anywhere in the world, and, when the telephone has been answered and the receiver replaced, you whistle into the mouthpiece with a specially-supplied whistle. This activates the device.

Europe is not only a busy manufacturing centre for all manner of surveillance and bugging equipment, but also a centre of supply for customers throughout the world. All maintain, with varying degrees of sincerity, that such apparatus is intended only for use by authorities although few, if any, are in any position to ensure that such goods, once they leave their control, will be used responsibly and legally. They are in business to sell things, and sell things they do. Law is the responsibility of the countries concerned.

In pointing out that the sort of devices I am describing could be used for criminal purposes, or in unethical ways, I do not ascribe blame to the suppliers, because it is not their business to make laws. Some, however, may see an element of cynicism, or at least of naivete, in their assumption that the snooping and surreptitious listening, made possible by the goods they sell, are always for a good and ethical purpose.

The catalogue of Maison Prati-Electro of Brussels, offers a wide range of listening devices for "Prevention — Watching — Protection — Detection". The advantages of the merchandise offered are further expounded:

> Avec quelque patence de la part de l'inquisiteur, cette écoute est révélétrice des délits, des intentions de délits, des trahisons d'employés ou de collaborateurs, des vols, des complicités, des actions sociales du type revolutionnaire, des commentaires de représentants aux clients, des fuites et indiscretions professionalles (lorsqu'on est tenu au secret), d'infidélités commerciales ou familiales . . .

There follow an enormous range of electric snooping gadgets, from FM transmitters to postage-stamp-size bugs, "drop-in" phone mikes, office ash-trays with micro-transmitterrs concealed inside, sub-miniature micro-transmitters concealed inside fibre pencils which actually write — and one mike-transmitter no larger than a lump of sugar, which can be stuck under a table, placed in a vase, or behind a picture, or anywhere. Woe to the erring wife whose husband, suspecting "infidélités familiales", buys one of these!

The line illustrations accompanying the photographs of the items offered for sale leave little to the imagination. A man sits at his desk, telephone to ear. A zig-zag, representative of a radio wave, goes through the open window straight into a waiting car. A snooper stands outside a window, a suction mike affixed to the glass, smiling beatifically as he listens in to the conversation inside the apartment. There is not space to list all the apparatus here; it could truly be called a cornucopia of spying devices. Inevitably much of it finds its way to industrial spies. Anyone may set up as a private detective, or as a security agency or consultant. The mere description is considered a sufficient qualification to buy such equipment, even though, for want of any satisfactory system of registration or vetting, many operatives engage in illegal activities. Many, indeed, are bona fide security experts with high ethical standards, engaged in counter-industrial espionage. On the other hand, some may with equal impunity, undertake spying missions on behalf of industrial clients.

There was a clear case of industrial espionage when the security staff of a well-known business machines firm got busy in the Paris Hilton Hotel a week before a rival firm was due to move in for a top-secret sales conference. Somehow, they had learned which rooms were to be occupied by the staff of the rival firm, and managed to install 'drop-in' telephone bugs. While the conference was in progress, they listened in to transmissions of the top-secret sales discussions.

It is by no means only 'Iron Curtain' countries where telephone tapping is commonplace in hotels, or where bugs are planted to pick up room conversations. The planting of 'drop-in' telephone bugs, which transmit noises from the room in which the telephone is installed, is certainly resorted to by hotels in London, New York, Paris, Amsterdam, Berlin and many other capitals — often, one suspects, with the full knowledge of the hotel management, if not indeed for their own purpose.

There is absolutely no problem in buying "drop-in" telephone bugs. These can be bought in England and, indeed, in most European countries, as well as the U.S.A. and Asia. They are even on sale in the duty-free shop at Schipol Airport in Amsterdam, Holland and at Hong Kong Airport.

In 1974 the fabulous yacht of Onassis, the Greek millionaire shipowner, was heavily bugged by a 'security expert' who managed to secure an invitation to one of the many lavish parties for which the multi-millionaire was famous. He managed to install microscopic bugs and telephone tappers in various cabins, even in the radio-telephone room. As the guests included people prominent in politics as well as the usual admixture of playboys, playgirls and showbiz personalities, with the necessary sprinkling of really prominent aristocrats and jet-set types, somebody must have reaped a rich haul of political, business and personal information. The real purpose, it is thought, was to eavesdrop on telephone and other conversations, with particular reference to Greek politics.

One deadly 'bug' is — literally — the size of an aspirin tablet. Its name describes its size — ¼″ × ⅛″ × ¼″ with a broadcasting range of from 200 to 800 feet and costing £1,000. It operates on frequencies up to 150 MHz.

The brochure of an English firm, L.T. Electronics Ltd., of Yately, Surrey, is a reminder of how sophisticated electronic surveillance material has become; and we know, from the rapid development of electronic equipment in every field, particularly in its incorporation of microelectronic techniques of engineering, that such apparatus will become smaller, more portable and infinitely more sensitive and versatile.

Take, for instance, a "telephone monitor". It records speech, and the dialled number, the month, day, hour, minute and second of the conversation! It is a super-eavesdropper, a total negation of the privacy of the telephone user. It is, admittedly, more expensive than the bugs advertised in the *Exchange and Mart*. This sophisticated piece of apparatus costs £8,900.00!

There is also a miniature telephone monitor which, "when connected to a telephone line pair and to any suitable mono or single track recorder, automatically monitors all incoming and outgoing calls made on the target line." This unit even records the source and time of incoming calls, even when they are not answered. It needs little power, a mere 6 to 9 volts DC and has a battery life of 2000 hours.

The 'family' of telephone monitors includes one mounted in a brief case, for use by connection "into a private or public telephone system, either through the exchange, or under field operating conditions — in every case in complete secrecy."

This highly portable eavesdropper will record on tape the telephone number dialled from the 'target line' (the line of the person or concern under surveillance), both sides of the conversations, and the month, day, hour, minute and second their discussion took place.

A handy supplement is a Display Recovery Unit which reproduces the conversations, and throws other details into visual relief, once the information has been stored on tapes. An inbuilt memory bank stores 100 complete sets of information and allocates each set a memory number for instant recall reference.

Incidentally, a small switchable gadget, a single channel frequency modulated transmitter kit, can transform any FM radio into a transmitter or receiver. These tiny adaptors are freely on sale, and at vastly varying prices. Some of the cheapest are extremely effective.

The catalogues of another United Kingdom company, Security Systems International Ltd., whose registered office is in the Isle of Man, and whose U.K. Sales office is in Cambridge, state with justifiable pride that their products are "for all Government security requirements".

They are indeed suppliers to police forces, and, with the amount of crime and violence prevalent today, it is good to know that our own depleted police forces can be strengthened by increased efficiency in their efforts to maintain law and order. Their offerings include the Processor, which takes the audio product of bugs and taps and eliminates blurring background noises such as echo, reverberations and other noise sources, whittling down the sound to those that are essential — say, conversation between two or more people. It can filter noise and pick out selected voices to the point where they are more readily distinguishable, and admissible as evidence.

Lesser used in industrial espionage are such larger microphones as the Shot-Gun Microphone and the Parabolic Microphone, both of which of which can pick up sound from a distance. It could be called the opposite of the aspirin bug, being as conspicuous as the other is 'discreet'. It would generally speaking alert the 'target' (the person or persons being spied upon) as in size the microphones can vary from one to four feet.

Both shotgun and parabolic microphones are used in the entertainment and sports industries. In effect, the parabolic microphone embodies a microphone within the bowl of a reflector, enabling sound to be picked up in a more concentratedly directional fashion than would otherwise be possible. Given the right conditions, conversations can be heard from a distance of 30 feet or more.

The shotgun mike, so called because of its vague resemblance to a Gatling Gun, is a clumsy but effective method of eavesdropping where there is a minimal chance of counter-surveillance being in operation. It can be bought streamlined and fully assembled from many suppliers, and is sometimes used by authorities. It is, however, fairly simple to make by anyone with a quantity of tubing, an inexpensive crystal microphone and an elementary knowledge of electronics. The tubes are of different lengths but held together somewhat in the form of a fasces (the Roman bundle of sticks, carried as a symbol of power). They amplify the signal, which can be further amplified, recorded or transmitted according to the requirements of the operation.

For fairly obvious reasons, it is not much used in the field of industrial espionage. It can hardly be used surreptitiously, and a mere glance at it would make its purpose obvious. One model really looks like a machine gun, mounted as it is on a tripod. Another consists of a single tube, instead of a bunch of tubes, with slots cut into the wall of the tube parallel with its long axis. The slots lower the boom or echo, but there is considerable loss of signal in the process. A shotgun microphone of really professional standard can cost between £500 and £1,000.

Public authorities, and both 'orthodox' and industrial spies, are aware of the application of laser to eavesdropping.

LASER is named after its nature — Light Amplification by Stimulated Emission of Radiation. It sounds dull enough, yet laser is undoubtedly one of the most potent and versatile of modern inventions. Laser is a new kind of light, demonstrated for the first time in 1960, so concentrated and power that it can produce a beam billions of times as powerful as the light of the sun. It is nowadays used for delicate eye operations, for welding steel and other metal plates, for innumerable secret and non-secret military uses, and for communications.

Its importance was immediately realised when Mr Gordon Gould, of Maryland, U.S.A., invented the laser beam. In 1959 he tried to interest the United States Army, which was, naturally, interested in its potentialities as a death ray. They immediately classified all Mr Gould's work and his patent application as secret. When a security check revealed that he had attended Leftist meetings in 1940 they confiscated his notebooks and forbad experts whom they had assigned to develop his machine from discussing their work with him. However, Mr Gould recently won an 18-years-old battle to win a patent. He was granted — after a long legal struggle — a patent recognising him as the developer of the system that used solid material, such as a ruby, to generate the laser beam.

The salient feature of laser is that it is 'pure' light. It is not diffuse. It spreads out so little that if projected on to the moon, it would light up an area of only two miles in diameter.

The man who *made* the first laser (as distinct from seeing and codifying the principle and idea, as did Mr Gould), was Mr T.H. Maiman, a scientist working for the Hughes Aircraft Company in California.

In the context of industrial spying, with which we are concerned, the importance of laser is that it can conduct sound. It is a kind of "superbug". When connected to a proper power source, a laser beam can be focussed on a window pane, which vibrates in accordance with the noises, including conversation, inside. This vibration modulates the reflected laser beam, which is returned to a receiver, demodulated, and the sound retrieved.

In the United Kingdom the principle is employed by a device known as the SI Surveillance Laser, which picks up conversations by its light beam from a window up to 600 yards away. This same system was used in February 1964 by the American CIA (Central Intelligence Agency) when spying on Lee Harvey Oswald, John F. Kennedy's alleged assassin — a fact which emerged only when that assassination was being investigated.

The SI Surveillance laser has also been used by C7 Division of Scotland Yard, both during the kidnapping of Dr Herrema and at the much-publicised Balcombe Street siege. It costs about £4,000 to buy, and is only supplied if appoval is granted by the Home Office. In theory therefore it should be impossible for an industrial spy to obtain — but then theory is not always fact.

Laser is not often encountered in cases of industrial espionage, but those interested in security and the countering of industrial espionage need, at least, to be informed of its potentialities — the more so, because it is developing all the time, and its present disadvantages in use for eavesdropping will probably be overcome. Laser apparatus will become smaller and smaller. It can even be operated by some kind of power-pack, ridding it of the necessity for a power supply, the power being 'stepped up' internally. Microtechnology may make it possible to reduce the size of the receiver — known as a photomultiplier tube — which, using a special decoder, demodulates the modulated light beam into audible sounds.

The increasing use of laser by industrial spies can and should be anticipated. The present disadvantage of the laser eavesdropper is that traffic, and the vibrations of the building itself, may be picked up by a window pane and drown the conversation which it is desired to record. There are technical means of separating such sounds, but they are tedius and expensive.

The first rumblings of the miniaturisation of Laser can already be heard. From Germany it is now possible to buy what is described as the SA515 Laser Microphone "for long range audio surveillance through windows" which enables "all conversations in a room to be monitored." It works for 45 minutes from its internal rechargeable batteries, or indefinitely from an external 12 volt supply. It can operate in ranges of more than a mile in good weather, and at about 500 yards in bad weather. And — yes, it has arrived — it is packaged in an innocent-looking brief case. Its laser beam gets right through double glazing and curtains, the usual precautions against eavesdroppers. It is the perfect tool for the industrial spy!

There are certain limitations to the use of laser, however as already stated. It works very well in a rural area, but not in a town or a city, because there is so much natural vibration caused by cars, lorries and aeroplanes.

As for the ubiquitous bug, we have not yet seen the peak of their mischievousness. In all microelectronics the tendency is for everything to get smaller and smaller. Already transmitters have shrunk to the size of a pea. We can expect them, in due course, to be as small as a rice grain, in which case such bugs could easily be encapsulated in the thin cardboard of a wall calendar, or concealed in or behind wallpaper. These will be powered by solar or daylight energy.

As in all conditions of supply and demand, there is fierce competition and innovation in the production of the equipment used in espionage and industrial espionage. Although — generally speaking — these may be considered two distinct branches of spying, no such distinction can be made as to the equipment and devices employed.

It is important for all engaged in security to recognise this, and not to deceive themselves with wishful thinking, which goes something along these lines: "These lists of equipment are given only a restricted and controlled circulation;

2. Only authorised and reputable security personnel will have access to these lists;

3. Such products as are offered for surveillance and counter-espionage will not be supplied to anyone who might use them for the opposite, i.e. an illegal, purpose;

4. Because the equipment is highly specialised, it would be difficult for any one but a security expert to use;

5. Because such equipment is extremely expensive, it would be beyond the pockets of crooks and undesirables".

All of the foregoing assumptions are demonstrably and hopelessly naive. First of all 'authorities' are themselves not necessarily ethical. Secondly, buying goods through intermediaries, or on the spot for cash, is always easy. Next, there can never be any guarantee as to use — a guarantee may be given, but it is nobody's business to see that it is observed, nor within their power to do so, even if the inclination existed. The biggest illusion of all is that expense would put much of the equipment out of reach of the industrial spy. As a broad generalisation, easily proved by past and current criminal records, anything on the market, however alledgedly restricted that market, will find its way into determined hands. The rewards of industrial espionage can be so spectacular that those determined to wrest valuable industrial secrets from their competitors will not cavil at the cost. Of course, this applies to *professional* industrial spies, and not to ad hoc information thieves, opportunists and suborned weaklings.

As regards telephone *tapping* — intruding on the private line and listening to, or recording, the ensuing conversations, and perhaps recording with the appropriate apparatus the telephone numbers dialled, the origin of calls and details as to times and dates and durations of conversations — there are innumerable methods of doing this, and I have not listed them all. All governments resort to it, a considerable, number of government departments do it, and an increasing, and already considerable, number of individuals and industrial concerns, do it, too. As regards the latter, I come across very many cases of private and unauthorised tapping in the course of my work.

Concerning *bugs* or electronic eavesdroppers (which is what they are) their range is not only enormous but increasing all the time. Almost anything can be made to contain a bug. At the moment there are felt pens which will write well but also act as transmitters; there are ballpoint pens with these dual applications. P.K. Electronics of Hamburg, in the Federal Republic of Germany, offer not only these but other ingenious bugging devices, from ashtrays to cigarette lighters, from calculators to candlesticks, wrist watches to 'ordinary' electric light bulbs. The latter will light your room effectively — and bug it just as efficiently, too.

A bug of a kind, widely used, is the 'bumper beeper' which is a small transmitter which can be fixed to the bumper or body of an automobile within seconds. It sends out signals which can be picked up within a distance of four miles, enabling the car to be tailed easily or eventually located. The battery power of these 'bumper beepers' lasts for several days. Some even have voice bugs planted in new cars before they sell them. Valuable information is often picked up in this way.

One amazing device (not a bug) produced for the delectation of industrial spies is a felt-tip pen (which writes as a felt tip pen) containing the world's smallest tape recorder. It provides 33 minutes of recording time on one track recording, and its minute cassettes can be replaced fast and easily. It even embodies the acoustic luxury of recording level control, making it of no consequence whether the sound source is near or some yards away. It has a very broad frequency response (100-4000 Hz) and operates for up to five hours on a 3 volt battery. It comes with a small playback unit, with loudspeaker, headphones, earphone jack, and fast forward and fast rewind facilities.

As a means of recording a conversation surreptitiously it would be hard to beat. I am not a technician and have therefore described the spy's apparatus in lay-man language. I am sure that certain experts will accuse me of a number of omissions.

The collection of information through the medium of stolen sound-waves is a large part of industrial spying activities. But what of *visual* aids to industrial spying.

As one would expect, in this technological age, visual techniques are also highly specialised and diverse. It is worth our while to consider a few of these, and the uses to which they can be put.

CHAPTER 6

Cameras — The Hidden Eyes

Ever since the camera was invented, it has been used to snatch information from those who would have preferred to keep it. Of course, ordinary spies — by which I mean orthodox spies — have always used whatever devices, methods or equipment which were known or available. Thus, when cameras came into use, spies were quick to use them too.

Prior to the introduction of cameras, thieves needing a visual copy of something had, to resort to sketching or painting. During the Boer War, Lord Baden-Powell, founder of the Boy Scouts and defender of Mafeking, was, as it happens, a spy of no mean skill and audacity. He liked to be pretending to catch butterflies, and would draw little sketches of butterflies whose markings referred to gun emplacements and suchlike details. Luck was also on his side, as he never had the misfortune to be captured and questioned by anyone who made a hobby of colleting butterflies. To a lepidopterist, his designs would have been instantly recognised as nonsense.

In the First World War, Lieutenant Karl Strauss, of the German Secret Service, drew a passable sketch of the new British Army aeroplane. True, photography had by then established itself, but photography was then in a somewhat crude stage, particularly as regards apparatus, which was almost impossible to conceal. Between the two world wars, many very good, tiny cameras, often marvels of engineering skill worthy of a watchmaker, were produced and, of course, used by spies. So, too, were movie cameras. Since then the potentiality and range of all photographic equipment has been widened immeasurably, the more so because it can be married to television equipment. The industrial spy (whose technical problems as regards photography are no different to those of his government-backed counterparts) has nowadays at his disposal a staggering armoury of sophisticated photographic equipment.

Some of it is, admittedly, costly; but the proceedings of successful industrial espionage can be so financially rewarding that cost is not always a factor. The purchase of costly equipment is regarded by the true professional as a necessary, indeed, an unavoidable, expense.

Putting it another way, anything that authorities can purchase can, one way or another, be acquired by an industrial spy. Certain firms will supply the more elaborate and ambitious telephone monitoring apparatus, for example, only to government departments and security agencies. This cannot guarantee that it will always be used ethically or for its original stated purpose. To take one instance only from the field of ordinary commerce, tanks, guns, planes, surveillance apparatus, armoured cars and communications equipment of every type have been sold, with the authority of governments, to friendly countries which later cease to be 'friendly' because of mere changes in policy, or an internal revolution.

The "old-fashioned" method of industrial espionage, by which an industrial spy either entered a factory or office secretly, or under some cooked-up story or identity cover, or by virtue of having obtained employment there in order to steal industrial secrets, and then proceeded to copy files by a pocket Minox camera or similar camera, was quite effective in its time, and according to the state of play, is still widely employed today. But the applications of photography to industrial spying do not end with the acquisition of stills. It may be necessary to follow someone and record his movements, and the people he contacts. It may be essential to have moving film to show a sequence of events, or the behaviour of apparatus and machinery. In manufacturing processes the sequence of events is always of importance, in respect of which a mere verbal description may not be adequate.

The reader should not be confused if I occasionally draw analogies from what is loosely called the spy world. I am concerned, as I assume you are too, with the menace of *industrial* spies, but the methods they use are sometimes similar to those of ordinary spies — so, too, is much of the apparatus they employ.

Photography has made great strides. It is now over two decades since the Russians shot down, over their territory, the American U2 reconnaissance plane on 1 May 1960, just before Soviet premier Khrushchev and the U.S. President Eisenhower were to meet at a summit conference in Paris. Only then did it emerge what fantastic cameras could now be made — a camera that could photograph the ground from a high altitude. Since then the sort of cameras used by

Gary Powers would be considered only suitable for the military junkheap. Nowadays for defence purposes, satellites are static at around 250 miles above the earth's surface, but can be brought down to sixty miles in order to take pictures. The resolution of these pictures are excellent and troop movements can easily be identified from this height.

The relevance of satellite development to industrial espionage is that the billions of dollars poured into its development have resulted in techniques which — as a commercial spin-off — have made available to ordinary purchasers inventions which would have been thought to belong to the realm of fantasy. The electronic calculator, now a commonplace piece of equipment, or the digital watch with its blinking figures are a case in point. Since the satellites had (and have) a military purpose, intended to survey and scan in great detail the countries of the world, much emphasis was put on the development of advanced cameras. By comparing photographs (often transmitted by television from the satellite) of the same place or object, changes can be discerned which may have taken place in a matter of days, or a day, or even within hours. A rocket silo, previously closed, is observed to be open; the packing cases on the deck of a vessel may be seen to have disappeared from view, or perhaps some of them opened; a wall, a factory, or emplacement, is being built — and so on.

One such satellite, Samos, travelled 1,200,000 miles over China and Russia, its cameras operating all the time. Millions of photographs were collected in this way and are, of course, being collected still.

Such programmes are beyond the pocket of even the maddest millionaire. But much of the 'spin-off' products are within easy reach.

Surreptitious cameras are now an inevitable part of the stock-in-trade of the industrial spy and, just as inevitably, a device used by those whose business it is to stop their dirty game. One silently-operating movie camera will film under all reasonable lighting conditions in colour, through a small rivet just beneath the strap of the innocent-looking small bag, of the sort that is now in common use to hold such things as wallets, cigarettes and other odds-and-ends. It can take up to 3,400 shots on one film and has an automatic lens to adjust for available light.

The TSS 600 automatic film camera measures about 8″ × 3″ × 3″, is fitted with an ultra wide angle lens giving a true 130 degree angle of view. This can take (again, silently) 3,000 individual pictures.

Such cameras can be hidden behind wooden panelling, or in box files. A row of box files on a shelf may include one with a camera whose lens lurks behind a small, round opening in the file's spine, a feature of most such files by which they can be pulled forward with one finger, and taken down. Many such cameras are built into books, a microscopic lens opening being somehow incorporated into the book cover. Such items can play a valuable part in detecting thieves, including those who steal files containing confidental information. Equally, if planted surreptitiously and skilfully, they can be used for industrial espionage.

Normal conditions of light are not necessary for secret photography. Infra red photography — developed largely for military purposes, though having many useful and innocent application in industry — enables pictures to be taken in complete darkness, by infra red flash and infra red film. But there are goggles by which one can see clearly in the dark, binoculars which reveal objects with great magnification even miles away, in what appear to be pitch-dark conditions.

The word 'noctovisor' has been coined (from *noc*turnal *vis*ion) to describe an increasing range of the PK 300-S 2nd Generation Professional Miniature Noctovisor (made by P.K. Electronic, of Hamburg, Western Germany) is small, lightweight and a wonderful aid to anybody conducting surveillance in poor or no light. Contrary to what many imagine, real, or total, darkness, is a very rare thing. This tiny pieces of precision apparatus would enable anyone to see quite clearly, with ten-fold enlargement and a 15 degree field of view, in what most people would assume was total darkness. But as long as there is some light from the stars or the moon, the picture appears as clear as daylight.

The PK 300-SS 2nd Generation Professional Noctovisor goes even farther, amplifying the existing light 60,000 times and so turning night into day, giving a long range in conditions of darkness. Even stronger amplification is offered by the PK 300 Residual Light Intensifier, which amplifies the 'residual' (i.e. almost non-existent and, to most people, undetectable) light 100,000-fold!

Concealed television cameras have increased in use as standards of honesty have declined, in Britain as elsewhere. Photoscan, a device which is reminiscent of a sea mine, being a kind of sphere from which protrude chunky antennae, each sporting a lens at the end, is a kind of ubiquitous all-seeing eye. They are nowadays a common feature in stores and public buildings; from a concealed vantage point proprietors can watch, not only the behaviour of customers but their own staff. Pilferers are understandably inhibited by the thought that they are being watched by means of television.

In the case of covert television coverage, such as would be useful in industrial spying operations, there are miniature television cameras measuring only $3 \times 3 \times 1.88$ inches and weighing only 11 ounces — and these, too, are being constantly reduced in size. Instead of the standard imaging or vidicon tube used in television cameras, these "solid state imaging sensors" assembled in a small 0.25 inch square are ideal (if that is the word!) for industrial spying. One has even been offered for sale concealed in the normal thermostat control of the sort found in countless homes and business premises. Such cameras at present cost about £2,000.

Fibre optics — literally bundles of glass fibres, each end of which has been processed and polished to form a perfect lens — are being used increasingly with television, movie and orthodox cameras, for they can spy through keyholes, look around corners and adapt themselves to all manner of situations and environments where the use of ordinary lenses would be inadequate.

The electro-optical solid state imager is tough in construction and consumes very little power. It is the 'creepy-peepy' par excellence.

A factor worth remembering, *apropos* automatic visual surveillance, is that its intended innocence of purpose, when employed by public authorities, stores, factories, transport centres and the like, may be defeated by an industrial spy who understands the surveillance system which is being used, and so gains access to its records for his own purposes. Banks habitually photograph by microfilm millions of cheques; close-circuit television surveillance systems in buildings are often linked to sequence cameras, which photograph every caller or customer and give the time and date of their calls. Rarely, in my experience, are such visual records conveyed and stored with anything like the secrecy and security they deserve.

Hidden cameras, as well as covert audio systems, are often installed nowadays when the building is being constructed. Apparatus has no longer to be smuggled in, or concealed, within a completed building. Cameras, bugs and recorders, and transmitters too if need be, are 'built in' behind grills, doors, pictures or anywhere else, and remain permanently out of view. Market Research firms which specialise in surveys whose real purpose is industrial espionage, find such a set-up of immeasurable advantage. Their callers and clients often talk freely and — as they imagine — confidentially. They often forget what they themselves have said, but the video apparatus and sound recorders have not!

In Detroit, U.S.A., many cased have been encountered of industrial secrets being stolen by camera devices. Long-range aerial photography, tele-photo lenses and even elaborate closed circuit tv systems have been employed to steal secrets of new car designs, sales drives, technical specifications are other heavily-financed projects. *Business Week* of October 31st, 1965 described as "one of the more notorious cases" described the discovery of a nine-camera television spying system found behind the overhead louvres in the design room of a Detroit firm. Even as long ago as April 7th 1962, the *Washington Post* reported that an "investigator" has used closed-circuit television, as well as a microphone, to spy (on behalf of a client) on business meetings held by a rival company in the hotel.

The equipment used in those days would now be considered fit only for the ark. Modern television, cameras and viewing devices of every sort have immeasurably increased in compactness, sophistication of design, and technical efficiency. And they have all become, without exception, lighter and smaller.

A camera offering much to the industrial spy is the PK 1650 Buttonhole Camera which is "recommended for secret photos". The noiseless camera fits easily into any pocket and its minature lens is disguised as a button. It uses a miniature film cassette with 15 exposures.

Another camera developed especially for surreptitious use is the PK 1565 Camera with Pin Hole Lens. Its description is accurate. The lens hood tapers outwards conically, reached a mere pin-point, enabling the camera to be camouflaged in very many ways, yet permitting accurate "surveillance photos" through an infinitesmal (and invisible) hole.

The "Black Minox", because of superb workmanship, reliability and very tiny compass, has always been a favourite with spies, orthodox or industrial. But there are on the market many rivals, specially made for clandestine use. One such is a micro camera encapsulated within a normally-working cigarette lighter of standard size. It gives absolutely clear exposures from one metre to infinite, by means of a special lens, and can be produced and used in even crowded places without attracting the least attention. There are other single lens cameras which go comfortably into the palm of the hand. The PK 785-S is one example.

There are many automatic surveillance cameras which, once installed, can be operated from remote control. When combined with a transmitting "bug", the user can decide for himself when to set the camera shutter going, or the film moving.

Although I have mentioned fibre optics as one possible new weapon in the industrial spy's armoury, I am, in this instance, looking ahead. At the moment they are probably used by a very few industrial spies who either possess or have access to, the necessary technical expertise. But they must be included in any assessment of the techniques to be faced by any individual or company wishing to protect its secrets. The real criminal takes the view that anything available to authority ought to be available to him. Generally this is true, in the sense that even expensive apparatus and equipment may be purchased, by fair means or foul, if sufficient money is available; it was assumed, for example, that thermic lances, which can cut through metal and stone like butter, were the monopoly of fire brigades, police forces and services departments who might need to use them and could bear the expense — but thermic lances were used in England by a gang of bank robbers. Such equipment is not to be bought in any ordinary store.

Even where equipment is used to a limited extent, or has in itself inherent limitations in use, account must be taken of its existence in all measures to counter industrial espionage.

The type of cine camera which is triggered off by a heat sensor — a device which picks up the heat of any human being within a distance of 100 feet — could, of course, be of equal service to an industrial spy, assuming that the sensor (which operates on a small PP3 battery and can last for three months of continuous use) could be adequately concealed and the camera also.

Cine cameras have obvious advantages over ordinary shutter cameras. They can be set to take picture-frames at stated intervals. They can take up to 3,400 pictures on one cassette. Still pictures merely prove that somebody was there, or that a piece of machinery or apparatus looked like that at the particular moment, when the still photograph was taken. *Moving* pictures, even a sequence of photographs taken at a few seconds interval, show the order in which actions take place. In the case of machinery, a moving film has obvious advantages for the spy, showing not only the sequence of movement, but the speed or particular functions, either of parts of the apparatus or of the apparatus as a whole.

I realise that the problems of setting up such apparatus illicitly must often be difficult. I know, too, that photographic records made with the aid of television cameras are often inferior in quality to those made by concealed cameras operating independently of television. Even so, I have instanced the case where a quite ambitious, illicit network of closed circuit television *was* installed. And all the apparatus used at this time would be considered cumbersome and old-fashioned today. The all-seeing eye may be anywhere there are industrial secrets to steal.

CHAPTER 7

Computers — Tools of the Industial Spy

A social and industrial revolution, comparable in its impact with the invention of machinery, offers a rich harvest to the legions of industrial spies who have found it profitable to keep abreast of modern technology.

There are, in fact, no inventions which cannot be put to bad, as well as good, use. An outstanding example is the computer or microprocessor.

Most people now realise that, trusted or suspected, loved or loathed, the computer is part of the daily lives of everyone in most parts of the industrially-developed world. They are in common use in government offices, local authorities, insurance companies, banks, public authorities of every kind, an increasing number of commercial companies and amongst a rapidly growing army of private owners.

The Times reported on 7th September 1980 that six million people in Western Europe will be using communicating computers as part of their daily work by 1987. Their report was based on a survey by LOGICA for the telecommunications of 17 Western countries. The current expansion of data communication is already twice as fast as the forecast of the first European survey made in 1972.

The United Kingdom has 185,000 computer terminals in use today, accounting for nearly a third of the Western European total. West Germany comes next to Britain with a usage of 96,000 computers system. By 1987 the survey claims that Britain will have 913,000 terminals. The study was commissioned at a cost of more than a million pounds by the Eurodata Foundation, representing 17 nations.

Even those figures are but a straw in the wind, for the report stops, deliberately, at 1987, when growth will be accelerated by the expansion of communication satellites, and the spread of computer networks to the home.

The spread of computers to home and schools is now well under way in the UK which is far behind the U.S.A. Two years ago PET was selling through 250 UK dealers at around 2,000 a month. Today I am told there are about 30,000 Commodore PET sets in use and another 10,000 of them in schools. It is expected on present showings there will be 100,000 of the latest version the VIC-20 commodore in use in 1982. Mr Robin Brabbeer senior lecturer in electronics at North London Polytechnic says that in five years time there will be about half a million home computers in use. In the United States it is estimated that 40 million home computers will be sold by 1990.

It is indeed an amazing revolution. Billions of pounds are transferred by computer over telephone lines or through terminals. The Federal Reserve Bank transmits over 35 trillion dollars to its member banks over unprotected telephone channels. Already in the U.S.A., large and mini-computers in daily use number over 600,000 systems. Already half of America's total output of goods and services and wealth (its "gross national product") depend upon the processing and transmission of data by, and to and from, computers, with or without their network of terminals into which information may be fed and transmitted to a central console, and vice versa.

The losses sustained by industry and individuals because of the inherent vulnerability of these electronic systems are many, many times those revealed and authenticated by research. Statistics show that computer crimes are far more lucrative than any other kind. Authenticated and recorded cases in the U.S.A. amount to a loss of $100 million a year. But magnetic records (which, putting in the simplest layman's language, is what computer storage amounts to) can be demagnetised, or partly demagnetised, or wiped out, or *not* wiped out when they are intended to be, so that finalised instructions to the computer can be repeated against the will of those owning or hiring the computer.

The *Daily Express* reported on October 11, 1980, that "electronic frauds have now reached a terrifying level". Some of these unpalatable truths were disclosed at a Government-sponsored seminar held in London for the official National Computing Centre.

It was disclosed in *The Observer* of 18 May 1980 that a secret organisation known, oddly, as CRANK — believed to have links with European terrorists working for the sabotage and disruption of computer operations, is operating in Britain. The City of London Fraud Squad was called in by a newspaper after the National Computer Council received an anonymous communication warning them that there existed an organisation committed to computer piracy and security cracking. The network of computer pirates stretched from universities to business companies, on both sides of the Atlantic.

It seemed that CRANK has access to the secrets of a whole range of computers — IBM 360 and 370, the ICL 1900 and 2900, the CDC 6600 and 7600, Honeywell Sigma's HP2000 and the E Digital Equipment Corporation's PDP 11 and DEC System L 10 and 20.

Investigation uncovers some odd and disturbing facts. The letter had, it transpired, come from a member of the staff of a national newspaper who was himself a member of CRANK. He had sent the letter to NCC as an act of bravado and defiance, forgetting that in his quest for economy he had allowed the letter to go through the company's franking machine. These are coded, so that the Post Office was able to identify the source from which the letter came.

"Pete" the correspondent who boasted of CRANK's success in cracking computer codes, claimed: "For the past five years we have constantly been finding 'bugs' (errors) in the TOPS 10 operating system, which allows *any* user to access *any* file on the system, including the protected accounting/password files."

Although the writer of the letter was traced by Scotland Yard's Fraud Squad, the national newspaper concerned would not prefer a charge, insisting on handling the matter themselves. One day they caught "Pete" red-handed at the copying machine; he had left behind in the machine the original of a CRANK newsletter he was copying. He was not discharged; merely reprimanded. Later he left for other employment.

It transpired that, by virtue of an informer friend within the Digital Equipment Corporation, he had been supplied regularly with 'bug fixes' — modifications which improved the manufacturers computers. This made vulnerable every one of the 200,000 installations, including the 10,000 in Britain alone.

DEC, based in Massachusetts, U.S.A., is one of the world's biggest suppliers of mini-computers, of which 10,000 are in use in the United Kingdom.

Naturally enough, computer companies minimise the risks inherent in computer use. Valuable information is transmitted to, or fed directly into, computers and microcomputers. Insurance companies keep records of their customer's insurances (which include details of the property owned by millions of people, their private and business addresses, and the nature of the insurance coverages) which would be valuable to a rival wanting to steal the customer away by offering slightly, or considerably, better terms. Banks hold records of millions of clients, showing the extent of their bank balances, of their deposit accounts, of the securities held on their behalf — along with an infinite amount of personal information which the bank collects on its own account, undisclosed to their customers, concerning their credit-worthiness, whether they are houseowners or property owners, what their salaries are. Inland Revenue authorities hold files concerning every citizen in the U.K., the U.S.A. and most countries.

Universities and laboratories throughout the world, and more especially in the western world, hold the results of every conceivable type of research on magnetic tape. Anyone able to "tape in" to the line, and to go through the sequential steps, or codes, by which the computer will divulge its information can help himself to as many secrets as he pleases. Or, as Dr. Donn Parker, author of *Crime by Computer*, has put it, any Government could design a computer powerful enough to break any code ever designed, and so uncover the secrets of any organisation it chose.

This speculation, however, does not apply exclusively to *Governments*. The National Science Foundation of America backed a research project into computer abuse, at Stanford Research Institute in Menlo Park, California. The results of the intensive enquiries, published in 1973, included 148 cases collected and investigated in the United States, Canada and Europe.

Although only some of these could be categorised as industrial espionage in the strict sense of stealing information with intent to sell it elsewhere, these cases add up to a salutory warning that no organisation or individual can afford to be complacent if they use a computer. False information fed into a computer; the tapping of lines into a computer; the insertion of *additional* information into a tapped line which itself is being legitimately used — all these devices are impossible to spot. There is nothing to *see* on magnetic tape. There can be no outward evidence that it has been electronically tampered with.

Some of this tampering can take on bizarre forms:

A bank depositor in the U.S.A. was smart enough to notice that, whereas his paying-in slips bore his own computer code in magnetic marks, the deposit slips on the bank counter did not. Otherwise, the slips were identical. The machine which processed the slips merely "read" the magnetic code and credited the account represented by that code — an address did not come into it. The address of a client can be identified from the bank's file of that number.

Therefore this wily client helped himself to generous handfuls of these blank deposit slips on every visit to the bank. Having accumulated several hundred, he marked them with the magnetic code with he had discerned on his own paying-in slips. Every time he went to his bank, he returned some of the formerly blank slips, which he had since marked, into the rack.

As a result, other bank clients using those slips were never credited with the moneys they paid in; the computer, obligingly, diverted their funds into his account. Within a matter of days he had accumulated $250,000 of other people's money. He drew $100,000 of it, disappeared, and has never been traced.

In Sweden, in 1970, two employees engaged in compiling a population registry copied the statistics and addresses which were on the computer tape and sold copies to customers, at a reduced price.

In 1971, in California, a company 'bugged' the telephone line of a rival and so obtained a copy of a computer programme. A criminal trial followed and the culprits, who had stolen valuable trade secrets, were convicted and, in the course of a civil suit, convicted and fined $300,000 damages.

In West Germany, in the same year, a secret agent for East Germany copied confidential data concerning over 3,000 West German firms onto computer tape.

"Computer Fraud and Countermeasures" by Leonard I Krauss and Aileen MacGahan quotes four examples of espionage within the computer industry.

1) XY Oil Company had a sophisticated seismic analysis system providing information necessary to make precise bids for tracts of land. They were always being beaten out on competitive bids against the QR Oil Company. Eventually, XY Oil hired a management consultant to tell them why they were always losing. The consultant learned that both XY Oil and QR Oil used the same computer service bureau where XY Oil ran its seismic analysis. QR had been using XY's system, obtaining the competitor's bid and then submitting one just a fraction higher.

2) Soviet agents were caught trying to bribe computer vendor engineers servicing a government installation. It developed that the service engineers always had lunch in the same restaurant as the Soviet agents. In the course of many lunches the agents were able to piece together enough of the conversation to realize that the customer reps had access to the computer installation they were trying to infiltrate. The Soviet agents offered a bribe and the service engineers reported it.

3) In another international computer espionage case, East German agents stole financial data on 3,000 West German businesses. The scheme was a simple one. The stolen data were stored

4) A drug company learned by the industry "grapevine" that a competitor was about to patent a new miracle drug which would make several of its existing products obsolete. In an effort to obtain the exact formula, an original approach was tried that took advantage of the common business practice of selling excess computer capacity on a service-bureau basis. The competitor with the new drug had excess capacity available on a rental basis. The executives who were trying to steal the formula posed as employees of a small business that needed use of the computer for occasional runs. They came into the victim's offices at night and ran their program. What that program did was dump all the victim's on-line files to tape. Back in their own computer centre, the executives browsed through the stolen files until they found what they were looking for. They then managed to patent the formula just a few days before the victim.

In 1972 a student in California achieved a Gargantuan information theft by copying 500 passwords from a file system, to get access to protected files. At the same two employees who were about to be retired from a company helped themselves to program listings describing secret industrial processes which were about to be patented. I should, perhaps explain that in the world of computers the "password" is the equivalent of a safe combination. It consists of a code of prearranged number of digits or signs, made in some sequence which must be precise for the computer to adduce the information stored. There are millions of possible combinations — but if an industrial spy either steals a tape, or taps into a line with a code which will unlock the records of customers and their codes, he can siphon off, into his own computer, records which may have taken hundreds of employees years to acquire.

That some of the cases I have quoted relate to fraud as such is highly relevant to our theme of *industrial espionage*; the same vulnerability which makes these supposedly secure communications and information "fortresses" open to the determined or merely informed intruder, makes them equally vulnerable and open to the industrial spy. If a mere crook can crack an entry code into a computer system, so can an industrial spy. If a criminal can tap into a computer system at any point (and there are many points, which I will specify), so can an industrial spy. This fact needs emphasis.

There have, in fact, been innumerable cases of computers being abused for the purpose — often achieved — of stealing industrial secrets. An employee of the University Computing Company (UCC) of Palo Alto, California, reputedly stole a programme from Information Systems Design, Inc. (ISD) of Oakland, in the hope of using that programme to lure a profitable client away from the competitor. Both were computer service bureaux. Since both used UNIVAC computers with remote processing terminals, and both terminals could be used over telephone lines, no access to the competitor's premises was necessary.

The case reached the high courts of the U.S.A. when I.S.D. charged an employee, who pleaded guilty of stealing a trade secret.

Only some mischance, some unfamiliarity with the side-effects of the technique used by this dishonest employee, revealed this piracy. Given more cunning and caution, and just a little more skill, it would never have been discovered. It is common knowledge that many such firms have set up in business on the basis of computer programmes stolen by much the same tapping devices and techniques.

These techniques are often childishly simple — to those who know them. There was, for instance, the amazing case of Jerry Neal Schneider of Hollywood, California, who at the age of 20, found that by fooling the computer he could make a quick million dollars. His story had an ironic twist, because his unethical expertise earned him so much publicity that he was quickly in demand by huge corporations wanting to know how best to guard against the sort of thing he did!

What did Jerry Schneider do?

He was giving a party at his home in Milbu, Hollywood, eleven years ago when the conversations wandered into computers. It was a subject on which, young as he was, Jerry Schneider was well able to discourse. Both in High School and in the University of California he had been marked out as an exceptionally talented technological student. He had won several awards. He had even, on occasions — usually during his holidays — been asked to help out on jobs by the telephone company.

He had been making a bit of pocket money by buying equipment from the Pacific Telephone Company, for resale. At the party he was giving, he remarked facetiously that anyone who knew the code to which the computer responded in the Pacific Telephone Company's office could make a fortune. Nobody took him seriously, least of all himself. It was some time afterwards that he found himself thinking — why ever not?

The computer which took orders for goods at Pacific Telephone could only be got into, or "accessed" by a code, which was changed frequently. One day Jerry managed to procure a stolen code book. From then on, it was simple. He could order what goods he pleased, using any telephone he pleased! He could as easily have made himself a fortune by phoning from distant Tibet, and absolutely nobody would notice that anything untoward was happening. Thus he obtained, and sold, a million dollars worth of equipment. It took him six months to do it. The District Attorney's office were convinced that he did this by tapping into the company's computer, and he himself has admitted that, not only did he do this, but that "it was very easy to do." He had set up his own company for the marketing of the goods he obtained from Pacific Telephones.

To Donn Parker, however, Schneider gave a story with interesting variations. He told him that he had posed as a magazine writer, and had been shown round Pacific Telephone's electronic installations with enthusiastic accompanying commentaries on what he was seeing. He told Parker: "I picked up a crumpled piece of paper out of one of the wastepaper bins, unscrewed it, and found the whole plan of the company's computerised operation laid out in front of me. All I had to do was call up each of the sites served and pose as somebody from the company to learn all I wanted to know."

The Pacific Telephone Company, as such companies are liable to do in circumstances such as this, played down the vulnerability of their system and their computers. Even so, they felt strongly enough to prosecute Schneider who received a light sentence of three suspended years' imprisonment and 60 days detention.

The wide publicity which this case received must be weighed against the estimate of the Federal Bureau of Investigation (FBI) that only one computer fraud in a 100 is detected, and only one computer crime in 800 is reported to the authorities. This alarming statistic means that there there are nearly 80,000 cases of computer "fraud" (or manipulation, for whatever reason, including industrial espionage) for every one that hits the headlines. The reported losses, therefore, are the wildest under-estimate.

The same holds good in the United Kingdom. The security overlordship of computers is so inadequate in Britain. The Swedish Social Security ministry, not long ago, flatly refused a request for data on the basis that, once swallowed up by British computers, any hope of its confidentiality would be lost.

The use of "software" in the world of computers poses yet another threat to industrial secrets. Software is the term for programmes anciliary to the main computer. It can be recorded on a printer, or a "floppy disc" (which is literally a floppy disc or record), whose electrical magnetic impulses will, when fed into the computer over a connection, tell the computer what to do, and when.

Anyone able to tap into the line leading into the computer can copy such a disc or taps, make additions and/or deletions, and so alter the normal procedures activating the computer and getting information out of it. In this way records can be altered or destroyed. Software can be copied, whether the software is borrowed illicitly or stolen or bought from a dishonest employee. This happened when what was the country's biggest airline, British Overseas Airways Corporation, was robbed of a computer programme, in the form of "software" by industrial spies. The programme, named "Boadicea", was intended to operate a world-wide network relating to the maintenance of aircraft, booking facilities and other secret organisational and operational plans. As the *Daily Telegraph* put it at the time; "The leakage cuts BOAC's lead, estimated at two or three years, over rival airlines in the use of computers".

The industrial spy nowadays has a wary eye on the banks; whether they have a wary eye upon him I have reason to doubt. Banks have computer installations which have cost millions of pounds (or dollars) to install but they depend for their operation upon a huge staff whose training has been highly specialised, and upon servicing from an unseen army of technicians whose electronic knowhow is a total mystery to all but experts. What they do, or elect not to do, can never be checked for credibility, or acceptability, with the care and detail that apply to written records.

It needs only a few dishonest, or gullible, employees to cause irretreviable industrial damage. Computer programmes which embody millions of pounds, or dollars, of research can be "siphoned off", not merely by tapping lines (of which more anon) but by the disclosure to an outside person of the code words that give entry, whether over a terminal or telex or telephone lines, into the computer data store. For a computer stores, as "files", collections of data which are transmitted, displayed or printed in a thousandth of a second once the entry code-word to the file is delivered electronically.

The vulnerability of banks, without which commerce simply cannot operate, is a matter of grave concern. Recently (in 1980) a London-based systems consultant participated in a competition, organised by a magazine called "How to Think like a Thief". Looking carefully into the matter Mr Leslie Goldberg won a £100 prize for a "do-it-yourself" guide to stealing millions.

Mathematics is Mr Goldberg's speciality. He found that, inherent in a new code system commissioned by the Committee of London Clearing Banks and scheduled to be adopted in 1982, were facilities for a "perfect fraud" which could have lost the banks millions of pounds. He discovered a flaw in the coding system, and data specialists at the National Physical Laboratory confirmed that the banks were unwise to adopt the code, known as the Standard Key Test.

Mr Goldberg discovered that, armed with equipment to intercept Telex or teleprinter messages, a criminal or industrial spy could modify them to make payments to his own account.

The amazing thing is that the key to unlocking the code was freely available from the Committee of London Clearing Banks as a help to manufacturers supplying communications equipment! Different test keys are used to help one bank check that a message it receives is exactly the same as that sent by another bank. The new standardised key could be altered without either bank being aware of it.

Mr Goldberg warned the Committee as early as 1978, but claims that the banks were not especially gracious about being told their system was so fallible. In general, authority does not like to be told of its mistakes, and in this case hundreds of thousands of pounds had been spent in developing the system.

An industrial spy would have a powerful weapon if he could extract the codes by which bank computers operate. He could discover the state of anybody's bank account. He could uncover the assets — liquid assets — of a huge company, and of their holdings in securities. He could throw the records of either into confusion by deleting essential information, or adding false information. He could discover the amount of moneys paid to them by their various customers, and, in so doing, help their competitors to sail in and get their business. Equally, he could divert moneys to his own account. Two crooks, having opened accounts in Zurich and Amsterdam, fed false information into the data bank (computer) of the Bank of America, Korea, drawing nearly $600,000. They had obtained a secret electronic code by which information is transmitted to and from the bank's computers. One of them, Daniel Grant, declared afterwards: "It's very simple. Money which has to be transferred urgently is sent either by cable or Telex. If you have the code you can send as much money as you like and the receiving bank is bound to pay out. It's as simple as that."

The extent to which big business rely upon computers as a record of valuable properties and money, Mr Henry de Pont of Wilmington, Delaware, U.S.A., testified at Senate Hearings that according to his researches, $10 billion securities have been lost, which could have been saved had they been recorded on computer. Chairman of the Senate Committee on Organised Crime, Mr McClennan, said in New York alone $300 billion-worth of securities were "going over to computer".

Those were the securities in just one vault. Their details were transferred to electronic taps. That can be multiplied by thousands. Information concerning these, as with bank account transactions, are transmitted silently to and fro, from office to office, bank to bank, country to country, ceaselessly, day and night. But, given the sort of methods I propose to list, *any* of the records thus stored can be and are retrieved illegally. In the U.S.A., the average bank robbery produces $9,000. The average embezzlement charge is round about $19,000. The average computer crime is $450,000. The emphasis on computer crime is understandable; whatever his branch of crime, whether it be industrial espionage or old-fashioned embezzlement the malefactor had, as his principal problem, the task of concealment — of not being observed, and of his methods not being detected. In the very nature of computer storage and computer operations, everything is concealed; the most dramatic incidents of piracy can take place without anything showing, or without any trace of them having happened.

There are at every stage of data processing, weak points which, we can be sure, have been carefully studied and mastered by the industrial spy.

Let us start with the main computer. It can be, and in the case of the larger and more important installations, which can cost millions of pounds, is, linked by various means to many other devices and systems permitting input, transmission, retrieval and receipt of information.

If to a bank, the route will be to and from the central computer to a transmission control unit, then to the company's private exchange or PBX, on to the telephone junction box, perhaps to another, then, perhaps to a data set, and thence to a terminal or smaller computer.

This is not the only route, or the only set of connections both within the company premises or complex, with its branches elsewhere (perhaps, as in the case of banks, throughout the country) which have terminals, and to such organisations and services with which it requires connections for the purposes of computer input and output.

In the single instance I have given, there are innumerable points of vulnerability open to the threat of industrial espionage:

The line between the main computer and the transmission control unit can be "wire-tapped;"

The connection between the transmission control unit and PBX can be wire-tapped;

The data, in its onward transmission to the junction box, can be wire-tapped;

At any point, perhaps over a distance of miles or hundreds (even thousands of miles) to the telephone junction box, the line can be wire-tapped;

Between the data set and the terminal the lines can be wire-tapped.

It is, and will certainly always be, a physical impossibility to watch and guard every inch of the way from point 1 (the main computer) to the terminal, whatever the distance between the two.

Wiretapping is a simply and effective technique, and the first to be mastered by the professional industrial spy.

Companies are often careful to guard the central computer, but are curiously slap-happy and casual about the terminals and the apparatus and lines in between. The industrial spy is not so stupid as to bother with the central computer if he can help it. Why should he? The "siphoning" of electronic information at any point along the lines of connection will give him all the secret information he needs.

But "tapping in" or wire-tapping, which is in most cases a matter of simple monitor and a pair of crocodile clips, is by no means the only means of illicit surveillance of private communications to and from a computer. There are the electromagnetic radiations from such apparatus, particularly the cathode ray tubes which are a feature of most computers; indeed, the seemingly harmless VDU (Visual Display Unit) screen is more of a give-away than anybody except an industrial spy realises. Its radiations can be monitored from a distance of half a mile, and converted with comparatively easy technical means into the data that are being transmitted.

The ordinary induction coil, albeit in slightly more sophisticated form and of heightened sensitivity, can also tap information *without connection at any point;* such apparatus is not only freely available throughout the world, but quite cheap, and so simply based that any intelligent schoolboy could make one. Many do! In fact as an example of schoolboy proficiency, the first messages from the Russian spaceship Soyuz were picked up by British schoolboys. Their experise was considerably more advanced than most schoolboys, and even of most electronic experts; by comparison, the construction and use of induction devices is, technically speaking, elementary.

The interception and demodulation or radiations from computers (the conversion of electronic radiations into simple, textual, visible language) can be achieved without leaving the slighest evidence.

There is a highly effective and deadly anti-computer technique, used increasingly by industrial spies thoughout the world, and now known for convenience of categorisation as "piggy-back entry".

"Piggy-back entry" is a very apt description of what transpired when computer information is being stolen in this way:

The line is tapped, anywhere along the route from computer to terminal. It is tapped selectively, that is, on the basis of information as to when, or within what period of time, a vital communication is to be made by a legitimate user of the computer or terminal.

It is quite usual for a line to be kept "open" by the users, between computer and terminal or between two computers; it is during this period, easily detected by the surveillance, that false information can be fed into the appropriate file, or modifications, even deletion, effected.

There is a deadlier aspect to this "piggy-back" technique.

PROTECTING COMPUTER SECRECY

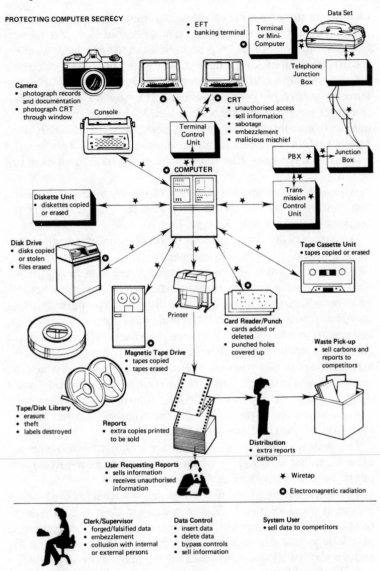

Data Set

• EFT
• banking terminal

Terminal or Mini-Computer

Telephone Junction Box

Camera
• photograph records and documentation
• photograph CRT through window

Console

Terminal Control Unit

CRT
• unauthorised access
• sell information
• sabotage
• embezzlement
• malicious mischief

PBX

Junction Box

COMPUTER

Diskette Unit
• diskettes copied or erased

Transmission Control Unit

Disk Drive
• disks copied or stolen
• files erased

Tape Cassette Unit
• tapes copied or erased

Printer

Card Reader/Punch
• cards added or deleted
• punched holes covered up

Waste Pick-up
• sell carbons and reports to competitors

Magnetic Tape Drive
• tapes copied
• tapes erased

Tape/Disk Library
• erasure
• theft
• labels destroyed

Reports
• extra copies printed to be sold

Distribution
• extra reports
• carbon

User Requesting Reports
• sells information
• receives unauthorised information

✱ Wiretap

⊙ Electromagnetic radiation

Clerk/Supervisor
• forged/falsified data
• embezzlement
• collusion with internal or external persons

Data Control
• insert data
• delete data
• bypass controls
• sell information

System User
• sell data to competitors

Operator
• copy files
• destroy files

Data Conversion
• change codes
• insert data
• delete data

Disgruntled or Militant Employee
• sabotage

Competitor
• sabotage
• espionage
• theft

Engineer
• install "bugs"
• sabotage
• access security information

Programmer
• theft of programmes and data
• embezzlement via programming
• bypass controls
• extortion — hold programmes for ransom

Computers store what are called "programme files". Built into such computers, or programmed into them, are certain secret sequences of command, sometimes long, sometimes short, which are a kind of security control, making it impossible to open the file (in electronic jargon) until the correct sequence of passwords and graphic, or numeric, signs have been transmitted. It is possible to so modify a computer's programme that these security precautions are wiped out electronically, without anybody being aware of it. Thereafter, access to files by illicit means is simplicity itself. The security safeguards have been eliminated. The guard has been put out of action.

Although the authorities were not especially amused, there is a certain irony — as well as a pointed warning — in the case of the boffins of Leavenworth, Kansas, U.S.A.

With the worthy idea of rehabilitation of its offenders while they were in prison, the U.S. Government set up a computer school in Leavenworth Prison. The tuition was of a very high standard, and the convicts were avid and enthusiastic pupils. Some cracked the code by which the Inland Revenue Service's computerised files could be "opened" (electronically) and, using the prison computer, inserted into the Inland Revenue Service's system details of completely fictitious files; their knowledge of computer technology was sufficient to alert them to the sort of characteristics which the computer would detect. Thus, IRS's computer received, by illicit means, from a computer in prison, returns from non-existent taxpayers who were (on the basis of the bogus returns fed into the computer of the IRS) entitled to a tax refund.

The prison computer was linked up with a private computer network called INFONET, which itself served many private and public businesses, as well as Government offices.

The information, passed silently and unobserved on to the magnetic tapes of the IRS, the computer then began sending cheques for tax refunds to the prisoners. It might have continued indefinitely, had one prisoner, who felt he was not getting a big enough slice of the pie, not revealed the plan to the authorities.

This rehabilitation-in-reverse was an object lesson, underlining the dangers inherent in computer systems, which, as the U.S. General Accounting Office declared when the Leavenworth scandal came to light, "have added a new dimension for potential crime. Computer related crimes in Federal programmes are cause for growing concern." The General Accounting Office revealed that in 1976 alone there were sixty-nine cases in which the Federal Government's computers had been plundered of their secrect information by unauthorised persons.

Not merely spies in the old-fashioned, ordinary sense, but industrial spies selling stolen information for gain, or hired or employed to outwit a competitor, are "tuning in" or "tapping in" to this Klondyke of private information. It is the invisible nature of this theft, or modification of records, which makes it especially dangerous and difficult to counter. As Clark Weissman, an American computer security expert once put it: "Sherlock Holmes can't come in and find any heel marks. There's no safe with its door blown off."

It has been found that passwords permitting telephonic or telex access to computer files can be hit upon be experimentation, thereby by-passing security controls. However, as C.C. Foster warned in *Data Banks, a Position Paper* (Computers and Automation; March, 1971 pp 28-30), "microcomputers can be used to break the code. Using a number of telephone lines, every possible password could be tried systematically. Computers equal to this experiment can be hired for as little as £14 a week. Assuming the password to be based on four letters, it would take about half a week, working 16 hours a day, to break the code. So for a very small amount of money one could plunder a file of information worth millions, or divert a bank's money to a fictitious name at an accommodation address!

The search for the password can often be limited, too, by the seeming fascination which "related" codewords have for most people, comparable with the passion for having evocative cable addresses such as, say, "At Rest" for an undertaker, or "winalot" for a bookmaker. Trying codewords related to the nature of an individual's interests, or a company's purposes, can often be narrowed down in this way.

There are, of course, many other points of vulnerability in the computer system apart from the system's input and output routines and apparatus. They are personnel — dissatisfied, or corrupt, or victims of blackmail; the various means of storage of data, whether on reels of tape, or "floppy discs" can be stolen, copied or altered. Programmes can be stolen, or made available to industrial spies or their confederates. All along the line there are people who may be vulnerable to bribery and blackmail, from the Methods and Procedures Analyst to the Programmer, from the Manager of

Technical Services to the Operations Supervisor. Even a Despatch Clerk can copy sensitive reports before sending them on their way.

Despite the strenuous efforts being made by electronics designers and engineers to make their systems secure from outside interference, it is, in the very nature of the dissemination and storage of information by electronic means, impossible to evade the attentions of the industrial spy.

What might be done, given vigilance, intelligence, determination, planning ability and a willingness to pay for the protection of information on a scale proportionate to the potential loss, is to limit the industrial spy's chances of success.

Which brings me to the question of counter-measures against industrial spying, generally.

Part II — Prevention and Cure

The Author

The Cloak.

The Polygraph in action.

Books are an ideal place to hide cameras and sensor equipment. Two books here are crammed full of automatic electronic equipment.

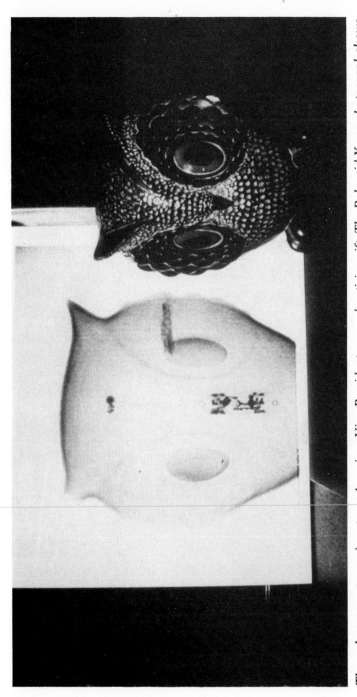

The owl ornament was given to an American Vice-President as an advertising gift. The Polaroid X-ray photograph shows the bug which it contained.

Psychological Stress Evaluator.

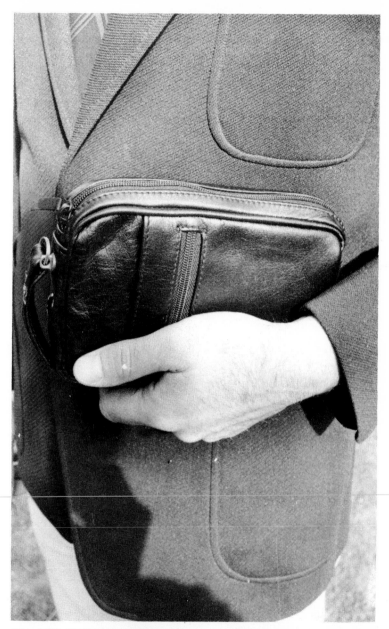

The TSS 400/500 series: This camera will film under all reasonable lighting conditions in colour secretly through small rivet on front of bag shown beneath the strap. Takes up to 3,400 shots on one film. Quiet and small — has automatic lens to adjust for available light.

Actual film print-out from security camera hidden close-by. Camera automatically activated by small infra-red body heat sensor. Up to three minutes of film was taken of the intruder.

CHAPTER 8

Formation of Company Policy

A company makes no bones about certain needs fundamental to its existence and viability.

At Board level, noboby would dream of suggesting that the company should dispense with insurance cover, or that doors to factories and offices should be left unlocked.

However, when it comes to the danger of industrial espionage, a strange complacency bedevils the thinking of otherwise well-organised and pragmatic folk. Why this should be, I do not know. But it is absolutely true, and the huge losses from industrial espionage, which increases in scope and audacity all the time, confirm that precautions against the theft of company secrets are regarded too often as a sort of extra, an indulgence advocated by nervous perfectionists.

Again, no sensible company would neglect its fire defences; the hydrants, escape ladders, sprinkler valves, fire extinguisherrs, hoses and framed instructions on what to do in case of fire are prominently displayed. Elementary "security" is often confined to the employment of an elderly security guard, not infrequently in dubious health and of limited stamina, whose tramping on circuit of the offices and factories and ground is deemed sufficient safeguard against burglary, arson, or armed robbery. I think there has been improvement in the willingness to bear the expense of what I may call "geographic" security, by which I mean the protection of premises against the more obvious forms of intrusion or attack, but this in no way offsets the numerous and sophisticated techniques of industrial spies.

At what level ought company policy be decided, and by what criteria is that policy formulated?

The answer to the first question is — at topmost level, in other words, by the Chairman and Board of Directors. For the moment we are talking of the formulation of policy, not of its implementation, although one naturally follows the other.

It may not be judicious to inform all upon whom you depend for the *implementation* of a security policy to know, necessarily, the thinking and planning behind the policy itself. For example, if you were tightening up security in anticipation of infiltration or espionage by a powerful competitor, only a handful of people could or should know this; how do you know that some member of staff has not already been suborned, or approached with an attractive offer to join the rival firm? Any relevation of the reasons underlying the security strategy or policy decided upon would alert the very enemy against which the protection was being invoked.

At top level however the following questions have to be posed and answered in unequivocal terms.

1. What is the scope of our present security arrangements — in terms of staff men engaged, their respective duties, their working hours, special qualifications and physical area to be covered?

2. Are the *physical* arrangements adequate in respect of the following security considerations: (a) Checking of locks on gates, doors and windows; (b) checking of telephone lines and intercommunication lines for evidence of tapping; (c) protection from direct access to computers — hardware — and their peripherals; (d) protection against unauthorised access to computer recordings, in whatever form; (e) issue, and recall when outdated, of official passes; (f) up-dating of pass procedures (for example, the old-fashioned type of card with a photograph affixed is no protection at all; such cards are often easily copied, or new photographs affixed); (g) burglar alarms, whether run on mains or batteries, checked regularly; (h) storage of 'classified' documents containing company secrets, formulae and plans.

3. Assuming that the physical arrangments measure up to acceptable standards (and they seldom do) *what of general policy*? What positive steps are being taken to guard against the theft of company secrets by espionage disguised as market research, or conducted through the medium of disloyal company employees?

4. As a fourth and vital issue arising, as a by-product, from company policy, to what extent may one's deadliest rivals in business be reported upon, assessed and competed

with? How much "competitive intelligence" is acceptable in ethical terms?

Standards of business ethics have slipped a great deal in recent years, and in my opinion are going to slip a lot more still. What is acceptable now in business would have been far from acceptable ten years ago, and with the advent of the microchip and the computer, the day is not far off when all major companies will have their departments of "aggressive" intelligence. Collecting information about business rivals will be deeper and more devious than ever before. Whatever else it may be called, the department will be really an industrial espionage department.

My forecast is based on the fact that I and many of my colleagues in the investigative field are being asked to steal secrets. It is one of the rules of The Association of British Investigators that, although industrial espionage may be quite legal, it is unethical, and therefore members of The Association should not indulge. A member may reject approaches, but it is common knowledge that despite the fact that the enquirer has it pointed out to him that the investigation he is requesting is virtually industrial espionage, he persists by trying other agents until he eventually finds one who will assist him.

Clearly, company policy regarding security, in particular so far as it is destined to prevent commercial espionage, must tackle three distinct fields; its internal security; its information gathering apparatus; its surveillance of company staff and vetting of new entrants to the company.

Document classification and control is a thorny problem. Broadly speaking, as in government departments, the more important and secret a document becomes, the more limited its circulation and the more stringent the keeping of records as to who had access to such documents, and when, become. There need to be at least three grades of document; secret, confidential and general. Obviously, in companies such as those concerned with the aerospace industry, such classifications exist already, and with even more categories; but as they work depend for their existence upon government contracts, their security tends to be as strict as that obtaining in government defence departments — which is not to say that they are strict enough. They manifest capacity to guard their secrets is almost a condition upon which government contracts are placed with them.

There are, however, a majority of large companies which content themselves with run-o'-the-mill routine security arrangements, concerned largely with keeping unauthorised people away and preventing the more obvious forms of theft, and which are casual to the point of incompetence when it comes to protecting their vital company secrets.

One policy point which every company has to decide is what information may safely be given to competitors. Information which is put into the public domain, or divulged to circles, such as the press, by which the public is informed, may be harmless in itself but mischievous cumulatively. At a press conference some hint of a new design may be made. A gossip columnist may hit upon the story of a prominent foreign designer being in Britain on a visit to the company's works; an estate agent's board announcing a huge site as "SOLD" to the company concerned can, in conjunction with the other two pieces of information, alert a rival to something big being in the wind. Careless phrases at an ordinary social gathering may unwittingly reveal a lot. A pretty young girl tells a motor car director "I love your latest model. I've had it a year now and, etc. etc. "Quick as a flash she hears him say "Ah yes, but the automatic steering of our next model really *is* something. . ." or words to that effect. Or he may hint at some faulty part having been modified, or some technical virtue having been enhanced.

Somehow, the documentation containing company secrets, and those secrets which are in the heads of employees, and of which they may speak or write unless aware of sanctions which can be invoked against them, has to be controlled.

In this regard, a first step is to write down the numerous categories of documentation, handbooks, reports, correspondence, work-flow charts, annual reports and the rest which may contain secret information in greater or lesser degree.

Every company has its own set of documentation categories, and their priority of content — comparable to the mischief that could be achieved by disclosure — differ from firm to firm. Bank deposits, cost accounting records, magnetic tape and tab cards, salesman's reports, executive correspondence, internal telephone directories, operation manuals, records of patents filed, minutes of meetings research papers, internal memoranda, tooling designs, drawings, plans, employee files, technical prints and records, production figures, contracts, quotations, records of purchases and payments, bills of lading, and shipping documents — to name but a few of the categories of documents encountered — may all contain vital information. Public relations departments are a continual source of leakage in many large companies. Anxious to maintain good relations with press, radio and television, requests for information may be transmitted from the outside enquirer to public relations staff, and from the latter — often under pressure of time and with little or no security clearance — to the appropriate department or member of the staff. Without some stated policy or permanent machinery for vetting the nature of outgoing information, the result may be public relations in reverse! It is quite amazing how much confidential information changes hands under the "Old Pals' Act". ("We do have a new design under way, Old Boy, but, off the record, we're not saying anything about it at the moment. I'll let you have the details as soon as I get a chance. We don't want the Yanks to steal a march on us. . ." Or this company, or that. .).

Hence the caution which needs to be unremittingly maintained in press releases, trade fairs, press conferences, association meetings, staff conferences, and speeches made by staff to seminars, public meetings and social gatherings; obviously what should or should not be disclosed can only be assessed by each individual company. But some general standards of assessment must be established at Board level, at which level, too, the administrative machinery by which responsibility for the control and custody of documents must also be decided.

Again and again I get evidence that such topics are the last on the agenda, if on it at all. What I may call the "locks and bolts" approach to security still prevails.

There are certain questions — admittedly hypothetical, some of them — which need to be asked in all seriousness:

O.K. says our cynic. Our premises are secure. The locks, the bolts, the fences, the gates, the guards, the guard dogs, the pass system and the restricted entry to certain sensitive areas are all to our satisfaction. We can breathe freely.

But can you? Is that enough? *Your* premises are secure? Good. Does that apply to the premises next door? What about air vents, drains, cellars and storerooms? A bank may think itself impregnable, but if the shish kebab next door, which has nothing worth stealing when closed except a few scraps of cold meat, boasts nothing better than a Yale lock on its door, there may be access — unseen — through *their* premises.

Is the pass easy to forge? Easy to print?

Has every pass been surrendered before being replaced by a current pass?

Is the pass, although encapsulated, really impossible to duplicate? Even though the photograph of the bearer is an integral part of the plastic pass, the same expensive apparatus that produced it could be possessed by a rival firm.

Is there any staff rule prohibiting the use of cameras within the company's premises?

What are the plans, the budget and the strength of establishment of the security staff?

Does the security staff include one or more people who have had practical experience of the safeguarding of *information*?

Perhaps the most crucial of all (and legally, as well as physically, the most complicated to enforce), what steps can effectually check upon the reliability of new staff, and what constraints can be imposed upon staff to prevent them disclosing or stealing information. This last, vital point is fundamental to any company's policy.

Some companies place a pathetic reliance on restrictive covenants. They require their staff to sign, prior to employment, or immediately upon engagement, contracts which appear to bind them on their behaviour whilst in employment and their actions when they leave, either to set up business on their own account, or take another job elsewhere (perhaps with a competitor) or retire.

Such documents are seldom worth more than the paper on which they are written. They are frequently ambiguous. Some phrases used are impossible to define in acceptable legal language, and would therefore be unenforceable in court. And where such phrases and terminology have an accepted meaning, they are often actually contrary to the law and for this reason no court would enforce them. Indeed, a company making charges against a present or ex-employee which proved to be unsustainable in law, could find itself mulcted of very heavy damages, or sued for unfair dismissal. Somebody in the company has got to understand, and understand well, the lengths to which it is legitimate to go in seeking to tie or muzzle its employees.

I know people in my business (the business of investigation) who have a restrictive covenant in their terms of employment whereby the employee agrees that if he ever starts business on his own he will not operate within an mile radius. The courts have ruled that this was wrong because it stops a man earning his living.

A company must be frank with itself; is it asking an employee to sign a contract containing clauses which sound forbidding but have no legal validity, merely to inhibit or frighten him into observing decent standards of loyalty and honesty — or has the contract been drafted with sufficient cognisance of existing laws, with the anticipation that the contract would be enforceable?

Let us look briefly at some of the considerations affecting such a contract, assuming that it contains, as they often do, restrictive covenants:

Under the Contracts of Employment Act, every employee must be given in writing the main terms of his duties to his employees and his rights. Thus, hours, pay, sickness benefit, scope of work, etc., will be set out. Save where there are nationally agreed forms of contract, it is open to either the employer or the employee to demand any terms he liked. Whether these become part of an agreement is a matter for negotiation.

Now it is reasonably standard practice to have a term restricting the future employment of an employee whenever there is something special in the business which needs protection. That something is often the clientele, for it goes without saying that the public gets used to dealing with whoever they deal with — the customer is used to a particular hairdresser, or public relations adviser, or travel agent, or anything else. Without any restrictions, the employee could work only long enough to get to know the employers' customers and then calmly leave, taking them with him. It is, in fact, done very frequently, with or without a restrictive covenant!

So it happens frequently. How often is there redress?

The short answer is — very seldom. Litigation is expensive, time-consuming, disrupting to the normal flow of business, embarrasing in the revelations of the inner working of the company, which rivals and customers may alike read about, and usually abortive.

"Covenants in restraint of trade" as the law call them are subject to one test only, namely the law test of 'reasonableness'. The law asks: Is the term reasonable for the protection of the employer's business?

To answer this question, three aspects of the matter concern the court: the geographical limit, the time limit and the scope of the limitation. And this is commonsense. The protection given to the employer must not be such that if the employee left he would have to change his occupation or starve because (at least prior to social security benefits and payments) the effect would be to tie a man to his employer for life, whatever the employer's behaviour.

That, says the law, is contrary to public policy.

Geographical limits. There can be no objection to a term which provides that the employee shall not set up business in the same line of business in the same town — unless that 'town' happens to be London, which has a population bigger than the vast continent of Australia, and an area as large as a county; or Birmingham, Glasgow or other large city. Why should an employee become a refugee from his own native town? Why should he be committed, for the sake of a job, to pulling up his roots, seeking a life in some other city where he may have no friends or contacts, selling his house, looking for a home, finding new schools for his children? Clearly, courts approach the problem of 'geographical limits' with considerable caution and with concern for the specific merits of each case. A hairdresser setting up in Hove may not compete with Brighton hairdressers to any appreciable extent. A specialist tree surgeon probably would. Whether a specified mileage will be upheld can be tested on the same principle (and not that it is from *the employer*, who is the person relying on the term, to satisfy the court it is reasonable).

Time Limit. 'For lifetime' will rarely be upheld, though circumstances could be envisaged in which it is reasonable, for instance where a man of 55 is taken on to deal with a highly secret and technically valuable process. In that case a working life of up to fifteen years would seem a generous estimate, while the exclusive nature of his work might be held to justify a lifetime's restriction. On the other hand, while a lengthy limitation is unlikely to be upheld, a shorter period might be, on the premise that the employer is entitled to a reasonable period in which to introduce his customers to his new employee and successor to the one with whom his customers previously dealt; those who might have been inclined to go along with the employee who is leaving will probably have met his successor in, say, the limitation period of three years. Thus 'a period of three years' might be upheld by a court.

Scope. Normally speaking, a restriction against going to work for any competitor might be held to be reasonable, but there are many circumstances in which it might not be. Suppose the only alternative employment of a similar nature (perhaps the only kind for which the employee is skilled sufficiently to earn a living) is with a competitor, such a restriction would, if applied, deprive an employee of his livelihood. Phrases such as 'similar' and 'work of the nature' are often used, and assumed to have enforceable validity but they are difficult — if not impossible — to interpret. No judge or jury would deprive a man of his right to earn a living on the basis of a vague or ambiguous undertaking, however willingly signed. Something against the law cannot be enforced, even if it form part of a contract.

In general, too, you cannot restrict anyone from doing anything personal to himself. For instance, you could not restrict a professional tennis player from playing tennis, or a comedian from doing shows, or a computer programmer from programming computers, because such a restriction cannot protect something belonging to the employer. The employer cannot claim that his employees are his own property.

Drafting covenants in restraint of trade is often a very tricky business. The court has no power to amend them; it may only accept or reject them. If it feels, say a '10-mile' restriction on a former employee's right to exercise his skills elsewhere is in inequitable, it cannot substitute 'five miles'. The clause is void. Incidentally, only that clause is void. So the rest of the contract remains valid.

What then, can a firm do when there is a breach of a *valid* covenant? I have already pointed out that the validity of a covenant is not axiomatic, even where both parties have agreed on its terms. But let us assume that the terms, on the face of it, are 'reasonable', are likely to be held by a judge to be 'reasonable' and that confident steps may be taken by the employer when he suspects that a breach of the covenant is likely to take place.

What can he do?

Firstly, such an occurrence is rare. Only where an employee knows that the restriction is unreasonable and unenforceable is he likely to show his hand. However, an employer with tangible misgivings about a coming breach, can seek an injuction to prevent it.

But, you may ask, if the agreement is patently unreasonable, why did the employee sign it, and how can the employee satisfy a court that he did not accept the implications of the contract?

The answer is that a man in need of work quite commonly goes along with the situation; he needs work, he needs money, he plays the situation by ear. He wanted the job badly, and the employer was adamant on the conditions on which he would employ him. In a situation of dire personal necessity and a monopolistic situation as an employer, some degree of duress, or at least extreme necessity, may be held to be implied. The law can say on such occasions: we don't care what is intended.

You cannot agree to do what is unlawful. Your agreement in law, is just as if the invalid clause had never been there.

The answer is that a man in need of work quite commonly goes along with the situation; he needs work, he needs money, he plays the situation by ear. He wanted the job badly, and the employer was adamant on the conditions on which he would employ him. In a situation of dire personal necessity and a monopolistic situation as an employer, some degree of duress, or at least extreme necessity, may be held to be implied. The law can say on such occasions: we don't care what is intended. You cannot agree to do what is unlawful. Your agreement in law, is just as if the invalid clause had never been there.

Litigation in hope of damages is at best an extremely speculative initiative. As in all claims for compensation, there is a need to prove that you have suffered loss, and what you have lost. You would need to show that your customers have gone to your ex-employee, and perhaps prove that they would not have elected to do so but for some inducement or prompting from him. Such proof would have to be specific. Alternatively, you would need to adduce facts to prove that you had lost markets and income because of his breach.

Clearly for a company wishing to prevent employees leaving and taking the company's customers or secrets with them, it is not as simple as it sounds, and woe betide any company which thrusts a clumsily-worded covenant in front of an employee and feels that it has thereby acquired the sort of rights and protection of the kind implied in signature of the Official Secrets Act. It has done nothing of the kind, and such a covenant must be most carefully drafted if it is to stand up in a court of law, whether in the United Kingdom, the U.S.A., or anywhere else.

The covenant must be 'reasonable' in all the circumstances. British courts are loath to tie down technologists, and for good reasons. The more highly specialised the technology, and the more advanced the degree of technical knowledge of the employee himself, the narrower the world in which he can hope to operate; no court would feel entitled to limit his prospect of earning a living, exercising his hard-won and rare skills and, potentially, depriving the community of whatever benefits might derive from the exercise of those skills. Such a covenant, however good the reasons, will inevitably be regarded with the most searching scrutiny and scepticism. This consideration has even greater weight in the U.S.A., where U.S. courts have inherited British common law, and where there is even more emphasis on the need for free enterprise and the need for anti-trust laws.

All that being said, it yet remains obvious that an employer engaging someone who will be permitted access to secrets fundamental to the company's existence, will wish, subject to competent legal advice, to safeguard themselves by way of covenants as best they can. If such a covenant does not restrict an employee absolutely, it is hoped at least that it will inhibit him and so reduce the number of dishonest and disloyal employees.

The company has to ask itself — what would a court consider reasonable in the circumstances in which we find ourselves? Litigation over the theft of our secret processes, or work organisations, or marketing plans would be pointless. It is always satisfactory to see a rogue imprisoned or fined, but it would not constitute redress for us; the damage would have been done. Once the formula for a new soft drink, or a secret process for making carpets wear longer, or a patent for making aircraft engines more silent or speedy, has been disclosed, there is not way we can repair the damage. Our mandate does not extend to other countries, let alone countries at loggerheads with the Western bloc. We would be undercut, we would lose our customers; and if we attempted to retaliate by a price war, we should find ourselves producing the goods without a profit. A court judgement is no compensation for a company's collapse.

What restrictions on an employee might be held to be viable in a court of law.

The drafting of the covenant as already stated must have regard to "reasonableness" — it must have every prospect of standing up in a court. There will always be an inherent gamble in these legalistic precautions, even so; none can forecast a court's judgement, least of all in a hypothetical case.

However, an industrial chemist working on a secret process could be restrained from taking up employment which would or might entail him using the secret knowledge acquired while in his present employ; from setting up in such work anywhere where his employers trade; from working as a chemist for a competitor who trades in the same markets (provided the 'market' was not the whole or most of the world, using the word 'world' in a rational sense).

The period of this restriction would depend upon the extent to which the employee would have access to secrets, and the exclusivity and importance of those industrial secrets. It is impossible to state any hypothetical figure. I can imagine secrets being so important that a restriction of fifteen years might be perfectly reasonable — as in some vital aerospace project, for example, whose designs and processes take years to bring to perfection, and more years to execute into the finished prototype. Leakage of the basic information to competitors, before the actual product could be finished and delivered would be absolutely disastrous. However, such a restraint could be made for ten years or even three years.

Anyone concerned with drawings might well be put under a much shorter restraint, since in other employment he would depend upon his memory of such drawings, which are often intricate, depend upon their relationship of parts, and, of course, upon the size and relative sizes of those parts. Memories dim, even assuming such a drawing could be held effectively in memory.

It would be utterly unreasonable to put such a restraint upon a store-keeper, however secret the contents of the store, unless he had access to something "saleable" to a saboteur.

Perhaps because the law developed largely because of its connection with craftsmen who are thought to be less mobile than executives, the geographical limit which can be placed on a craftsman tends to be much less than that which can be lawfully placed on an executive. The higher the executive, the wider the limit, which is reasonable. Top executives fly all over the world to represent their companies. They make contacts everywhere. If so disposed they can, therefore, do their companies far more harm than those who are less mobile, less well connected, and not so well informed.

Consider the case of a researcher. By definition, his job is and will continue to be, research. Admittedly, much of this research will be general research in his chosen field, but some of it will be specific research in a field related to the activities of his employer. Much of the facts and information he handles would not be available to him except in connection with his job, and because of the resources and research facilities of the firm employing him. Much of his information derives from his basic training and education prior to joining the firm — information which is inherently him, and much of it in the public domain. But some, clearly, derives from the fact that he occupied a position of trust. An obvious example is that of the pharmacist employed to conduct research on behalf of or within the organised complex of a drug company. The restriction which may reasonably be imposed is that he is left free to continue his research but cannot pass on the company's trade secrets and cause the company financial damage.

To summarise: you cannot prevent a man using his head; you can prevent him using something put there during his employment with a company and which is propriety to them, whether such use be for himself or for a third party — that is the thinking which should influence the phrasing of a restrictive covenant.

Having said which, I repeat that such documents offer limited protection. It is more important to check carefully on the bona fides, character and track record of those who are to be employed in positions of trust. To what lengths is it desirable and and legitimate to go for this purpose?

CHAPTER 9

Vetting

Of all subjects which are unpopular with managements, and imply much heart-searching and ambiguity of feeling, none poses so many problems as that of vetting the staff.

To clear the air at once, I must emphasise that no apology is needed or should be given for "vetting" (enquiring as to character and background) those who are to be entrusted with important responsibilities.

I feel that many managements are often either tactless or timid. Ham-handed enquiries into a man's life, especially if conducted in such a way that people who are questioned sense an air of mystery which they might interpret as suspicion, are inexcusable. A man's standing and character are as important as the status and stability of the concern employing him. Skill, tact and firmness — generously admixed with commonsense — are required of those selecting staff or checking on their credentials and suitability.

I mention this because no duty is performed well if coloured by a sense of guilt or apprehension; many concerns merely go through the motions of checking on the character of their employees. If the job is highly specialised, and the prospective employee seemingly highly skilled in a field where there are few people with such qualifications, the temptation may be to say, or merely think: "He looks a nice enough chap. Not the sort to pull any line with us. We don't want to seem intrusive with our enquiries, and frighten him away — or make him withdraw his offer of services — by offending him."

Organisations other than Government Departments are already under a severe handicap when it comes to checking the credentials of prospective personnel; yet they cannot afford to increase the risks involved in engaging the wrong people for posts demanding discretion, loyalty and responsible custodianship of company secrets.

Although every company has its own particular field of activity, and special requirements, there are certain general rules which must be observed if the company's secrets are not to be at risk.

1. The category of information involved in the work must be related to the individual's track record, mental capacity and general character;

2. Assertions as to experience cannot be taken for granted; they may well be true, but people change jobs more frequently these days than was once the case, while the whole business of giving references (where they are given) is very unsatisfactory. Frequently companies give an unsatisfactory employee a glowing reference simply to speed his departure through the factory or office door. They feel it saves time, legal arguments or even trade union retaliation. The delinquent employee pursues his activities with another company;

3. Company secrets are not the property, generally speaking, of the directors and management. A company is a legal entity and to fail to protect company secrets that are essential to its properity is to play false by shareholders. An immense amount of invested money comes from trust funds from which pensions have to be paid, while the majority of private shareholders are quite small people financially, often investing their savings in a few hundreds, or perhaps a few thousand, shares. In a sense, those who run public companies are custodians of their shareholders' savings, and to employ dishonest or vulnerable people for the handling of company secrets (or who can ascertain them without hindrance; is to break faith with the shareholders.

Private firms (as distinct from Government offices) are at a disadvantage. The Government can draw upon many services for information on prospective employees. There is little problem, if pushed to it, to look at a person's income tax returns, equate his life style with his declared financial resources, track back on his education, inspect records of marriages, birth and deaths, Service records (where the subject has been in any of the Forces) and, indeed, to enquire from previous employers, in writing or by interview, into the subject's moral character, domestic arrangements, family background, hobbies, memberships of organisations, and so on. All this can be done under the ample protection of the Official Secrets Act. The subject will not be shown the reports, and therefore those who are interviewed about a prospective employee will feel free to talk in confidence. The process introduced by the Labour Prime Minister Lord Attlee after the disastrous Burgess-Maclean affair was called (and is still) 'positive vetting'. In general it is conducted in a responsible and tactful way, and only in respect of people who have asked for employment of the kind which, they know, will involve detailed enquiries before they can hope to be employed.

Private concerns do not have all these files and records of individuals at their disposal. They must therefore, in a thorough, careful and legal way, follow methods of vetting less privileged than those available to Government departments. It is time-consuming, yet the fact remains that, from existing file records, any government possesses a very detailed biography of every citizen in the land, assuming that it is willing to collate the records reposing in different buildings from the Census Office to Registrar of Births and Deaths, Department of Health and Social Security, Service records offices, hospital and medical records, educational reports, passport office records, and the like.

That a company is entitled to screen or vet its employees is unarguable. Whether it undertakes this task itself, or delegates it to a competent and discreet security agency, is another matter. From the outset of his application for employment it should be made clear that no appointment can be authorised until a sufficient time has been taken to gather, in adequate depth details of the prospective employee's record of past employment, his credit standing, educational status, personal character, domestic status and general social background. The prospective employee should be asked to state specifically that he is willing for this to be done as a necessary preliminary to any positive offer of a job.

Both parties must take this security checking seriously — the employer particularly. The employer, by inference, will feel more relaxed and confident when he has confirmed for himself that he may safely and confidently permit his new staff member to have access to company information; the employee has the satisfaction of knowing that he is held in confident regard. Not that the vetting of staff is the beginning and end of security protection against industrial espionage; but it is a preliminary and fundamental ingredient of it.

It should be emphasised to the applicant that vetting does not imply suspicion; a firm which is not selective in its employees is not likely to be a happy or efficient one, and the individual is not singled out for such enquiries, which apply to all or at least, to all engaged on the level of responsibility proposed.

Some security experts favour a kind of gradation, which affects the duration and thoroughness of vetting. While accepting that certain exceptional degrees of secrecy demand an unusual depth of enquiry, the general rule ought to be that thoroughness and completion should always be the standards applied. Better be sure than sorry. The whole object is to *prevent* industrial espionage — not merely cope with it when it happens. An irretrievable situation caused by loss of vital secrets is not made better by inane and useless expressions of surprise and regret after such theft — "Whoever would have thought it of him!"; "I'd have staked my life on his honesty"; "And to think we've played golf together for years, and he was two-timing us all the time!"

The first and obvious question, raised of course to eliminate any possible doubts on the subject, is: has the prospective employee any convictions and, if so, how serious were they, what was the court's decision, how long ago did it happen, and has there been any cessation of dishonest behaviour?

Clearly, security officers, company executives and security companies do not have access to police records; nor, in my opinion, should they. It is an unfortunate fact that some security companies pack their boards with ex-detectives and ex-police officials who use the experience and contacts within the police service, gained during their past employment, to extract "grace and favour" information from official files. One would hope and expect that such behaviour would be illegal, and prompt punishment meted out for such presumption; but this is not the case. Two private investigators were charged at the Old Bailey with obtaining information from official and bank records by misrepresentation, found guilty and sentenced; but the Appeal Lords later quashed the sentence, establishing that to obtain information from police, government and private organisations is not an offence, even where misrepresentation is made. The curious thing is that, while the enquirer goes scot free, the police official or government employee may well suffer demotion or dismissal for contravening the Official Secrets Act or the Police Act.

There is also the Rehabilitation of Offenders Act, 1974, to be considered. It is too detailed to summarise here (HMSO: ISBN 0 10 5453374 9) but, in effect, enacts that many convictions may be deemed to be "spent" after specified periods of time, and that it may prove legally dubious to induce an applicant to disclose previous convictions or offences:

> Section 4 (2) states: Subject to the provisions of any order made under sub-section (4) below,
> where a question seeking information with respect to a person's previous convictions, offences, conduct or circumstances is put to him or to any other person otherwise than in proceedings before a judicial authority:—
> (a)   the question shall be treated as not relating to spent convictions, and the answer thereto may be framed accordingly; and
> (b)   the person questioned shall not be subject to any liability or otherwise prejudiced in law by reason of any failure to acknow-ledge or disclose a spent conviction or any circumstances ancilli-ary to a spent conviction in his answer to the question.

In brief, a person is not bound to disclose a spent conviction nor, if one is discovered, will it be deemed a proper ground for dismissing or "excluding a person from any office, profession, occupation or employment, or for prejudicing him in any way in any occupation or employment."

Imagine the investigator's dilemma when he discovers that an applicant has a criminal conviction which is pertinent to the position he is seeking, yet that conviction is "spent" under the Rehabilitation of Offenders Act. Should he break the law and tell his client, or should he allow an employee to be put in a position of temptation where in similar instances in the past he has succumbed. In such instances I always advise my client to obtain a certain newspaper giving him the date of edition in which the report of the conviction appeared. The client can then read a public document and make up his own mind.

Nevertheless, an employer is entitled to full information on the background of any one likely to be given access to company secrets. Where there is reason to suppose some past demeanour may have happened, the files of the local newspaper may reveal it. Searching files, again, is time-consuming, even though, by law, every news-paper must be filed at the vast British Library at Colindale. A search, not to be prohibitive in time and money, would need to be based on some approximate date.

Enquiries have, clearly, to be conducted with extreme tact and discretion; one is not entitled to ask questions of employers, neighbours, tradesmen and the like which could be interpreted as implying doubt about a man's integrity.

What information may fairly be sought about an employee?

Obviously, his full name, date and place of birth, marital status, number of children, the name of his spouse, his mother and father's name, social security number, home addresses for the last 20 years, present address, details of education by year, school and its address, and records of his employment since he started working; supported where possible with documentation ie. birth certificate etc. The most recent employer should be given first. This information, especially, should be thoroughly and neatly set out — by address, job, department, and from the month of a year of commencement to the month of the year of cessation.

References will be required, giving the name, address and occupation of the referees.

There is something to be said for standardised applications for employment, and for form letters sent to employers and others seeking information about the applicant; it enables the information *as stated* to be put into tidy and easily accessible form. But the confirmation of information is what matters most.

It is not unknown for criminals and, indeed, industrial spies, to create the very "company" which they give as a reference. It may well be a public telephone box, accommodation address, the home of a friend, or an office or bed-sitting room hired for a temporary purpose.

Personally, I prefer to call upon people whose names have been given as references. One can see what sort of an address it is, whether there is evidence of company activity (if a company has been mentioned). A search at Companies House in the City of London, or their headquarters in Cardiff, will reveal when the company was formed, for what purposes it exists, the names and addresses of the directors and company secretary, and the annual reports the filing of which is a statutory obligation. An assessment can also be made of the referees.

Records of bankruptcies will reveal if the individual has been declared bankrupt at any time. If he has left a trail of unpaid bills wherever he goes, a credit rating will soon reveal his status.

So far as his track record of work is concerned, he needs to know precisely what his duties were and how — in the sense of giving satisfaction to his employers — these obligations were discharged. Did he have access to that Company's confidential documents and procedures? It goes without saying that if he spoke too freely about his previous employers' affairs when seeking his new post, his lack of discretion would be noticed, and a sensible employer would foresee that his own confidential information might likewise be bandied about.

Perhaps the applicant (especially if he is an industrial spy) has given as previous employers firms or companies that have ceased trading. This is also a good ruse for a person with a criminal record to cover that embarassing period of time that he spent in prison. Again, under existing company law, notification has to be made of a company ceasing to operate; details of an inactive or wound-up company can still be consulted, and the addresses of the directors ascertained. In such a case I would make it my business to call upon the previous manager or one of the directors, to confirm that the applicant had worked during the period stated, and discover what view was taken of his services, and the circumstances in which he left that company's employ. It is even more useful to ask if the director can remember the name of the man's immediate departmental chief at that time, or of his foreman.

The right to privacy has had a good deal of airing in most Western countries, in the United Kingdom and in the United States particularly. There is much apprehension about the keeping of files on individuals and their private lives, and one needs to ask what definable boundaries exist, if any, between legitimate enquiry and a respect for the privacy of the individual.

So far as industrial espionage is concerned, the issue is a simple one; this sort of piracy, the stealing of valuable industrial secrets, is growing alarming, and a company is entitled to take reasonable steps to protect itself against it, *in advance*. The vetting of employees to this end is in the interest of all employees, from executives to working bench, for a single renegade can jeopardise the livings of all the rest.

I am not in favour of obtaining by covert means details of anybody's bank account; in the legitimate pursuit of enquiries relating to important staff appointments, banks can at their discretion, answer such a query as "would you consider Mr . . . . . good for a credit of, say, ten thousand pounds?" Banks are not obliged to answer queries other than those which the law enjoins; in certain circumstances they may be compelled to disclose details of their clients' business to the Inland Revenue or the Police. Those cases are exceptional.

Vetting requires not simply the compilation and confirmation of information regarding the applicant; it requires analysis. It is the quality of the information that counts, not merely the quantity. What sort of picture emerges from it all? Is he is a man of sober habits, happily married, a good husband and father, a prompt payer of his bills, owner of his own home, keeping up a standard of living dignified and adequate, but void of extravagance? Does his income account, logically, for his life-style? If he is living far beyond the scale of his earnings, he must either have made plenty of money in the past and conserved some of it, or inherited it, or been engaged in some profitable activity which he has not disclosed.

If companies are not to obtain police information by surreptitious means, yet have a moral obligation to their employees and share-holders to avoid employing in key positions people who may have run seriously foul of the law, what resources are open to them? It is not unknown for security staff to be recruited from men having criminal records. Perhaps certain applicants might be invited to obtain a letter from the police confirming that they know no reason why he should not be placed in delicate work. This is the system practised in Sweden, and seems quite effective in preventing criminal types from infiltrating into departments where there are important secrets. Oh, that it was so in the United Kingdom.

The checking of educational records is absolutely essential. Putting "B.A." or "D.Sc" after one's name proves nothing. Often prospective employees claim to have attended particular colleges and universities, or to have acquired degrees, and enquiries have sometimes revealed that some schools did not provide the courses which, it was claimed, were taken there. A check with the educational authorities, and a perusal of examination results, may be necessary.

Firms in the U.S.A. tend, in the questionnaires which prospective employees are required to complete, to go beyond the degree of personal detail expected in the United Kingdom. Apart from date of birth, height and weight (and sex, of course) are recorded. So, too, are any special physical defects, hobbies, car ownership, rank and branch of service in the armed forces of the United States, date of discharge, and reasons for discharge. This policy should in my opinion be adopted in the UK.

The neighbourhood checks, as carried out in the U.S.A., and in the UK for U.S. companies are unusually thorough. The type of home in which the applicant lives, its value, local enquiries as to the type of work neighbours believe him to pursue, his relationship with authorities in general, his general reputation, moral character, drinking habits (if to excess), and so on. His membership of civil or civic organisations is noted. Not merely is it asked if the applicant "has ever been in trouble" but whether any member of his family has been in trouble also. They also check on the wife, who could have a lover working in a rival company.

The questionnaire often sent to previous employers as part of pre-employment investigation really gets down to assessing the work the applicant did and how he performed it. The company is asked to give (from their records) the applicant's date and place of birth; if these differed from those proffered by the applicant in his search for a new job, the disparity would need to be explained — whether the man gave different accounts of himself, or whether the company which previously employed him was slipshod in keeping records.

Previous employers are asked to state the man's starting position, and the nature and grade of his work at the time that he left. Other details required are whether he supervised others, and if so, how many; a list of previous employers as shown in *the company's* records — again as a check on details the man has supplied in his latest application; — the degree of "security clearance" he had been given, if any; his job rating (from "superior" to "below average") and his job performance; his co-operation with staff and colleagues, his emotional balance, general appearance, capacity for leadership, attendance record, any on-the-job accidents, or difficulties related to his job. Finally, were his services satisfactory and would he be re-employed if he wished to be?

References are taken up with the same thoroughness. These enquiries frequently include information about the applicant's spouse. In the upper echelons of business there is usually a social side — company functions, seminars, conferences, business trips and so on — and it is fairly common for a man's wife to participate in some of these, thereby coming into contact with company officials and perhaps executives of rival companies. Her discretion, temperament and character play their part in her husband's acceptability for work of a specially responsible category.

Educational enquiries are seldom perfunctory. The school's name, address, telephone number, grade, and the name of the school officials interviewed are the first requisite details. But there follows a barrage of other questions: between what dates was the man a pupil? Where did his parents live? What were his main subjects? Did he graduate and if so, what degree did he receive? What was his standing in class — and his position out of how many students? What extra-curricula activities did he follow? Clearly, baseball would be an acceptable answer, while glue-sniffing would not be. What did his teachers and faculty advisers think of him? What was his health record like? It is usual even to ask for the names of teachers and professors who taught the individual in their classes.

However, these are the rigid and comprehensive steps taken in the U.S.A. by a conscientious and security-conscious company. The majority are not, as the estimation in the *Daily Mail* of January 2nd, 1980, of the extent of computer crime in the United States — a staggering £100,000 million! — shows. And computer crime is only one aspect of industrial espionage. It is true that few individuals could emerge from such a searching enquiry without at least a tiny blot on their copy book somewhere; indeed, by these criteria, the late Sir Winston Churchill would only with difficulty have climbed beyond the level of office-boy. As he cheerfully admitted in later life, his academic career could scarcely have been less distinguished. But the object of security vetting is not to find the perfect man, but to detect in time a man whose defects of character would make him an unsuitable person to be privy to the secrets and procedures entailed in his job.

In many countries and notably in the United States, however, there is a vast amount of legislation aimed at protecting the individual's right to privacy, and preventing his character being assailed by malice or misinformation in the course of employment enquiries. In the U.S.A., those conducting a security clearance have to keep in mind the stringent provisions of the Fair Credit Reporting Act (FRCA) and Investigative Consumer Reports (ICR). The FRCA insists that organisations supplying reports on individuals must insist on them being used for "legitimate business purposes". There is little comfort in such wording, whose vagueness could well lead to difficulty in a court of law. The individual must, of course, be notified beforehand of the intention to institute such intensive enquiries; further, if he should be denied employment as a result of adverse comment made during enquiries, he may demand in writing to see the report. I wonder if these inhibitive considerations are explained to the many people — previous employers, neighbours, friends, educational authorities and others — whose comments, if damaging, might earn them a black eye! We may assume that interviewees are not told that the subject will be given the right to see reports whose contents reflect adversely on his character — otherwise I imagine that they would be constrained in their replies to queries.

In the compilation of reports, on the basis of which the decision to employ or not is taken, care should be taken to weigh the facts against the source. If the interviewee is a relative or friend, some degree of loyalty may be presupposed, and perhaps an inclination to forget those aspects of character on which a non-friend would be more outspoken. Nor should it be taken for granted that everyone interviewed is truthful, reasonable or without prejudice. Disparities of basic facts, such as different accounts of jobs said to have been held, or birthdates, or addresses, are another matter; if the fault lies with the applicant, the conclusion may be inescapable that, if he is disposed to deceive other people, his latest prospective employer would prove no exception.

*   *   *

Are mechanical or scientific aids of value in assessing the potential reliability of an employee?

Are "lie detector" tests of use in eliminating applicants whose integrity is doubtful?

Are psychological tests of value?

Can graphology be used to locate undesirables?

All these questions are relevant, since one, more or all of these resources are frequently used in evaluation of an employee whose duties would entail access to classified material.

Not one of these methods, or all of them put together, can be a positive safeguard against industrial espionage but, in combination with the enquiries I have mentioned, may be usefully revealing.

The Polygraphy or stress evaluator is one of the most commonly used pieces of apparatus. In skilful and knowledgeable hands it can be of value, but it has limitations. I do not go along with the assertion of the American security consultant, Charles R. Carson, who has spent 26 years with the Federal Bureau of Investigation and 20 years as a Special Agent before starting his own business in New Orleans, that "a polygraph test is the best method for determining dishonesty levels. These tests must be given uniformly to all applicants considered for employment in high temptation areas". He is also on record as saying that "the polygraphy establishes the truth of answers to pertinent questions." Again, this is too exaggerated a statement of the polygraph's dependability.

The polygraph is a tool. Any tool can be used well or badly. The results it produces may be evaluated with competence or ineptitude. To place excessive confidence in its use is to court the very risk it is intended to eliminate, for if the machine gives the applicant an honesty clearance, or is assumed to have done so, a confidence may be placed in the applicant which, on the basis of polygraph tests, may prove quite unmerited.

What is a polygraph? Briefly, an apparatus for measuring human stress.

Stress can be caused by (1) anger; (2) anxiety; (3) physical disability and the physical or mental frustrations arising from such handicap; (4) unusual physical exertion, and (5) a sense of guilt.

These variations of stress are widely felt at some time or another by all human beings, and the physical reactions to such largely psychosomatic states can, indeed, be accurately recorded. But it is in the reasoning, and the interpretation of physical reactions in mental terms, that skill and care are required. Stress can be caused by any one of the five main causes I have listed; in a polygraph test, the operator knows that some tests are bound to be inconclusive, since factors other than guilt or a desire to deceive may account for his physical reactions.

The polygraph measures blood pressure, heartbeat, the rate of breathing and the amount of sweating on the hands. There are devices by which these changes are recorded by the machine; a blood pressure cuff, something like a ligament, around the upper arm, forearm or wrist; an electrode at the fingertips, a band or so around the chest.

Under stress, the heartbeat quickens. Breathing may become deeper and quicker or, conversely, more shallow and slow. Skin changes can be measured by electrodes at the palm or fingertips; moisture increases electrical conductivity, so when a person sweats, as happens in moments of stress, the changes in electrical current are recorded on paper.

An employee, or applicant, cannot usefully be subject to an *immediate* polygraph test. There has to be careful preparation. Any atmosphere of mystery or menace may put him in a state comparable to a visit to an amateur dentist by a patient with a broken molar. The stress is induced, not inherent! Thus, there had to be a pre-testing interview, in which the applicant is made aware of, and shows himself to be willing to undertake, the tests; for the interviewer to re-cap on the facts of the matter, and to form some estimation of the kind of man with whom he is dealing. The interviewer will explain the purposes of the tests.

An important preliminary — but with the polygraph working — is to try out one or two 'control' questions.

The object of a control question is to make the subject lie, and note his physical reactions at the time. Thus you have a recorded polygraph reaction to what is, unquestionably, a lie.

To illustrate the point. If I were to question a subject, using the polygraph, without a preliminary interview, or the precaution of 'control' questions, I would have no positive clue as to the source of the stress reaction. Of course, I suppose, if he had stolen a packet of paper clips, and every time I mentioned 'paperclips' to him the machine went haywire, I could very easily interpret this was proving his theft. What if he were in a seething rage of being suspected of such a thing, and that, consequently, the mere mention of the subject put his blood pressure up?

So the control question gives some indication of his reaction when lying. You might, for example, place a row of dominoes face down (or, say, just ten of them). You tell the subject to pick up one at a time, look at it, and, when the examiner, who does not necessarily know which one he has picked, asks him if it is such and such a number (making his way through the series of numbers) the subject has in every case to answer "No".

But, clearly, by going through all the numbers the examiner knows are on the table, *one* of his questions, such as "Is it two sixes?" must be right, and the subject's answer a lie. The stress reactions recorded by the polygraph at this point are noted, and used as the criteria by which to detect a lie when the subject is under test and the examiner has no other means of knowing whether the answers he is receiving are true or false.

The polygraph is not a lie detector. Although that is the name by which it is commonly known as. It measures physical stress which may or may not be connected with guilt. Nor does the polygraph establish innocence. Despite these limitations, it can be useful as part of a general investigation.

In the United Kingdom the polygraph is often regarded with suspicion by those invited to be subjected to its tests, or with an enthusiasm, sometimes considered excessive, by others who see in it a short cut to enquiries. Thus, in August, 1974, Mr J.K. McLellan,

Chief Constable of Lanarkshire Constabulary, told reporters that he considered that there was something about a polygraph worth investigating. "We must convince people that to have a polygraph test would help us eliminate them from our investigations, not involve them." I never did find out the result of his findings and he is now dead.

Two years earlier a Detective Chief Inspector who went to the United States on a Winston Churchill Memorial Trust Fellowship reported: "I see the polygraph as being an inestimable help in the detection of crime and hope that the ethical objections to its use in this country" (i.e. the United Kingdom) will soon be overcome."

In 1975 the Labour Member of Parliament for Nuneaton, Leslie Huckfield, asked the Secretary of State for Employment whether there would be legislation introduced to prevent employers from conducting personality or lie detector tests on potential employees. He considered the nature and depth of the questions excessive and unnecessary. The Secretary of State replied that he did not consider legislation necessary as there was no evidence of lie detectors being used in tests for selection purposes in Britain.

The polygraph or so-called 'lie detector' has been used in the United States since the early 1920's when Dr Jon Larson, then a student at the University of California Medical School and working part time with, used an instrument to record simultaneous changes in blood pressure, heart rate and respiration patterns. There is, therefore, nearly half a century of empirical and experimental knowledge behind the modern use of the polygraph, and I must make it clear that, in acknowledging its limitations, I do not advise against its use or usefulness. In World War II, when it became essential to "screen" people needed in intelligence and top secret military appointments, the polygraph speeded up the process. In the United States today almost every police force makes use of the polygraph. None do in the UK.

It would not be true to say that *no* industrial firms make use of it in selecting applicants for employment, in an effort to minimise the risk of engaging an applicant who might indulge in industrial espionage, but certainly they are very few. Even today the majority of companies regard industrial espionage as a risk which endangers others but not themselves — if, indeed, they give any thought to it at all!

For my part, I prefer the Psychological Stress Evaluator. The type I use is the model PSE 101 made by Dektor of the U.S.A., which detects, measures and displays graphically certain specific, stress-related components of the human voice.

Superimposed on the audible voice frequencies are inaudible frequency modulations (FM) whose strength and pattern relate inversely to the degree of psychological stress in the speaker at the time of speaking.

These *involuntary* modulations of frequency result from minute oscillations of the muscles of the voice mechanism. Known technically as physiological tremor or micro-tremor, they can be shown in the laboratory as a normal accompaniment to the activity of any voluntary muscle, occurring at a rate of 8-14 cycles per second.

In other words, however, good an actor a man or woman may be, there are elements in the aural makeup of their spoken words of which they are unaware, which they themselves cannot hear, and which reflect their true thoughts. Of course, according to the strength, intelligence or cunning of a subject, the element of control varies. Most of the functional indicators of stress are attributed to the Autonomic Nervous System (ANS), while physiological tremor as seen in the voice mechanism appears to be controlled by the Central Nervous System (CNS). As the ANS gains dominance in a stress situation, the micro-tremors are suppressed.

Stress induced by fear, anxiety, guilt and conflict facilities the detection of attempted deception. A tape recording preserves the speech pattern, containing the voluntarily formed words which contain the involuntary speech components. The Psychological Stress Evaluator processes the voice frequencies and displays the inaudible, stress-related FM patterns on a moving strip chart.

Clearly, the polygraph and the PSE have their uses, though neither, in my view, should be employed without the permission or in the case of the PSE, knowledge of the subject. The advantage of the PSE is that it does not have to be wired up to the subject in any way.

In many states polygraphs are licensed, and similar restraints often apply to "other devices" such as the stress evaluator, sometimes called the voice analyser.

The makers claim a 95 per cent accuracy for the PSE's evaluations. Considering the complications and complexities of human nature, this record of success seems to be very high and therefore questionable.

The PSE's obvious advantage over the polygraph is that the

whole operation frees much of the stress; there is an unwelcome 'brave new world' atmosphere about connecting electrodes to a man's body, a rigmarole which is quite likely to induce the very stress whch it is intended to detect. The PSE permits the test to be carried out in a relaxed, comfortable and effortless way, free of the foreboding with which a vast number of people regard 'mysterious' machines and apparatus. The disadvantage is that it only tests one sense whereas the polygraph tests three.

The PSE chart is traced by a heated stylus on heat-sensitive paper for ease of operation and permanence. The tape recording can be charted in four different modes of display, for general or detailed evaluation. Used intelligently, the PSE has been known to give 100% correct diagnosis. A Maryland County Police Chief Polygraph Examiner proved 26 out of 26 cases to be correct by corroborative confessional subsequent investigation.

A recent newcomer to the field of vetting, offering a quite different service or system, is The Stanton Corporation, of Chicago, Illinios, U.S.A., which has affiliated offices in most major American cities, in Canada, South Africa, Manilla and Australia.

Ironically, the Corporation's literature hints at past personal experiences of industrial espionage! It seems that an honesty test by a rival concern was (by their account) "patterned after the Stanton Survey by an ex-employee of Stanton . . . items in the test were altered just enough to prevent copyright infringement suit." With commendable restraint, and possibly with an eye on the libel laws, Stanton's brochure does not pin-point the alleged culprit by name.

Now — as to the nature and merits of their system.

In effect, they supply their clients with a pro-forma 'survey' or detailed questionnaire, and the sum total of the answers is then analysed by them with a view to establishing the potential employee's honesty or otherwise.

The Corporation's brochure asserts that "To any good judge, any good interrogator, known people give themselves away by what they say and how they say it. Stanton found out that people give themselves away by what their choice of words is. Not handwriting, but PHRASEOLOGY."

It is claimed that hundreds of words have been catalogued for their "true meaning". I must confess that the examples adduced seem wanting in logic, and too dogmatic. I am not at all sure that three out of every four people who venture the comment "this is a nice place to work" to an interviewer are, as stated, dishonest.

However, it is claimed that applicants with a history of criminal behaviour will answer key questions differently to those with clean records. The claim is made on the basis of two random samples drawn from a group of 30,000 applicants who had been processed at the Stanton Analysis Center. The applicants had sought jobs with a total of 320 clients and were being checked for suitability as employees. By a system of points-scoring it was established to the satisfaction of Stanton that the mean score of applicants with criminal tendencies was twice or (as with another sample) nearly twice as high as those who were honest.

The employer is invited to get the applicant to complete one of these questionnaires, assess the score according to the answers given, and then telephone Stanton for "instant analysis". Alternatively, the employer may elect to make his own analysis on the basis of the completed questionnaire. Alternatively, the survey can be mailed to Stanton, who will analyse it and respond with a telephoned report.

The Corporation give an impressive list of executives in banking, industry, retail stores and the security industry. I have not tried the system, and cannot usefully comment upon its merits, except to observe that such a system — based upon an analysis of *written* answers to questions — must presuppose the truthfulness of replies, otherwise any system of scoring by points would be impossible. Is such a supposition were safe to make, an elaborate questionnaire of this nature would be quite unnecessary.

Personality tests are another technique of staff selection used extensively in the United States and, to a lesser degree, in Britain. They depend upon interviews with and written statements by the applicant, whose family and professional record will be noted and discussed. There are very many tests for assessing intelligence, reflex actions and emotional attitudes, too numerous to list here. There are various 'schools' of psychology, including those of the best-known psychologists, Jung, Freud and Adler, who are by no means agreed on the fundamentals of the profession.

Yet an applicant's track record, not merely professional, but human, is of enormous importance. Behavioural science does produce patterns of human behaviour from which conclusions of human behaviour in the future may be fairly surmised. A man who shows by his comments that he has always been critical, or suspicious, of his superiors may be revealing an innate jealousy of anyone whose achievements or status exceed his own. There is a swift and easy transition from jealousy to dislike, and from dislike to hatred. One can imagine a perceptive executive saying to himself: "I don't want his sort of jealousy and resentment smouldering in my company. Once he feels a sense of grievance, he will, by his previous record, want to score off in some way — against the individual above him, or against the company". In short, this character trait could be considered a security risk.

His general flair for leadership and responsibility will be examined in any personality test. Work produces many a crisis. Things do not go to pattern. Somebody may be ill, or leave, or become involved in an accident, and his responsibilities may in a second be increased enormously. If this involved being jockeyed into a level of responsibility where there were strong security considerations, would he be equal to it?

The time to ask this is before the contingency occurs, and before the man is engaged.

In the Services, "headshrinkers" were often the butt of much ridicule or even dislike. But some of that criticism came from inadequate people who knew inwardly that, subject to expert scrutiny, they might be found inadequate for the ranks they held, or wished to achieve.

Most professional psychologists consider it an ethical requirement of a personality test that the subject should be made aware of the conclusions reached and, if he so wished, be allowed to challenge them.

I have, as a matter of interest, submitted to a psychologist test myself — happy in the knowledge that, whatever the conclusions, I would be unlikely to sack myself! I was gratified to learn that my examiner considered me "at the lower end of the superior range of intellectual ability as compared with the population of UK managers" though this phrase seems to me to be having it both ways (*lower* end of the *superior* range). I agree that I am "habituated to working much harder than most" and commend such habituation. I am not sure what is meant by the statement that I "have nowhere to go which does not destabilise his life in some way." If what is meant by this is that decisions imply risk, this is a common factor of human life and does not worry me overmuch. Allowing for these somewhat negative reactions on my part, I would say that parts of the psychological assessment, prepared for me by the psychologist, did contain some useful and perceptive points.

*   *   *

Graphology is another technique by which the future dependability of an employee may be assessed.

As a tool of analysis, graphology has long established itself. Long before World War II the Saudek Institute of Graphology had established itself as an institution where handwriting was submitted for analysis before posts of extreme responsibility were assigned.

The potential integrity of a person can be assessed with considerable accuracy. Handwriting, in its characteristics, cannot be disguised in fundamental ways, nor do physical disadvantages affect the significant features of an individual's handwriting. For these reasons it is used extensively in Europe and in North America as a personality selection technique. An estimation from the March 1979 issue of *Dun's Review* suggests that more than 85% of European countries use graphology for this purpose.

The founder of the Institute of Psychology of Handwriting in Budapest, Dr Klara Roman, evolved a system of "graphological psychograms" in the course of twenty years research, and has since established the system in the U.S.A.

The main factors looked for in writing are left slant, right slant, middle zone height, right trend, left trend, horizontal expansion, angularity, word spacing, right margin, organisation, alignment control, narrowness, tension, connectedness, simplification of form, rhythm, bunching and joining of words, exaggerated curlicues and flourishes.

The various characteristics are given a score, and the final analysis, on the basis of a quite complicated chart, assigns different values to intelligence, work possibilities, creativity, dependability and other human qualities and skills.

Not all graphologists follow this Hungarian system. Richard Saudek, a pioneer in this field, set out his theories in a textbook which is now a classic of its kind, in the thirties.

Graphology is taught in many schools, colleges and institutes and there are many practising graphologists in all European countries and in the United States (which has a *Directory of Handwriting Analysis,* published by Marjorie Westerguard of 31246 Wagner, Warren, MI 48093).

Certain characteristics of handwriting have been confirmed by comparison of features in groups of people having the same characteristics. Thus, lines sloping up and long t-bars often denote ambition; upright writing with over-ornate capital letters and fussy flourishes may imply arrogance; backward sloping writing often indicates an over-cautious disposition and — watch it! — writing which slopes upwards very steeply, combined with uneven middle-zone letters may indicate deceit.

Again, as a guinea-pig, I have had my handwriting analysed by a scientific graphologist. The 5,000-word report was highly perceptive. I was flattered to be given high marks for tact, adaptability, imagination, development capacity, energy, enterprise and drive but mildly surprised to find myself a low score of 40 in self-reliance (after making 30 parachute jumps!) and earning only 45 points of a possible hundred for "accuracy and detail". A little ego-deflating!

My report was extremely detailed, and accurate in most of its conclusions. Had this been a report prepared for somebody wishing to form an appraisal of my character and potentialities as an employee, it would, in my view, have been a balanced and fair report. There is nothing speculative or show-business about graphologists. It is an exact science which has proved its worth for more than half a century, and has behind it an immense wealth of accumulated facts which support its principles of analysis.

A graphological test, combined with psychological interviews, stress evaluator tests and the intensive enquiries I have outlined, would, undoubtedly, limit severely, if not entirely, the number of miscreants achieving posts of authority in important companies and institutions.

Cost is, however, a factor. It costs about £750 to physically check on a man's career and background thoroughly; it really does take time and trouble and is worthless unless conducted by experts who have tact, tenacity and patience. The other tests I have mentioned would add even further to the cost.

I must again repeat that cost ought not to be the main consideration where the issue is the protection of company secrets. Their loss simply cannot be valued, and frequently cannot be repaired. Economy on security is the worst and most dangerous economy of all.

CHAPTER 10

Counter Measures and Security Planning

What precautions can a company take against industrial espionage?

Some are simple. Some are complicated. Many are quite cheap. Most are very expensive.

Clearly, a company has to ask itself: what, in relation to our running costs, our turnover, our capital investment and the potential loss or depreciation of any of these things through industrial espionage, can we afford to spend as a precaution against it?

It is not wholly a financial decision. A man may be very good at figures but less than imaginative when it comes to assessing the determination of his competitors, the effectiveness of existing security arrangements, and an estimation of the various point of vulnerability from a security point of view.

The management, if it really deserves its name, has to say to itself: we have got to reduce the possibility of industrial espionage to the absolute minimum of chance — as near to a minimum as intelligent planning and precautions can make it.

Even so, the acturial voice must be heard, though not as dictating policy. There is little point in over-insuring to the point that the profits whose theft one is trying to avoid are thrown away by needless extravagances.

Let us try to envisage a conclave of top executives — not too many of them, as the whole point of such operations is to prevent leakages and retain an element of surprise in precautions against industrial espionage — meeting to discuss how to combat industrial espionage.

There are certain elementary questions they would have to ask themselves:

1. How secure — from the standpoint of access to strangers — are our offices, workshops, and premises generally?

166

2. To what degree and in what categories ought we to classify documents in this company? What information is general, limited, confidential or top secret?
3. How secure from interference are our
   a) Computers
   b) Computer files
   c) Correspondence files
   d) Drawings and designs
   e) Company's legal documents
   f) Company accounts
   g) Telephone lines, Telex etc.?
4. Do we restrict access to these different categories of information to particular sections of our staff; if so, which classifications to which staff?
5. But if we *do* restrict access to certain categories of information to certain members of the staff, is it sufficient a safeguard, merely to exclude them from the circulation list of these documents whose security classification is above their level of security clearance? We may not *proffer* them access — but have we taken adequate steps to ensure that physical access to areas where confidential information is visible or available, is denied them?
6. Can we answer the foregoing questions ourselves, on the basis of the information at present available, or do we need
   a) to appoint extra security staff
   b) employ an outside consultant?
7. If the answer to question 6 is (b) — that we need a consultant, how do we go about choosing one?

Let us take the last question first. It has been decided to choose a consultant.

As a first step he will probably recommend an "electronic sweep". This is an elementary but vital first precaution. Of little use to discuss improving your security precautions if every word you say is being transmitted by a hidden bug, or recorded surreptitiously!

What you do *not* do is to flip the pages of the business telephone directory or the Yellow Pages. It is too easy in the United Kingdom to set up as a security consultant and, if you choose unwisely, you could end up with an ex-policeman who has been thrown out of the force for misbehaviour, or a criminal who needs only a stock of printed paper, a table and a room anywhere (even at home) to set up in business!

If the Company solicitor cannot obtain a name from a fellow solicitor or other legal source, the best course is to enquire of a professional association such as The International Professional Security Association, The American Society of Industrial Security, The Association of British Investigators or The Institute of Professional Investigators — (see appendix for fuller international list) unless you happen to know of a company which has encountered a similar problem, solved it to their satisfaction with the help of a security consultant, and so can recommend a concern from personal experience. I repeat: you must be sure of the bona fides of the security consultant whom you decide to engage, otherwise you are not slamming the door in the face of industrial spies, but possibly admitting them! A dishonest security consultant might well plant bugs for his own benefit, or misuse for profit the information about your company which you are attempting to protect.

You have probably done well to engage a professional, because the equipment he will bring with him is not only varied, highly specialised and expensive, but of a kind which — even if your company possessed it — would be useless in the hands of untrained people. The equipment required includes:

1) Electronic sweep or de-bugger
2) A telephone analyser
3) An ordinary AF/FM radio
4) A small metal detector
5) A harmonica or oscillator
6) A portable X-ray unit
7) A radio mike, and
8) a tool kit.

You will need to meet him in an outside office and not in those to be searched, for obviously you do not wish your instructions to him to be overheard should the premises be bugged. During the sweep, utmost silence must be maintained, for should the room be bugged any conversation between you will be overheard.

Do not take a "it's beyond me. Just get on with it and tell me what you find" attitude — ask to see the various pieces of equipment and enquire what they do and be shown how they work. It is not unknown for security consultants to arrive with impressive-looking boxes of tricks which do nothing useful. Coloured lights flash, wheels go whirr and indicators vacillate wildly, but it is sometimes in aid of earning him a fee and not protecting your property. However, I prefer to think that, at this stage, you have exercised the caution I commended and chosen a thoroughly professional operator.

Probably your consultant will have with him a radio microphone similar to those used on the stage and in television. The Home Office will give a licence for this type of radio transmitter to be used in this context. Be very wary if an actual bug is produced as a demonstration, for it is extremely unlikely that a licence will be issued by the Home Office and the consultant will be technically breaking the law himself by contravening the Wireless and Telegraphy Act 1949, in that he is using a transmitter without a licence. A person who is prepared to break the law is a person to be avoided.

It is important that you insist that either yourself or a member of the staff be with the consultant during the whole time the sweep is being carried out. The object is to ensure that in searching for bugs he is not planting them himself. After all, in engaging him to prevent the theft of valuable company secrets, you are admitting that there are company secrets worth stealing.

If, therefore, a consultant was dishonest, a bug planting by him might be done for one of two reasons: (a) to eavesdrop on your company affairs with a view to selling the information, or (b) to ensure regular and further business, for immediately after planting the bug he would "discover" it and you would realise how right you were to have the sweep carried out. You need not be constrained by the thought that the professional will object to this mild supervision because, if he is a professional, he will well understand the reasons for it. If there is more than one operative, then more than one member of your staff must be assigned, to deal with each.

So a physical search has been decided upon. Even here, you need to be specific. Which particular areas of your offices, workshops or other premises are important enough to justify the sweep? Remembering the incredibly small size which microtransmitters have now reached, and that they can be placed almost anywhere — air vents, ventilating shafts, electric switch recesses, pictures, clocks, radios, ash trays, books, files, walls, ceilings or anything else — it is clear that, short of pulling the building down a *total* check is impossible. It would involve x-raying every brick, nook and cranny on every level! So there it is; where does the check start and how far is it practicable for it to go?

But, in the area selected for sweeping, the search will be very thorough. Every inch of the room is searched for a foreign body, all wires traced to their source. It has to be remembered that a remotely-controlled transmitter may have been planted, and that it may be switched off during the sweep. And there may be a wire leading to a miniature, sound-activated tape recorder somewhere. Devices to cope with that sort of threat can be costly. What is known in the United States as a Non-Linear Junction Detector costs about £1,500 or $3,000. (depending on the rate of exchange).

Look with suspicion on new paint (especially if it does not precisely match!) or refurbished plaster. They should be scanned with a metal detector and if a positive result is obtained the plastering should be dug out to check that it covers no bug. All bugs contain some metal element and can be detected by using a metal detector.

Telephones come in for special and rigorous attention. Each must be dismantled by unscrewing the base, and carefully examined. Both the mouth piece and ear piece unscrewed and the cylindrical objects inside will be carefully checked for bugs which are used to tap telephones, and which I have described in an earlier chapter. The lines should be traced as far back as possible to the point where they leave the building, and checked individually.

No assumptions should be made as to *where* bugs might be. Not only likely but unlikely places should come under scrutiny. Underneath surfaces of desks, the space behind curtains, perhaps up near the curtain rails where nobody ever troubles to look, behind books, or in boxes, filing cabinets — the possibilities are endless but eliminating any of them one by one is worth while.

Presents and advertising gifts should not be excluded. Remember how the Russians fooled the American Embassy in Moscow by presenting them with a large eagle, embedded in which was a bug? It did its job for quite a while before the Americans, with all their wealth and expertise, detected it. Similarly, ash trays, reading lamps, gift calendars, even a complimentary calculator, may all contain bugs. This is quite an easy procedure, using such equipment as the Inspector, which produces a Polaroid instant x-ray photograph of the object.

The electronic search demands the very best equipment and it is because of this that I have recommended the employment of a first class security consultant in preference to staff, doubtful starters or pin-money amateurs. There are many cheap pieces of apparatus on the market, both in Europe and North America, which purport to satisfy all anti-bugging requirements, such as a small hand-held model which necessitates a manual sweep of all the wave-lengths. It is time-consuming, although it may achieve its object. One German maker offers a miniature transmitter detecting device which can be carried by politicians, business men and others as a sort of electronic bodyguard; but this detector also picks up local radio stations, the noise of electric typewriters, TV and radio sets and a whole range of electronic noise. The business of sweeping, scanning all walls, furniture, ceilings, floors and objects with the antenna, in a regular pattern of six inches apart, is time consuming but should never be hurried, for then the job would not be done properly. You should be careful not to suggest impatience by your manner, or imply that the operator is dragging it out; it cannot be done hurriedly.

There are many excellent anti-bugging devices on the market, such as the Scanlock Mark VB, a high speed, automatic apparatus, easily portable, which detects and locks-to-signal as it detects bugging devices. Its advantage is that it gives the best of both worlds — it can be used as an automatic detector or a manual device, providing comparatively high speed checking of important areas such as board rooms, conference rooms, etc.

What attitude should be taken if this, the first step in reshaping the company's security precautions, reveals the existence of a bug?

This is an issue for discussion at board level.

Industrial espionage as such is not an offence, but the use of a bug is. The law is being broken, and as a law-abiding citizen you should consider reporting the matter to the police. Yet occasions do arise where such action, and the ensuing publicity, make it plain to the world that the company has been the victim of industrial espionage, perhaps to the extent (so far as any shareholder, customer or the public in general are concerned) that the company's viability is held in question. In other words, it might seem to the directors, and might actually be the case, that the damage done eventually to the company's reputation and fortunes would be much greater than if they had been silent and, so to speak "kept it in the family".

It is unlikely that the security consultant himself would report the matter to the police. He might well recommend such a course, thereby easing his conscience and leaving the initiative to you. It is worth remembering, when the pros and cons of such a situation are weighed up, that it maybe equally against the law to conceal the knowledge that an offence against the law has been committed, depending upon the legislation of your own country.

What to do with the bug itself when it is uncovered.

There are several courses:

a) It can be torn from its source and literally jumped upon. This is a human and almost automatic reflex action, but it should be anticipated and avoided. A dangerous situation, I need hardly say, requires a cool head.

b) It would be more strategic, and productive, to mount a phoney board meeting at which bogus plans were discussed, **invalid** assignments given and misleading formulae or patterns accepted or rejected. It would have to be done in a very natural way, which would require adequate preparation and even a bit of rehearsal, since to flounder and bumble during the actual eavesdropping would give the game away. The plans, and other details adduced at the phoney meeting, must have the semblance of feasibility — it must not be a 'caricature' of a meeting. This presupposes some modest acting ability on the part of those concerned, but as anyone who engages in business has to dissemble his real feelings very frequently, it ought not to be too difficult.

c) The bug henceforth can be the subject of observation, with a view to seeing whether any attempts are made to retrieve it or change the batteries, which have a limited life. Such pieces of equipment should be disposable, for obviously the installer risks discovery when he initially plants the bug, and runs an even greater risk of discovery if he returns to retrieve it. One would expect that few industrial spies would bother to do this; but, in my experience, spies are greedy people. They never have enough money.

Management should ask itself, when a bug is found, when it may have been planted, and by whom. Have there been visits by telephone engineers,, window cleaners, cleaners, other visitors? Which of them, if any, were left alone in that room long enough to have been able to plant the bug (a job taking only minutes)?

It should not be automatically assumed that, because a bug has been discovered, the chase is over. There may be another one and even another one. A shrewd industrial spy knows something of the laziness of human nature — knows that the average man, having found one, assumes that it is *the* (only) one.

Even if you do find who planted the bug, redress may be impossible. I once kept strict watch on some premises, waiting to see if whoever planted a bug (which had been uncovered by our sweep) would return to it. Two such visits took place, each by a different man. One came to change a battery, another to recover the bug. We tailed them to see where they went. Alas! Both were employees of a rather notorious 'security' agency well known for their devious means of obtaining information by the planting of illegal bugs. This did not tell us on whose behalf they were acting, and we did not think it would be very fruitful to ask them! Our main interest (on behalf of our clients) was to discover what rival company was out to steal their industrial secrets. We never did find out. I am not ashamed to admit this failure, as we had conscientiously carried out all that could usefully and legally be done. Neither I, nor any of my employees, will break the law in order to uphold the law. Those who do bring discredit on the security industry generally, and discourage companies from securing the services of experts whom they may badly need.

Let us now get back to the board room. And let us consider again the points on which they need to be clear in formulating their company's security policy.

The first point — whether the premises are secure from outside intrusion — is primarily a matter of nuts and bolts, equipment and adequate surveillance. As to physical security, the range of locks and bolts, safes and protected doorways and gates is now enormous and made all the more effective by the development of electronic controls. Television cameras hidden behind the opening of an ordinary file can operate silently when a sensor is triggered by a stranger breaking a circuit — or even by the heat of his body. Alarms connected with the police station can be similarly activated.

Yet, the bigger the premises, the more complex becomes the vexed question of security controls and passes.

Even where the security establishment seems to be adequate in strength, a lack of alertness or slavish acceptance of routine often makes security a purely nominal affair.

The company must ask itself: our staff come and go, salesmen and area representatives who do not work here have to come and depart frequently; clients and customers come and go, so do messengers, and representatives of all sorts of ancillary services; delivery men bring goods, while others come to our loading bay to collect ours. We are visited by telephone engineers, postmen, cleaners, window cleaners, caterers (perhaps), advertising and public relations men, journalists, Inland Revenue inspectors, representatives of the

Department of Health and Social Security, VAT and chance visitors from abroad.

As to visitors, what checks have we that they are each what they purport to be, that they are expected in a particular department, and leave our premises when they have achieved the purpose of their visit?

As to passes, now — are we satisfied with the passes we issue to staff? Are they reasonably forge-proof? Are the conditions of issue stringent enough, and, when the holder is away on holiday or from sickness, does our company take custody of his pass or leave it to his uncertain care? When the time comes for reissue (assuming that passes are valid for a stated period, say of one or two or more years) do we account for every single pass previously issued?

There are broadly two kinds of pass. The old-fashioned sort were merely printed cards, with perhaps the photograph of the holder affixed with gum, staples or eyelets, possibly embossed by some countersunk seal or overstamped with a rubber stamp. The crudeness and inadequacy of these bits of board makes them useless from a security point of view. The printing is usually simple to copy, the staples, eyelets available to anybody, the rubber stamps easily procurable and, as for the embossing by a hand press, raised characters impressed by the smooth, inkless tip of a ball point pen can fairly easily duplicate the effect.

Such forgeries easily convince security guards, who often grow bored with their job and merely go through the motions of their supervisory duties; it is rare indeed for such a pass to be carefully and critically inspected. At the height of the Second World War, I am told, a soldier wearing *enemy* uniform swept into the War Office in Whitehall, flourishing a bus ticket which served as a pass! This story is probably exaggerated but illustrates my point.

There are passes which not only identify the holder, but encapsulate the holder's photograph in a sealed laminated case, which cannot be opened without damaging the whole thing. In any case, the photograph is not affixed as a separate thing, but is an integral part of the whole plastic pass.

Classification of documents? This depends upon the extent of the company and the nature of its products. The maker of cream biscuits would be entitled to feel that he needed simple categories; makers of space-age weapons would take a quite different view. In any event, the security category assigned should not be stated on the file, but indicated by the file's colour, or a coloured label whose significance is known only to a few. To take a hypothetical case, details of a new prototype of a jump-jet aircraft would obviously be TOP SECRET. So would correspondence, documents, contracts, sales records and orders, photographs, plans and even the sales literature of sub-contractors. All these are obvious bait to an industrial spy.

Following this top category, with its restricted access by a few selected executives and specialists, would come SECRET. Next, perhaps, HIGHLY CONFIDENTIAL, then CONFIDENTIAL, and perhaps, lastly, RESTRICTED.

But secrets do not become protected by the mere affixing of impressive labels. Scrupulous checks have to be maintained on the date and time of issue, the authority on which this issue was made, and to whom, and for what period. Equally stringent checks have to be made on the return of such files and documents.

Every member of the staff should record his or her name on the folder or file.

But what about *access control*? Having graded staff according to the degree of access permitted, how is this to be affected? Supposing, for instance, that Grade A staff (a tiny minority of executives and specialists) are permitted access to TOP SECRET documents, or allowed to venture where these are kept; that Grade B staff have access to SECRET documents, and so on down the scale of responsibility — what system of control will ensure that the junior clerk does not go wandering into the filing department, or chat on some irrelevance as he leans against the designer's drawing board?

The answer lies best, I believe, in access control. This consists of an encoded magnetic card with fits into a contraption which reads the card. These are not foolproof against forgery, but extremely difficult to forge. Their printing and magnetic lettering might well be revealed by expert examination, but it is doubtful if the code would be known.

The Paris Hilton, together with other hotels, for instance, now has a system of access control for every room. Instead of having the normal key, they now have a paper-type card which is programmed by their computer so that when you hand your card in — or even if you do not hand your card in — once there is a change of guest, the access control to the bedroom is programmed on a different card. In the old days, if you booked into room 501 and left without returning the key, you had thereafter a means of entry to that room if and when you wished to assert it. It was rare for managements to waste time chasing lost keys, and even more rare, on grounds of economy, for them to go to the trouble of changing the room lock. Not surprisingly, a great many robberies have occurred because of this slackness and inefficiency, and I do not doubt that a good many industrial secrets have been stolen in this way also, as executives left their document cases and memoranda strewn about (especially at conferences, where almost every minute of non-conference time is spent on socialising).

The best system I have so far encountered, offering a formidable degree of security, is provided by Mastiff Security Systems Limited of Leatherhead, Surrey. The system makes it impossible for any unauthorised person, or staff person not authorised, to enter particular zones of special security, such as computer records department, computers, and so on.

Let us be clear on terms. ACCESS PREVENTION means the physical guarding of premises when they are not in use — out of working hours. This is a matter of locks, bolts, burglar alarms, patrols, guard dogs and the rest.

ACCESS CONTROL means the protection of high security areas *during* working hours.

Ordinary locks constitute a security risk inside a building, because where the door has to be opened and shut frequently, the temptation is to leave it ajar because the rigmarole of unlocking and re-locking seems hardly worth while ("I'll only be a minute") with the Mastiff system. In effect each member of staff carries a tiny radio which emit a signal recognised by the lock of the door they are authorised to go through — it will open of its own accord. A refinement of the system is that, even when an authorised person goes through a door as permitted by the *Mastiff* an unauthorised person coming up the rear and slipping through at the same time would be detected by the system which would sound a local alarm and lock the door ahead. To prevent people inadvertently taking the token home, an exit alarm can be fitted which is activated by token holders passing a check-point.

This certainly gives a very high degree of security control and, combined with adequate vetting of staff, the provision of passes as near forge-proof as possible, and the physical protection of the premises, can *if worked to rule*, get as near to perfection as we are likely to get.

Photocopying departments, require strict supervision as regards access. Throwing faulty copies into a wastepaper basket; making extra copies for fun, or merely for the purposes of industrial espionage! The solution would seem to be to limit access to the photocopying department.

With differences of detail, the Borer System also offers a high degree of access control.

The Borer System combines data processing and recording for access control time-recording, shop-floor data collection and personal credit (with which we are not, in this work, concerned). The co-ordinated system is very advanced in its combination of facilities, of which access control is an important feature.

The key to the system is the coded card which serves as a means of identification for a variety of purposes. The information capacity of the card is very large, and its invisible and non-magnetic coded content cannot be copied or destroyed. A unique and secret code is used by every company employing the system. As with Mastiff, cards can restrict the holder to particular areas and so can be graded as required. An individual recognition number is allocated to each card holder.

There are various points in the building where a card can be inserted. The access control ingredient of the service checks the cards for area and 'time validity' (period of validity), checks the card number against the 'embargo list', checks the security code, registers the card data and time-of-day for future use, returns the card and — if all is in order — releases the door lock. It also raises the alarm if an unauthorised entry attempt is made.

The feeding of data into central computer is subject to many checks, including shop-floor checks. It checks the contract number, quantity and other production details, and gives warning if erronious information is given.

It does a lot more besides, but we are concerned at this point with access control. These two systems are not the only ones available to industry today, but illustrate my point. There are other systems, and no doubt more will be developed.

It is possible to have an access control system which is programmed to be activated by a palm print. Grisly though it may be, if the stakes were high enough a criminal could kidnap and chop off the hand, which would then serve as a key! Many a murder has been perpetrated for gain, and is no less likely to happen in fields of industrial espionage, where the rewards are very big indeed, as in any other field of criminal activity. In these days of terrorism and violence anything can happen.

There is another system of access control, in limited use but not in general supply at the moment, which is programmed to people's individual voices. It seems to me that a determined industrial spy, having armed himself with a forged pass, the lopped-hand of the rightful user so that the palm print will be acceptable to the palm-print reader, and a tape-recording of the man he is impersonating, might some time gatecrash any holy of holies.

Such piratical efforts to get at the industrial secrets may seem fanciful, but are they? *The Industrial Security Times* of November-December 1980 claims that in 1979 only 4% of known industrial espionage cases in Europe can be accounted for by one businessman trying to score off on another. The rest, it is asserted, were instigated by "national, state-controlled secret service institutions".

Since these are seldom limited in funds or resources in terms of both equipment, scientific know-how and manpower, the farthest-fetched hypothesis is more likely to be valid. Henry Stanhope, Defence Correspondent of *The Times* (of London) on January 17 1981 revealed that the United States has announced the successful test of a laser beam which can destroy intercontinental missiles in flight. A technical secret like that, affecting the whole military balance of world power, must certainly attract the persistent curiosity of foreign powers. Expense would certainly be no object.

The estimate of 4 per cent as representing the number of known cases of 'private' industrial espionage (as distinct from governmental) is, of course, very much an estimate. It is based on known (i.e. reported) cases. Most cases are not reported even when discovered. And most, I imagine, are not discovered. But that industrial espionage is predominantly initiated by industrial spies working on behalf of, or actually with, foreign governments, there is no reason to doubt.

This merely underlines the urgency of informational security. It is an illusion to suppose that, if industrial espionage is uncovered, there is then any effective remedy. The birds have usually flown, and cannot be pursued or sued in their own countries. Hence the basic precept of anti-industrial espionage: BEFORE, NOT AFTER.

*   *   *

What of telephone security? The Company will need to survey its telephone installations and decide over which lines, and under which controls, confidential information will be passed. Top secret information will probably never be entrusted to a telephone line, as the technical problems involved in combating telephone tapping are formidable. There are, certainly, a wide range of encoders and decoders; there are types of electronic apparatus which warn if the line is being tapped; and there are scramblers, which turn any telephone conversation into gobbledegook but which emerges in your companion's earpiece as ordinary speech, if he has a comparable apparatus.

There is one telephone, known as the Cloak, designed to meet the challenge to the phone's privacy. It costs nearly £2000 and it is claimed that it can ensure the confidentiality of 'phone conversations by defeating such commonly used eavesdropping methods as tape recorder activators, telephone transmitters (parasitic or battery powered) and infinity transmitters. It is doubtful if it can ensure against a tap on the line. Some telephone lines extend for miles — under city streets, over mountain ranges, across rivers. It is a physically impossible job to test every inch of that transmission line. The same is true of telephone conversations transmitted by microwaves. In Britain and the U.S.A. and no doubt most other countries that are highly industrialised, such electronic communications can be plucked from the air by the right sort of apparatus. It is well-known fact that most embassies use such apparatus.

The old-fashioned "scramblers" have, however, been vastly improved upon and computer technology combined with micro-electronics have produced some very useful protective devices. One such is the Top Security Ruggedised Portable Voice Security System, Model SC 3700. It is a mobile apparatus which is first set near to any telephone, from which the number is dialled and communication established. The moment that is done, it is placed in the coupler and conversation is continued through its integral handset. Millions of codes are possible, and the speech spectrum can be divided into the five bands; it can hook up to AV, FM or SSB radio, wire lines, satellite and repeater links.

The company will investigate the merits of the various telephone security systems available and settle for that which fits its needs and its pockets. With all such complicated apparatus, some assurance as to maintenance service must be sought, and there needs to be some certainty that there are staff available within the firm capable of exercising effective technical supervision of such things. Do not expect the house electrician to cope!

The disposal of documents will certainly feature in any company's security planning.

Embassies, from time-honoured usage, burn unwanted documents, of such as they wish not to fall into the hands of a hostile force, such as when an embassy is besieged. Few offices or factories have a real fire nowadays, even less the old-fashioned anthracite-burning stove which was ideal for paper disposal.

Automatic shredding is the only answer. Routine disposal, by merely filling sacks with unwanted documents (which, amazingly enough, still goes on) and letting the refuse collectors take them away, is nonsensical from a security point of view.

A company can either instal its own shredding facilities, or contract with firms of shredders who send collectors at stated intervals, collect unwanted documents in tough canvas bags, rather like kitbags, which are padlocked by the customer, the key being put into yet another bag, to be returned with the shredding material to the contractor.

What vetting processes the shredding companies apply to their staff, and what safeguards are applied to prevent any of the documents not going straight and unexamined into the shredder, I do not know. But I have not heard of any instances of a shredding company being found out in carelessness or corruption. They will not, however, allow a customer or his representative to accompany the paper that is to be shredded, which would be — for those who wished and could afford it — the ultimate safeguard against unwarranted access to confidential documents.

Many firms, of course, possess their own machines, but the larger the company the greater the variety of sizes and weights of material they wish to destroy. There can be price lists, contracts, tenders, confidential reports, correspondence and so on. They come in a variety of bindings as well as of materials; some may be stitched, others stapled, some sewn or bound. They would defy many of the shredders on sale. And there is the question of the *volume* of paper waste. It may be neither practical nor economic to attempt its shredding internally.

For smallish businesses, however, there is a wide range of commercial shredders to be bought. Some companies find the shredded paper useful for packing. I am told it is excellent for bedding down racing horses and greyhounds, but have never tried it.

The basis of the shredder is that the narrow, parallel strips get all mixed up and cannot be reassembled. This is not a hundred per cent true. Given opportunity, and the necessary patience and time, those parallel strips can be realigned and the document restored. But you would have to be quick off the mark; once shredding paper has been overlaid by a lot more, it would, unless a particular document were in a special colour contrasting with the rest, be like looking for a needle in a haystack to attempt to retrieve it.

Clearly, documents intended for shredding by machine within a factory office, or awaiting collecting from a contracted shredder, need to be safe-guarded from tampering.

The security precautions of the professional shredders are quite strict. Every client is assigned a code number, as well as the specially designed and lockable canvas bags designed to hold up to 150 lb or more of paper. Each bag carries a code number. On a regular service, a security van, accompanied by two guards, arrives at a client's premises each week. The bags are sealed in the client's presence and a receipt is issued.

The closed van makes for a special depot which carries no identification or clue as to its purpose. The bags are opened under supervision and their contents fed into the shredder, after which the client is issued with a certificate of their destruction.

Shredding machines or disintegrators must be chosen for their intended use — which includes the volume of waste, the type of material to be destroyed and the hours of operation. Careful thought must be given to this choice. A machine with capacity far beyond requirements is unlikely to be cost-effective. Too modest a version may be inadequate to the demands made of it.

Volumatic Limited market an excellent disintegrate which pounds into a fine powder, typewriter ribbons, carbon papers etc. papers etc.

Business Aids of London offer a good selection of modestly-priced machines. Ofshred of Huddersfield supply heavier duty machines at prices ranging from £300 to £600. Rexel of Aylesbury have machines for reasonably heavy traffic at between £200 and £600. Roneo Vickers of Croydon offer two types within the same range, while Sharpenset Engineering Ltd of High Wycombe offer a machine at around £250. Industrial Shredders, which had been taken over by Reliance Security Ltd, have a wide range of apparatus. As, at the time of writing, we are in the middle of a raging inflation, I cannot guarantee the prices quoted.

Sometimes firms have to unload an enormous quantity of highly valuable and secret documents, for reasons of space. Having had their records microfilmed, they face the problem of how to dispose of papers whose misuse could damage or even ruin them. Shredding under stringent security safeguards is, clearly, the only answer.

*   *   *

It goes without saying that no company's security planning can be reckoned complete without clear and comprehensive provision for computer security.

I mean, by "computer security", the taking of such steps as are reasonable, practicable and economically feasible for the protection of the information stored in the computer or computers.

This is not just a matter of physical access. The principles of physical security already described could limit access to security areas to authorised personnel only. But this is by no means the end of the story, as the facts about computer crime and vulnerability in Chapter Seven make clear.

The computer, as we all know, has become a ubiquitous and permanent tool of government, administration and commerce. Whether this should or should not be so is now an academic question. Millions of files are held on the Metropolitan Police Computer, on the records of the Swansea car registration centre, of the Companies House records at Cardiff, at the Department of Health and Social Security, the Ministry of Defence, of banks and local authorities and building societies . . .

We are reaching the stage where no company of any consequence will be without a computer, which will file on magnetic tape the names of customers, details of orders, contracts, the personal files of members of the staff, of banking operations, and everything ancilliary to the company's existence and operation.

To what degree can computer information be secured?

The American expert August Bequai, a practising attorney in Washington, D.C., specialising in all legal aspects of technology, has declared that "a computer can be safeguarded but never made fully impregnable."

There have been recent instances of this, some grave, other comical. A Belgian citizen pleaded guilty in a federal court in the U.S.A. to attempting to pay $500,000 to obtain secret computer technology for the Soviet Union. Under a plea bargain with federal prosecutors in Alexandria, Virginia, Marc Andre Degeyter confessed to arranging for the illegal sale of secret data that would act as a decoding device in a widely-used computer programme made by Software AG in Reston, Virginia. He paid $500,000 to an FBI agent posing as an employee of the firm.

On 5th June, 1980 Leeds and Northrup of Pennsylvania fired one of its computer project leaders/programmers named Joseph Hershman, and within a very short space of time went to remove his passwords from the files. To the company's surprise they found that data relating to their Max I computer control programme has been erased. Further enquiries revealed that, within a few hours of his dismissal, Hershman had gained access to his ex-employers' IBM 370/158 and had deliberately erased programmes relating to Max I, one of the company's most vital classified programmes.

In this instance the company did not dither or dissemble but took prompt and decisive action: they took legal action against Hershman in the Montgomery County Court. They had two reasons for doing this, (a) to discover what further data Hershman might have altered or erased and (b) "pour décourager les autres". (To discourage others).

Electronic crime has been sweeping America, youngsters often tapping in on computers using computer terminals in their own homes. Brian Catlin and Christopher Adams, both 17-year old students at Fremd High School in the Chicago suburb of Palestine, shut down the computer system at Lepaul University from September 17 to 19 1980 (enrolment week) "as a challenge."

As Chicago Police Investigator Douglas Ellis put it "someone said it couldn't be done, and they spent approximately a year proving that it could be. Computer courses were shut down, research data could not be retrieved and accounts were in chaos.

By way of humour, the students called themselves "Vladimir" and "System Cruncher". They used a terminal hooked up to their home telephone, and used a code to gain access to Lepaul's computer.

Donn B. Parker, whom I have already quoted has said that "over the next ten years" computers will be increasingly vulnerable. "If students are able to do these things," he warned, "what could a foreign power do with sufficient resources and intent in our increasingly fragile electronic fund transfer systems and other critical systems in the country?"

Manhatten police refuse to reveal his name, since the culprit is only 13, but a boy of that age tuned in to a computer and erased about 10 million items from its memory bank! The "precocious genius" found that, using the Dalton school telephone, he could keep calling the computer communication's ex-directory number. He had discovered the entry password by a mere process of elimination — going through scores of words until — hey presto! — he had hit upon the right word.

The complexity of computers is less forbidding to students in the formative (early) educational stages because there is no temptation to equate computer terms, which the machine can accept, with ordinary spoken or written language. Thus it is that quite young people can grasp with easy computer technology which might well baffle an older and more experienced man. Industrial spies would not fit this category — they are either technically knowledgeable themselves or in league with those who are, since a knowledge of how computers work and interlink with terminals and software is essential to any breaking of their secrets. The significance of the successful cracking of computers by young students is that the vulnerability of computers is exposed.

Even more disturbing is the known link between certain terrorist groups and foreign powers, and industrial spies. A spy will sell his secrets to the highest bidder, unless he is hired by one specific master. Millions of pounds are fed into terrorist groups from many sources — mostly governmental — through a series of intermediaries. To extract information from defence or government computers, or from firms whose secrets have a profitable resale value on the international black market, can provide funds for those terrorist movements. Organisations which do not stop at terror are not likely to stop at anything else.

Therefore we can forget humorous quips about sixth form pranks. In fact, although a sense of mischief has often been the motive, the schoolboys did the world a favour by reminding them of the unfulfilled obligations of computer security.

Mike Comer, author of *Corporate Fraud* and Editor of *Computer and Fraud Security Bulletin*, recently told the magazine *Computer* that he considers "the potentiality for computer fraud is very great."

The *physical* protection of the actual computer areas has been covered by the various methods I have described. Such a summary is hardly possible on the question of computer security — preventing the unauthorised access, via telephone or terminals, to data records and programme details. From the outset, a company reviewing its overall precautions against industrial espionage must assume that efforts could be made to "crack" the entry codes to their computerised data records, and thereafter extract information, infuse false information or erase inconvenient information, at the intruder's pleasure.

The first and obvious task is to list all the risks and then examine all the defences in the light of that list. For this step the advice of computer experts is obviously needed, and for balance one needs to ensure that not all of those experts are employed by the company selling or maintaining the hardware! I do not imply that large computer companies would attempt to mislead, but they would be unusual salesmen if they emphasised — perhaps even mentioned — the more serious hazards involved in possession of their equipment.

A big literature has grown up on the subject of computer security. A bibliography of computer related crime, *The New Criminals* has been compiled by The Institution of Electrical Engineers (IEE), published in March, 1978, and may be highly commended. The National Computing Centre has published a useful work, *Security For Computer Systems*, while the U.S. Department of Commerce, through its National Bureau of Standards, has compiled *Guidelines of ADP Physical Security And Risk Management*.

The technical aspects of protecting computer systems have been the subject of many useful seminars such as those organised by the National Computing Centre and the Institute of Chartered Secretaries and Administrators, which were led by senior personnel highly experienced in the topics discussed. Four separate seminars were organised in several cities (London, Bristol, Manchester and Stirling) and each was directed at a separate level or department of responsibility. Seminar 1, on Defining Responsibilities was aimed at senior managers who used, or were about to use, computers, and senior data processing staff. Seminar 2 was intended for data processing managers, senior systems personnel and programming staff. Seminar 3 was concerned with Monitoring the Effectiveness of Security Measures while the fourth seminar touched on the question of adequate insurance cover.

Like all of those seminars, and many similar that have been held since, much useful ground was covered, but the fact remains — the best insurance against the theft of company secrets is intelligent planning based on innate caution. It is possible to insure against most contingencies, such as damage to computers, theft of tapes, and so on, but the chances of persuading an insurance company to insure against industrial espionage (including theft of *information* from computers) are not only remote, but potentially so expensive as to be impracticable.

To repeat. Your own security arrangements, initiated with proper thought and kept constantly under critical surveillance, are the best insurance of all.

Part III —
Industrial Espionage and the Law

CHAPTER 11

Laws
The United Kingdom

The law as affecting industrial espionage in the United Kingdom is complex, contradictory and, as things stand at the moment, usually ineffective.

The *Law Society's Gazette* of 28th January, 1981, expressed the view that ". . . it is perhaps true to say that many lawyers are ignorant of English law's ability to protect secrets'. It is equally true indeed, as the article states, that "intellectual property gets some protection under the Copyright Laws and those governing patents, and that, in certain instances, "the law can protect private and State secrets as well as trade secrets".

I would not equate the two classes of secrets. State secrets are mostly covered by the Official Secrets Act, whose harsh provisions make it an offence even to *contemplate* the disclosure of State information. No such edict protects the secrets of individuals and companies.

The inadequacy of English law was emphasised in a case that came before the Old Bailey in 1973 when two brothers operating as private detectives, were alleged to have obtained information from Scotland Yard, Government offices, banks and other authorities by falsely claiming to be police or civil servants. If banks or other authorities rang them back, on the extension given to them, the switchboard operator, reading from a list, would announce "Barclays Bank" or "Post Office" — or whatever authority was being impersonated at the time.

One of the accused was sentenced to twelve months' imprisonment, and his brother to nine. The Court of Appeal cut the sentence of one brother to nine months, suspended it, and fined him £500; it suspended the other brother's sentence, fining him a similar amount.

The House of Lords quashed the convictions, set aside the sentences and awarded damages.

Lord Dilhorne, in his speech, said the brothers had obtained confidential information about customer's bank accounts by pretending on the telephone that they were working for another bank. Information was also obtained from the Criminal Records Office, The Ministry of Defence and other authorities.

However, their Lordships decided that there was no such offence as "conspiring to create a public mischief", the offence of which they had been convicted.

Lord Diplock, another Law Lord, expressed the opinion that "this branch of the law is irrational in treating as a criminal offence an agreement to do that which, if done, is not a crime."

Lord Diplock added that "this reproach to our criminal jurisprudence is engaging the urgent attention of the Law Commission."

The Law Commission's "urgent attention" continued for nine years. They drew up a draft law on Breach of Confidence, which was published on 31st October, 1981. This promises rather more redress to those whose secrets have been disclosed without their permission. It is considered that wide-ranging powers, should the draft law (see Appendix) pass into the Statute, would make the securing and exploitation of unauthorised information more hazardous. Yet, even so, the Commission makes it clear that where the disclosure of information may be deemed "in the public interest", it will be allowed.

The report confirms what many — including myself — have long considered the case: that the existing common law on breach of confidence is unsatisfactory, inadequate and should be abolished. The proposed legislation would stipulate civil liability for the misuse of information acquired either in confidence or "by certain specified improper means." These include the use of theft, violence, electronic bugging, tape recorders, telephoto lenses or "interference" with documents or with computers that store information. The latter could well cover a whole range of computer offences — merely abstracting information illicitly, or altering existing computer data records, or adding something to them.

The proposed law would make an employee or hired person suspect to an "obligation of confidence". It would also, for instance, be applicable if an industrial spy were to bug a boardroom and then sell secret information this obtained to trade rivals who turn it to commercial account.

The law would offer added protection (over and above that provided by existing laws, including the Official Secrets Act) against the disclosure of official information — except where the object was to prevent crime.

Dr Peter North, one of the five-man commission, made it clear that the proposed law would not hamper the police in their fight against crime — which often demands the use of sophisticated surveillance and photographic equipment.

The report, known as the Breach of Confidence Report, was commissioned by Lord Hailsham when he was Lord High Chancellor, and it may well be that by the time this book is in circulation we shall be nearer to some control, or at least limitation, of industrial espionage.

For some time it had been hoped that a curious piece of legislation known as the Anton Piller Order might be a useful weapon against industrial spies. It was certainly intended to be, since it arose from a case involving computers, heard by the Court of Appeal in 1975.

Anton Piller, a German manufacturer whose company makes novel frequency converters for computers, obtained an order against an English company which was allegedly infringing copyright in engineering drawings.

The Anton Piller Order is most curious legally, since it amounts to being a civil search warrant, permitting authorities to enter a man's house or other premises and look for incriminating material. To obtain such an order the plaintiff applies to the Chancery Division of the High Court in *camera* and *ex parte* (that is without the knowledge of the alleged culprit and privately) for an order that the defendant "do permit him" to inspect his premises, and to seize, copy or photograph material bearing on the alleged infringement. The defendant can also be required to provide information such as the names and addresses of his customers and suppliers.

The order was rightly described by one judge as "the extremity of this court's powers", so severe that it was intended to be rarely used, and then only on the strongest possible *prima facie* evidence that information valuable to the plaintiff has been stolen, and is being used, or is likely to be used, in such a way and on such a scale as to endanger his livelihood or reputation. In practice it was used quite a lot, since it promised to be a speedy and effective remedy in certain cases of piracy, such as the illicit copying of video tapes and other copyright infringements.

However, prior to the recently-published report of the Law Commission, the House of Lords (on May 8th 1981), in the case *Rank Film Distributors Limited and Others v Video Information*

Centre (a firm) *and Others,* handed down a decision that made legal history — and rendered the Anton Piller Order almost useless as a protection against industrial espionage.

The case was heard before Lord Wilberforce, Lord Diplock, Lord Fraser of Tulleybelton, Lord Russell of Killowen and Lord Roskill.

They upheld an objection by proposed defendants to an action for infringement of copyright in films that an Anton Piller Order, made *ex parte* by a judge on the film company's application, would require them to answer questions and disclose information which would put them in danger of self-incrimination in criminal proceedings for conspiracy to defraud, and so violate the privilege against self-incrimination, which was one of the basic liberties of the subject.

Lord Fraser observed that if, as the House held, the objection was well founded, the usefulness of the Anton Piller type of order, developed in the Chancery Division and widely used in recent years to prevent acts of industrial piracy, would be "much reduced if not practically destroyed", while Lord Russell suggested that legislation might be the most effective way to protect owners of valuable property rights.

The evidence was strong and clear that the defendants *had* engaged in the distribution and sale of pirated copy video tapes on a very large scale; the main question their Lordships had to consider, however, was whether the two defendants could avail themselves of the privilege against self-incrimination in order to deprive the plaintiffs of an important part of the relief which they sought.

Lord Wilberforce added that it might seem to be a strange paradox that the worse, the more criminal their activities could be made to appear, *the less effective was the civil remedy that could be granted.*

And so, although the Anton Piller Order has proved useful until then in actions brought in England, New Zealand, South Africa and elsewhere, it was by this particular judgement rendered largely ineffectual as a weapon against industrial spies.

Happily, and in accordance with the hope expressed by their Lordships in arriving at their decision, there does seem now that steps may be made soon towards more effective legislation.

One eminent lawyer whose opinion I sought on some aspects of industrial espionage thought that the industrial spy could fairly be called a kind of "intellectual shoplifter". He added — significantly enough — that the term shoplifter has fallen into disfavour, since it implied a psychological rather than a criminal phenomenon, and was eagerly seized upon by culprits who pleaded absent-mindedness, psychological disturbance or impulse. Shoplifting is a euphemism for theft. Industrial spying is theft — the stealing of secrets against the wishes and without the knowledge of their rightful owner.

Sales literature of companies often stress that their product embodies a patent design or process, or a secret design. Such information offers a firm incentive to an industrial spy, whom the law may not deter, and may actually assist. Patents and "secret designs" cannot be equated. The first is public the second restricted to those considered to be responsible enough to have access to the secret. A patent is public. Anyone can go to the Patents Office in London (and their equivalents in other countries) and read all about it.

Unless bribery is used to suborn an employee, an industrial spy will probably need to get into private premises. The legal restrictions on physical access to other people's premises are not as onerous as some suppose. Anyone may unbolt my garden gate and walk up my garden path; anyone may walk into the head office of a manufacturing concern; anyone may wander through a factory gate and, subject to security checks (if any, and if effective) may wander also through factory workshops.

Just as physical obstacles are often negligible, so are the legal obstacles. There are no legal barriers to access; trespassers, despite the forbidding notices so often displayed, cannot be prosecuted, at least, not for trespassing alone (except on secret or military establishments). They might conceivably be the subject of a civil action for which damages would be limited to the specific degree of damage caused. However, if you can prove that a trespasser has come and is likely to come again to your premises for some nefarious or illegal or dangerous or harmful purpose, you can bring an action for trespass and seek an injunction in that action restraining him from entering your premises — and not only him, but his servants or agents, that is, anyone acting on his behalf or in his stead.

Broadly speaking, the laws affecting the whole problem of industrial espionage in Great Britain are:

1. *The European Communities Act 1972*
2. *The Theft Act 1968*

3. *The Official Secrets Act, 1911*
4. *The Copyright Acts, including the Copyright Act of 1911, the Copyright Act of 1957, the Copyright (Amendment Act) of 1971 and the Design Copyright Act of 1968.*
5. *The Prevention of Corruption Act, 1916*
6. *The Wireless & Telegraphy Act 1949*

Mr Alan Campbell, Q.C., consultant to the Council of Europe's Sub-committee on Penal Law and Criminology, has stressed the need for more realistic and effective laws against industrial espionage in Britain. He has stressed that the techniques nowadays employed in obtaining information by industrial espionage may involve the use of electronic and photographic devices (such as I have described in previous chapters). Relevant criminal law hardly recognises the existence of such means. It is enshrined in the Theft Act of 1968 and said Mr Campbell "is based on an almost Biblical concept of theft." It assumes that only *tangible* objects can be stolen, and requires proof by the prosecution of intent to deprive an owner or possessor permanently. The law provides reasonable protection for patents and copyrights, said Mr Campbell, but "not for the intellectual components of the wealth of industry."

I entirely agree that the "intellectual components" are insufficiently protected, and have long advocated that, instead of depending upon lack-lustre authorities who have limited legal powers to prevent industrial espionage, industrialists should make themselves more self-reliant as regards secrets protection, or, at least, take positive steps to employ those, or contract with those, who are experts in this neglected art.

Although I heartily endorse Mr Campbell's useful advocacy of a tightening-up of legislation in respect of industrial espionage, I would not agree that existing laws on patents and copyrights are wholly satisfactory in practice. There have been successful prosecutions in respect of pirated tape recordings, gramophone records and so on, but with millions of radio cassette recorders and videotape machines around, adequate surveillance is surely beyond any known capacity. Tape recordings of radio shows, television shows and recorded material may lawfully be copied *for personal use*, but how to ensure that they are never used for other purposes? Again, there is copyright in printed material, and a school which used its photocopying machine over-lavishly found itself in breach of copyright and could not use what it had copied. Notwithstanding that and similar judgements, an enormous lot of photocopying of copyright printed material does go on in schools, institution and commercial concerns.

Possibly, Mr Campbell meant to imply that the Patent and Copyright laws offer better protection in their fields than the jumble of confused and contradictory legislation does in respect of industrial espionage. Indeed, he makes the point that laws regarding trespass are in favour of the industrial spy, with his tape recorder, Minox camera, bugging devices and electronic gew-gaws for intercepting or tampering with computerised information.

As for Patent Laws, they are sometimes of help when patent infringements are detected and contested, yet they are, in some respects, of actual *help* to the industrial spy. A patent must be specified in detail, and those details are public — available to the public. They may be referred to and copied — and are. Legal authorities do not agree as to the extent of protection the law affords, although one eminent lawyer has informed me that "the law recognises 'intellectual property'."

Since no-one is allowed by law to make a profit out of stolen goods, one would wish that the same principle could be applied in cases of industrial espionage. But it is legally more complex than that. I may have a recipe for an exquisite liqueur, the only one of its kind in the world. Indeed, there are recipes for such drinks as Drambuie or Green Chartreuse whose secrets have been closely guarded for centuries. Supposing I have such a recipe, and it is stolen. If it had been written on a scrap of paper, and that paper taken from its place and copied, I might be able to charge the individual with stealing paper to the value of a half penny. But the law might claim, if I asked for damages because of the loss to my business of somebody else making and offering for sale a similar liquer, that I still *have* my property. I still possess the information. It just happens that somebody else has it having obtained it dishonestly — but illegally? There's the rub!

The Theft Act might help in some cases. It is an offence under Section 16 of that Act to obtain a pecuniary advantage by deception. Thus, if a spy were obtaining designs, for instance, with a contract ready for the sale of them, he could be convicted of an offence under S.16.

The law which says that no-one is allowed to make a profit out of stolen goods is based on the legal maxim which says that no-one can pass on a better title than he has. For example, some people purport to "sell" cars which they have on hire-purchase, but, since such cars become their property only when they have completed the entire payments any sale before then is merely theft, and the purchaser, however honest and however unwittingly party to a theft, has no title to it.

The same principle applies — in theory — to the theft of information. Unlike the stolen motorcar, you cannot get it back. But it is like the car in that the persons using it are not entitled to it, nor can they keep the money they make from using it. The owners of the information can claim an account of all the profits made in an action which is sometimes quaintly described as for 'unjust enrichment.' It is seldom practicable to sue the thief; he may have been merely an instrument to steal the information. You are entitled to sue the principal — if you can identify him or trace him.

Clearly entry into premises by force may constitute burglary and the like. Burglars, however, do not normally give advance notice of their intentions, and only amateurs leave evidence of their identities. Forcible entry into premises for the purposes of planting bugs or taking away documents is a criminal offence.

The general law of contract applies where an employee is induced to betray his employer's secrets. The employee may be breaching his contract, and anyone who induced him to do this may also be liable for damages, if discovered. If a company has induced somebody else to suborn an employee of a rival company, the 'inducer' is liable to compensate the company from which the secrets were obtained. It takes little imagination to realise that such considerations are unlikely to deter the true industrial spy. As to compensation, he may be thousands of miles away by the time the duplicity is uncovered, while any attempt to seek redress from, say, an Iron Curtain country, would meet with a stone wall of bland denial and obstruction.

Putting it another way — what the law says, and what it can achieve are two different things. Statutory protections are useless if the process of implementing them is too slow, tedious, ineffective or outrageously expensive.

The whole realm of patents, which some fondly suppose will protect their secrets, is a legal quagmire into which none dare venture without a sure and expert guide. There are two kinds of patent in Britain, the British patent and the EEC patent. In the U.S.A., the U.S. Patent Office is the sole granting authority. So far as Britain is concerned, patent protection is based on a number of statutory provisions embodied in the 1977 Patents Act and EEC directives.

The first principle is that a patent lasts for 20 years, after which it lapses and cannot be renewed. The second is that it covers only something made exactly according to the specification which must be filed as part of the patent application. The situation is made more difficult when one bears in mind that patent provisions vary from country to country and procedures vary likewise. For example, in some countries, an invention is protected from the time when the application itself is filed whereas in others you have to wait until a patent is granted. When a patent is granted (if it is granted) the protection is valid only in the territory of the granting authority. As industrial spies acknowledge no boundaries to their activities, a spy from country A will cheerfully purloin patent secrets from country B. For instance, a British patent does not cover Turkey.

The confusion which reigns as to the merits or demerits of industrial espionage is best illustrated by the decision in 1979 in the case of *Oxford v Moss* (1979) which established the alarming premise that the information in that case (the contents of an examination paper) was not "property" protected by the law of theft; it is an argument which could be applied to industrial information. The decision that information is not of itself property is confirmed by other judgements, notably by the judgement of Lord Upjohn in *Boardman v Phipps* (1966). Since the Theft Act says that theft means the dishonest appropriation of *property* it follows that industrial secrets, however precious to their rightful owners, are not covered by this Act.

However, action is possible in certain individual cases. The House of Lords held in the *R v Scott* case of 1974 that to conspire to rob another of his legal rights amounted to a conspiracy to defraud. A similar interpretation was given to other cases. Conspiracy is both a crime and a tort (an actionable wrong).

The Official Secrets Act 1911 gives exceptional protection, so far as legal restraint and redress are concerned. It is an offence, not only for those in Public employ to disclose information without authority, but even to *contemplate doing so*. One head of the Civil Service once maintained that the disclosure of any information not specifically authorised to be disclosed was a breach of the Official Secrets Act. By this standard, it is strictly an offence to reveal that the troops in World War One were issued with plum and apple jam.

We all know, of course, that not all offences are as trivial — e.s., Anthony Blunt.

The Law Society's Gazette dated 28th January 1981 commented:—

> "It is clear that any type of information may be secret, although trade and commercial secrets are the most obvious type. For instance, *Seager v Copydex (No. 1) Supra*, concerned the protection of a type of unpatented carpet-grip, which had been developed by the plaintiff and conveyed to the defendants in the course of marketing negotiations . . ."

The question of what constitutes confidence, and the extent to which it may be deemed reasonable for the 'confidence' to be observed, is in law dependent upon the relationship between the person vouchsafing that confidence, and the person permitted to be in receipt (or custody) of it. The law has to decide to what extent confidentiality is implied or specifically agreed upon. This is seldom a simple matter.

British law concerns itself with breach of confidence only when the fact that such a relationship is confidential is clear and unequivocal. In the case of *Coco v A.N. Clark Engineering Ltd*. the nature of the relationship between employer and employee (or confider and confidant was spelled out in an attempt at clarity:

> ". . . if the circumstances are such that any reasonable man standing in the shoes of the recipient of the information would have realised that upon reasonable grounds the information was being given to him in confidence, then this should suffice to impose upon him the equitable obligation of confidence — *in particular, where the information is of commercial or industrial value.*" (my italics).

That such a relationship springs, as the Law Society puts it "from a straightforward contractual relationship" is implicit in many legal judgements, such as those concerned with the relationship between an inventor and the manufacturer.

There are a few uncertain remedies open (at the cost, perhaps, of ruinous or speculative litigation) to those whose commercial secrets have been stolen. In the *Coco v Clark* case I have mentioned cursorily, with no attempt to go into its details, no injunction was granted against the use of the information which had changed hands; the court's attitude was that the issue seemed to them one of information having been used without payment, not of information which should not have been used at all.

Sometimes the law permits an action to succeed for damages based on 'value of information taken', but it is obvious that this again may be highly speculative conclusion to an action concerned with the theft of commercial or technical information. Success demands the provision of sufficiently detailed evidence to enable the judge or jury to assess with reasonable accuracy the damage caused by the loss of the designs know-how or secret commercial strategy and organisation. What such a loss may entail cannot usually be assessed in terms of orders and contracts lost; trade has its vagaries, international finance its ups and downs. Beyond tangible orders cancelled, and negotiations broken off in mid-stream as a result of the industrial espionage, how can one be so sure what sales and contracts *might* have transpired if the secrets had remained with their legitimate owners?

There have been rare cases (*Ansell Limited v Allied Rubber Limited* is an example) where items made with 'stolen' secrets have been destroyed by Court order, but this is rarely done.

The laws affecting industrial espionage are far from satisfactory, and there is plenty of scope for reform. That is should be possible to steal secrets which may ruin a company without fear of legal retribution and yet be liable in law for the mere purloining a file whose intrinsic value is, say, ten new pence, makes little sense and of less justice.

Following the publication of *The Younger Committee Report on Privacy* in 1972 (CMD 5012), the Law Commission produced Working Paper No. 58 in 1974 on the fundamental question (fundamental in respect of industrial espionage) of breach of confidence. It was recommended that the law should be reformed to cover effectively actual loss, which could be a basis for a claim for damages and a second category, of "distress". This latter category, in my view, would alleviate considerably the damage done to individuals and firms whose task of trying to convince a judge or jury as to the *extent* of potential damage done is, for reasons I have mentioned earlier, quite impossible. I do not expect to go into a court with a crystal ball in order to bring to heel somebody who has stolen my secrets; the secrets should not have been stolen and their theft may well have caused me distress, particularly if the secrets are the product of years of research and specialised experience. I expect legal redress without the trouble and expense of speculating as to what profits *might* have accrued to me but for the piece of industrial espionage. I hope fervently that the recommendation of the Law Commission will bear fruit — but the revision of law, especially bearing in mind the enormous burden of legislation imposed on Parliament and the detail of the Committee work involved in all stages of the preparation of Bills, is a lengthy business. Moreover, to introduce such a head of damage into English law would mean setting out along a path which English law has always declined to follow.

The laws governing the right to broadcast — are basically simple; unless you have been granted a licence to broadcast, you may not do so. To use a 'bug' for as little as thirty seconds or less, transmitting without official permission is to break the law.

The laws concerning *telephone tapping* (listening in to a telephone conversation or conference, three or four way, without consent over the telephone system) are more ambiguous.

Amazingly, although telephone tapping is abhorrent, a social nuisance, an affront to privacy and a favourite method by which industrial spies pursue their profitable mischief, it is not illegal!

That the Government can tap telephones was, of course, quite cheerfully admitted by the Home Secretary for the first time in 23 years, in the official report (*The Interception of Communications in Great Britain*, Cmnd 7873, April 1980. The previous report was the *Birkett Committee of Privy Councillors Report* in October 1957 (Cmnd 283, October 1957). The 1980 report was in many respects vague and unspecific, for the fairly obvious reason that the subject was aired openly only under pressure and against official reluctance. The short report was the fulfilment of a promise made by the previous Home Secretary, Mr Mervyn Rees, in 1979, after a judgement by Sir Robert Megarry in *Malone v Commissioner of Police for the Metropolis* on February 28, 1978.

It was Malone's contention that 'phone tapping (by whomsoever) was a violation of Article 8 of the European Convention of Human Rights, to which Great Britain is a signatory.

Malone had based his application to appeal to the European Court on the case of *Klauss and Others v Federal Republic of Germany*. There 'phone tapping had been carried out by the State, but the European Court decided that Germany has satisfied the minimum conditions, since in Western Germany interception of telephone calls is covered by legislation. The whole business of phone tapping is subject to supervision by a parliamentary Committee, for the right of complaint against suspected interception, while the subject of the interception had the right to be informed when the interception had ceased.

Mr Justice Megarry dismissed Mr Malone's action holding that no unlawful conduct had been established. He held that, since the European Convention of Human Rights was no part of English law, the Convention did not, as a matter of English law, confer any direct rights on the plaintiff that he can enforce in the English Courts.

On April 1 1980 Mr Whitelaw, the Home Secretary, told members of the House of Commons that he did not propose to introduce new legislation but would provide for an "independent continuous check". These would be heralded by a White Paper embodying the views of a (then) unnamed judge. Since then (on 3rd March 1981) the findings of Lord Diplock, Chairman of the Security Commission, have been published, and state that there is nothing wrong with the way telephone calls were intercepted by the Police, Customs and Excise, and the security services. Lord Diplock will continue the "independent checks" mentioned by the Home Secretary, although his future findings will not be published. A fuss has been made by a sufficiently large group of Conservative M.P.s to make the Government think again.

The statistics of interception given in the White Paper are sparse and, according to vociferous and possibly well-informed critics, a gross understatement. On 31 December 1958 there were 237 authorisations (95 telephones, 142 letters); in 1968 there were 273 (155 telephones, 118 letters) and in 1978 there were 308 authorisations (214 telephones, 94 letters). The new report by Lord Diplock adduces no statistics.

The meagre figures made many feel that they hardly accorded with facts published in a long article by Duncan Campbell in the *New Statesman* on February 1st 1980, revealing that a tapping centre existed at 93 Ebury Bridge Road, London SW1 with the capacity to tap 1,000 lines simultaneously. The underlying inference was that either the centre was grossly overmanned and too ambitiously conceived, with an eye to telephone tapping on a vast scale, or the actual extent of phone tapping by the authorities had been vastly understated.

The *Law Society's Gazette* (21st May, 1980) says: "the interception of communications plays a major role in police efforts to control and prevent major organised crime and drug trafficking".

Having stated that premise, the *Gazette* asks what can de done if one's phone or a client's phone, is being tapped? *Prima facie* it amounts to a breach of article 8 (1) of the European Convention of Human Rights (the basis on which Malone, mentioned earlier, brought his action against the Commissioner of Police of the Metropolis), but the Law Society notes that the Convention has never been formally incorporated into English law. In fact, the Convention asserts what it considers desirable, not what can or may not be done. Besides, the second paragraph of the same article, qualifies the first by permitting interference with the right of communication "in accordance with the law" if such interference may fairly be deemed "in the interests of national security, public safety or the economic wellbeing of the country, for the prevention of disorder or crime, for the protection of health or morals, or for the protection of the rights and freedom of others."

It is quite clear from this that a member State has merely to state that the phone-tapping possibly rubber-stamp authorisation was issued in accordance with State laws.

So — official agencies of the State may, subject to authorisation from the appropriate quarter, tap the telephones of anybody (including, of course, the switchboards of companies) as a legal right.

But what of the unseen army of phone-tappers whose object is industrial espionage? The mere mechanics of phone-tapping are really very simple. But are they illegal?

Amazing to relate, as I have said, phone-tapping in Britain, carried out without authority and (of course) unknown to the persons or person being overhead, is *not* illegal! I am aware that the really adept and 'dedicated' professional industrial spy would not be bothered by the legality or otherwise of any procedure that achieved its intended purpose — the theft of information. Even so, the state of the law in the United Kingdom in respect of tapping in on somebody else's telephone is far from satisfactory.

Consider the case of *R v Senat & Cho Him Sin* (1968) 52 Criminal Appeal R.282.

Private investigators had tapped a telephone in the course of matrimonial enquiries. The evidence obtained was used subsequently in a criminal trial and the appellants were convicted. Counsel for Senat argued that as telephone tapping was "contrary to public policy", the evidence so obtained ought not to be admissible. Lord Parker, Lord Chief Justice, made short shrift of that argument making it clear that telephone tapping by private individuals, though an invasion of privacy, was not then unlawful. He said that the Government was considering legislation to protect that privacy. "Considering," in Governmental language, is not a euphemism for speed. As things stand, 14 years later telephone tapping as such remains lawful!

Of course, there is the Theft Act, S. 13. This section makes it an offence dishonestly to use or divert electricity. Well now, I do not propose to tap anybody's telephone but, if I so wished, I would send a letter to the Post Office saying that I intended to tap a telephone. I would enclose £1, stating that the money was intended to cover any electricity I might use. Even in these expensive times, I would have to be "on the line" for a very long time to use up my pound.

By this means, I would be circumventing Section 13 of the Theft Act, since I clearly had no intention of using electricity "dishonestly", or diverting it. Incidentally, it is an offence under Section 65A of the Post Office Act of 1953 to use the public telephone system with intent to avoid payment. If you sent them the money beforehand this section could be ignored, since you will have proved that you intend not only to pay but to pre-pay.

There is a legal precedent for this, in the case of *Boggeln v Williams* 1978 I WLR 8 where the defendant had been convicted under S.13 by magistrates, but the Crown Court had allowed his appeal against conviction. The prosecutor appealed to the Divisional Court.

The facts are relevant to our general issue of phone tapping and its legality. The Board had cut off the defendant's electricity supply. He happened to know how to reconnect and how to wire in the meter so that it recorded what electricity he was using. He wrote to the Board saying what he was going to do, and he did it.

"The question for the Court," said Mr Justice Lloyd, "was whether an intention to pay for electricity knowingly used without the authority of the electricity board was capable of being a defence to a charge brought under Section 13. "The fact," he concluded, "that the defendant did not believe at the time when he reconnected the supply that he had the consent of the Board does not of itself make the defendant's conduct dishonest in law."

Mr Justice O'Connor said there were two elements: "use without authority and to do so dishonestly."

But "dishonesty," although often quoted in the Theft Act, is purely a question of fact and has to be decided by the jury. The Court has frequently said that there must be no attempt to define "dishonesty". Legally it is too vague a word.

The latest edition of that legal tome, Archbold, in the matter of the case of *Boggeln v Williams*, suggests that Mr Justice Lloyd was wrong in applying a subjective test. That note relies on the case of *Rex v. Greenstein* (1975) 61 Cr App R 61 where the Court of Appeal makes it clear that belief in your own honesty cannot be the test.

Lord Justice Lawton delivered a judgement in the case of *Rex v Feely* (1973) 57 Cr.L.R.312 which puts the matter in a quite different legal light:

> "In our judgement, a taking to which no moral obloquy can reasonably attach is not within the concept of stealing either at common law or under the Theft Act 1968."

So in reply to my query to a distinguished lawyer as to my position, were I to send the Post Office money, and announce my intention to tap one of their telephones, he informs me that:

> "Applying these authorities and dicta — bearing in mind that *Boggeln v Williams* has not even been adversely criticised, let alone reversed, I come to the conclusion that what you propose to do is lawful."

I hastened to reassure my friend (probably unnecessarily!) that the case I had put to him was a hypothetical one, and that I had no intention of tapping anybody's telephone. But it did indeed interest me greatly to learn that, had such an intention been in my mind on my hypothetical basis, I could have put it into action without fear of the law. Good news, perhaps, for industrial spies, but less cheerful for those anxious to protect their vital secrets. In fact, as we know, an industrial spy would *not* inform Telecommunications of his intentions, but the fact still remains that he possesses the right to tap telephones if he does not steal electricity.

Legally speaking, the position regarding computers, those electronic storehouses of information, is marginally **different**. Unlike the telephone, which is hired and under the legal control of Telecommunications, a computer is "property". Attempts to secure access to it by burglary or trespass could — if detected — involve charges. But an attempt to prove the theft of electricity, where access to the computer lines was obtained outside the premises and away from the computer, would raise problems. For the computer to be working at all, it would be using electricity anyway, and no extra electricity would be involved in "tapping in" to its secrets.

If all this makes me sound like Job's comforter, please do not blame me, for I do not make the law. I merely try to repair some of the damage caused by its shortcomings.

I felt it worth while, in exploring the extent of industrial espionage, the labyrinth of present legislation here and abroad, and the constant fight to up-date the techniques to counter it, to enquire what the Metropolitan Police are doing about it. For this purpose I was granted an interview with Chief Inspector Ashdown regarding the industrial espionage unit set up within the Metropolitan Police.

It is not so called and, indeed, has no specific name, being part of the Art and Antiques Squad, which is a part of Department CI. I have no idea whatsoever as to the connection between industrial espionage and arts and antiques.

Department CI was formed nearly ten years ago and the Industrial Espionage Squad some time later. Its terms of reference and its policy are not defined, differing for each case. The Squad could be called in at any time, but is usually only involved when a crime has been committed *in the pursuit of* industrial espionage. It would seem that crimes which are a by-product of industrial espionage may be countered more vigorously than industrial espionage itself. The unit, I was told, has equipment for sweeping for bugs, but the equipment was un-named.

The unit is local in scope, has never operated outside London, though prepared to advise other police forces if necessary.

The strength of the unit was un-stated, while I understand that its personnel are drawn from all the members of the Fine Arts and Antiques squad where a matter of industrial espionage is involved. Most cases are still sub-judice, but one can be mentioned in which they were involved — this was the case of *Regina v Raymond*, where an attempt had been made to bribe someone to produce a computer programme. The squad obtained a conviction of a fine of £400.

The Unit does not advise in a crime prevention context. It was suggested to me that many cases do not come to the notice of the Squad, being dealt with at a local police level, especially if a crime has been committed. Mr Ashdown told me that very few cases had been investigated in the year and declined to define a few. I got the impression that it was a very small number. He also indicated that his Squad investigated more cases of film and video piracy, and this was very much on the increase.

My conclusion is that this service is a nonentity and a non-runner. The public, and I mean by the public the commercial world, are not particularly interested in utilising its services, and I would not be surprised to hear that it had been disbanded.

CHAPTER 12

Laws
The United States of America

Although, in certain fields of activity connected with industrial espionage, the United States of America can claim to be more thorough in its restrictions and more prompt with its penalties than is the case within the United Kingdom or Europe generally, the network of both Federal and State legislation is in many respects uneven, in some cases ineffectual and in other respects frequently ambiguous.

The rapid developments in technology and the unpredictable impact of certain new inventions, such as laser, for example, mean that existing laws are being constantly out-dated by events. New techniques become available and, before the manner of their potential abuse is realised, are exploited by criminals; only when these depredations become known and enormous do the creaky wheels of legislation start turning.

Legally, the most powerful restraints in the general field of industrial espionage concern bugging. Under Title III of the Federal Omnibus Crime Control and Safe Streets Act of 1968, there are set forth in 18 USCS, paragraphs 2510-2520, in considerable detail, a whole range of things a citizen may, or may not, do to other citizens, and what law enforcement agencies may or may no do.

The specific listing is as follows:—

SECTION	TITLE
S2510	Definitions
S2511	Interception and disclosure of wire or oral communication prohibited
S2512	Manufacture, distribution, possession and advertising of wire or oral communication intercepting devices prohibited
S2513	Confiscation of wire or oral communication intercepting devices

206

S2514	(Repealed)
S2515	Prohibition of use as evidence of intercepted wire or oral communications
S2516	Authorization for interception of wire or oral communications
S2517	Authorization for disclosure and use of intercepted wire or oral communications
S2518	Procedure for interception of wire or oral communications
S2519	Reports concerning intercepted wire or oral communications
S2520	Recovery of civil damages authorized.

Broadly speaking, it is an offence to sell a bug, to buy a bug, to use a bug or even to possess a bug. Legally, a bug is a very hot potato — with the reservation that modern bugs are considerably smaller than a potato and far more easily concealed. Section 801 sets forth (at far greater length than I give it) that inter alia (d) "to safeguard the privilege of innocent persons, the interception of wire or oral communications where none of the parties to the communications has consented to the interception should be allowed only when authorised by a court of competent jurisdiction."

Section 2510 (I) describes wire communication as meaning "any communication made in whole or in part through the use of facilities for the transmission of communications by the aid of wire, cable or other like connections between the point of origin and the point of reception furnished or operated by any person engaged as a common carrier in providing or operations such facilities for the transmission of interstate or foreign communications."

Section 2510 (2) defines "oral communication" as "any oral communication uttered by a person exhibiting an expectation that such communication is not subject to interception under circumstances justifying such expectation." Hardly a masterpiece of clarity!

Section 2511 is more readily understandable to the non-legal layman and sets forth explicitly the details by which "interception and disclosure of wire or oral communications" are prohibited:

Any person (a) who wilfully intercepts, endeavours to intercept, or procures any other person to intercept or endeavour to intercept, any wire or oral communication, or (c) "wilfully discloses, or endeavours to disclose, to any other person the contents of any wire or oral communication, knowing or having reason to know that the information was obtained through the interception of a wire or oral communication . . . (d) "shall be fined not more than \$10,000 or imprisoned no more than five years, or both."

Section 2512 of this appropriately-named "omnibus" prohibits the manufacture, distribution, possession and advertising of wire and oral communication intercepting devices."

The "omnibus" act effectually covers interference with and interception of communications to and between computers and their terminals, as well as telephone tapping and bugs. The penalties for infringement are severe — if the culprits can be first detected and, secondly, brought to justice — but, as I have already pointed out in my reference to computers, they are vulnerable at a very great number of points, and electronic eavesdropping, erasure of records and illegal addition to existing records can be achieved without creating any noticeable disturbance. However, the Act does serve as a brake; there are deterrents to the manufacture and sale of bugging equipment, for instance; though the crime position is bad, especially as regards industrial espionage in the United States, it would probably have been worse but for the legislation enacted as a result of widespread abuse in the sixties, the period of the birth of this new form of crime.

Bribery, a common tool of the industrial spy, is a weak spot in the counter-industrial-spy armoury. Most States in the U.S.A. have no commercial laws which adequately control this.

On my frequent visits to the United States, where I am a member of numerous American organisations concerned with security, I gained the impression that the machinery of law and order enforcement is to some extent fragmentated and un-coordinated. I had attributed this to what seemed to me to be the duality of control, the existence of two separate law enforcement entities, namely, Federal Laws and State Laws.

I had supposed that this was due to the fact that the country's vast size (the size of a continent) precluded the effective implementation of nationwide regulations, but this, I am informed by a distinguished American lawyer whose skill and judgement I respect, is to misjudge the situation. As he puts it to me:

> "It is submitted that the federal laws are designed to have a different scope and impact from the various state laws in view of the nature of the federal power and the constitutional granting of federal powers. An inspection of Provision (a) of the "Findings" provision of 1801 indicates that the federal power utilised to legislate in the "wire interception" area, stems from the Interstate Commerce clause of the

Constitution. It is the interstate nature of the prohibited activity that gives rise to the federal criminal law prohibiting wire interception and interception of ordal communication. Accordingly, rather than the size of the continent being the chief underlying reason or rational for the duality of federal and state law, it is rather the scope of the federal power. The state laws in connection with wiretapping are designed primarily to prohibit intrastate interception of communications generally. Moreover, Congress did not intend by the enactment of federal laws to preempt the field of wiretapping so as to supercede or exclude state legislation in the field. (*United States vs. Hoffa* (CA7 Ill) 436 F2d, cert den, 400 US 1000, 27 L Ed 2d 451, 91 S Ct 455, 457).

In passing Title III of Omnibus Crime Control and Safe Streets Act, Congress preempted the field of interception of wire communications to a certain extent, however, States have been deemed also to be permitted to regulate wire taps, provided their standards are at least as stringent as those of the federal act. (*State vs. McGuillicuddy*, (1977, Fla App D2) 342 So 2nd 567). Therefore, although the limitations set by S18 USCS S2516 are to be observed by State authorities, the State is not prohibited from imposing even more restrictive requirements than are set out in the Federal Statute. (*Application of Olander* (1973) 213 Kan 282, 515 P2d 1211).

Accordingly, a number of states have passed comprehensive wiretapping and electronic surveillance acts. In 1977 the Maryland General Assembly enacted a comprehensive act patterned after Title III of the Omnibus Crime Control and Safe Streets Act of 1968, consolidating prior wiretapping and bugging provisions in the prior Maryland law.

In order to understand the underlying rationale behind the Omnibus Act it is necessary to understand the historical background associated with wiretapping and criminal law. During the first half of this century, the Supreme Court did not regard wiretapping as a search and seizure within the context of the Fourth Amendment, since wiretapping could be conducted without physical invasion of person or property. The Court in *Katz vs. United States*, rejected the physical invasion theory and laid the groundwork for the enactment in the following year of the comprehensive federal wiretapping statute. The Katz Court refused to "retroactively validate" an unauthorized wiretap even though the investigating agents had carefully circumscribed their search. Only if a magistrate issued a Presearch Order establishing precise limits for the search and later had been informed of all that had been seized, would the agents conduct have been proper under the Fourth Amendment.

S2511 (2) (c) in the Federal Wiretap Statute states that "it shall not be unlawful . . . for a person acting *under color of law* to intercept a wire or oral communication, where such person is a party to the communication or one of the parties to the communication has given prior consent to such interception. The Maryland statute, clearly delineates those persons who may intercept under such circumstances, limiting the scope of such interceptions to the enumerated felonies under S10402-(c) (2) of the Maryland Law. Under the Maryland Act, only a "investigative or law enforcement office" may intercept a conversation upon the consent of only one party. In Maryland, such an interception may be undertaken by a person who is not a law enforcement officer, only if (1) The person is a party to the communication and (2) all of the parties have given their prior consent. By making both participation and consent mandatory, the Maryland Law has imposed stricter requirements for civil monitoring than Title III of the Federal Code. Monitoring is further restricted in Maryland "to provide evidence of the commission of the offenses of murder, kidnapping, gambling, robbery, bribery, extortion, or dealing in controlled dangerous substances, or any conspiracy to commit any of these offenses.

A recent Law Review article, published in the University of Baltimore Law Review, namely Volume Nine, Winter of 1980, Number Two, interestingly points out that Title III of the Omnibus Crime Control and Safe Streets Act of 1968 had given the Court's authority to approve covert entries of private premises for the purpose of installing eavesdropping devices.

With reference to the "diversity of state law" under different categories affecting "industrial espionage", that there are a number of effective criminal laws, both federal and state and civil laws, both statutory and case law rulings, which effectively protect the interests of persons, businesses and corporations. an example of such criminal legislation is the Maryland "Theft" Law, which has recently been enacted in the State of Maryland covering theft of a wide variety and encompassing all of the laws previously falling in the category of "larceny" including but not limited to larceny, larceny by trick, larceny after trust, embezzlement, false pretenses, shoplifting, and receiving stolen property. The new "theft" criminal statute contains a broad definition of "property" which has been defined under the statute to mean "anything of value" including but not limited to: (1) Real estate; (2) Money; (3) Commercial instruments; (4) Admission of transportation tickets; (5) Written instruments representing or embodying rights concerning anything of value, or services, or anything otherwise of value to the owner; (6) Things growing on or affixed to, or found on land, or part of or affixed to any building; (7) Electricity, gas and water; (8) Birds, animals, and fish which ordinarily are kept in a state of confinement; (9) Food and drink; (10) Samples, cultures, microorganisms, specimens; (11) Records, recordings, documents, blueprints, drawings, maps and whole or partial copies, descriptions, photographs, prototypes or models thereof, or any other articles, materials, devices, substances, and whole or partial copies, descriptions, photographs, prototypes, or models thereof which represent evidence, reflect or record secret scientific, technical, merchandising production or management information, designed process, procedure, formula, invention, trade secret or improvement; (12) Financial instruments, information, electronically produced data, computer software and programs in either machine or human readable form, and other tangible or intangible items of value.

Therefore, under the Statute, it is clear that computer software and programs, electronically produced data, intangible information of all nature, trade secrets, inventions, improvements, formulas, and indeed all production and management information are thus covered under the new theft statute. Moreover, civil law affords a great deal of protection to the business community in general. Unfortunately, businesses, large and small, fail to adequately protect themselves by civil contracts, inclusive of extensive employment contracts, prohibiting the divulgement of trade secrets and other "property" of the employer.

The reason, of course, that there are no federal "theft" statutes is a historical one in view of the fact that there is really no "substantive" federal criminal law. In other words, Title 18 of the US Code, prohibits only federal laws within the ambit of federal power. There simply is not a mechanism for legislating "substantive" federal law, save and excepting those areas of an expanding nature which fall within the federal ambit. However, a growing number of States in the United States have adopted the modern "theft" type of statute which specifically covers industrial espionage".

I have quoted my lawyer friend at length because the points he makes are valuable, and for any who want further information I can do no better than refer them to the laws themselves, despite the difficulties to the layman of understanding legal language, which is necessarily involved because of its need for precision in providing for every eventuality.

It is always perilous to attempt to compress the laws of any country, but the diversity of laws within the U.S.A. relating to wire and telephone tapping is impressive.

Thus, in California, wire and telephone tapping are covered by Section 643J of the California Penal Code. Similarly, it has, like New Jersey, New York and Texas, Trade Secret laws whose provisions vary and cannot be effectively summarised, which can be invoked where specific violation can be proved to the satisfaction of a court, and the guilty parties be identified and found.

In Pennsylvania, Illinois and Massachusetts it is often possible to seek redress for the theft of trade secrets under their larceny laws, which define and emphasise what trade secrets are and that stealing them is an indictable offence. In certain other states the larceny laws give some, but more limited protection insofar as, while the statutes make it an offence to steal trade secrets, the onus is on the prosecutor to prove that what was stolen was of value. No doubt this can often be done, but as I have said in a previous context, the hypothetical rewards of *potential* sales and exploitations of a formu-

la or method or design must remain, in their very nature, specula-
tions of a kind a judge and jury may or may not accept.

Computer fraud is tackled more imaginatively (in terms of legal
effectiveness) in some states than in others. Clearly, gaining access
to a computer and either extracting or adding information is an
intrusion. The computer's owners, or those persons affected by this
intrusion, have not consented to the access to their files, and would
not so consent were they aware of the industrial spy's activities.
Interference with a computer in order to extract information, erase
data or infuse new material is therefore tantamount to burglary.
Certainly, the instrusion is not effected by breaking and entering,
but the intention is the same and the effect is the same. Instead of
prizing open a door with a cold chisel, the burglar has used codes
and secrets to open up an electronic file not intended for his use.
Certain states recognise this principle in their statutes concerning
burglary, notably California, the District of Columbia, Delaware,
Florida, Massachusetts, New Jersey, New York, Pennsylvania,
Illinois, Texas and Virginia.

The forgery laws in certain states can also be invoked where
secret information has been extracted from computer records —
California, the District of Columbia, Delaware, New York, Pennsylvania and Texas.

In many states the protection of computer files, and in particular
the protection of computer programmes, is very unsatisfactory.
Patent laws offer much protection, but courts are reluctant to hold
that a computer programme can be held to be the monopoly of the
deviser; the assumption is that another computer enthusiast, given
the same equipment, facilities and brain-power, could have de-
vided, by empirical or deductive thinking, an exactly similar programme. An analogy for this would be the fact that, in early history
when countries were divided one from another, precisely similar
skills developed — i.e. weaving. To invoke the Patent Laws in
protection of purloined computer programmes is at best highly
speculative and at worst doomed to failure. In fact 70 percent of all
such actions in this field have failed. However, expertly interpreted
and applied, the copyright laws can sometimes be used to protect
programmes.

In the world of commerce the damage which can be done by
industrial espionage does not always take the obvious form of
stealing designs, formulae, production layouts and future plans.
Accumulated experience of a specialised kind, available only in the

job held by an employee, is often more valuable than a patent. So often it is not a question of what apparatus or mechanisms or processes are used, but under what conditions, within what restrictions, in what order, and to what timing. Pharmaceuticals, oil refining, nuclear and other industrial processes are examples of this.

The work "know-how" admirably describes this kind of cumulative experience. An admirable definition of "know-how" is provided by a judgement (68 U.S.P.Q. 317 64F. Supp. 420 (DCC.Md.1946)):

> ". . . know-how, that is to say, factual knowledge not capable of precise separate description, but which when used in an accumulated form, after being acquired as the result of trial and error gives to the one acquiring it an ability to produce something which he otherwise would not have necessary for commercial success."

It follows from this that the suborning or bribery of key employees is often more disastrous than the simple theft of patents, processes and the like. But, as I have endeavoured to emphasise throughout this book, prevention of industrial espionage is better than attempts to avenge or remedy it. Litigation, not merely in the U.S.A. but almost everywhere in the Western world, is a costly quagmire into which none but the brave, the wealthy or the merely foolhardy dare venture.

CHAPTER 13

Laws
The EEC Countries & Europe

The legal position respecting industrial espionage within those countries comprising the European Economic Community slowly — very slowly — clarifying and codifying in respect of different areas and aspects of industrial espionage, and to differing degrees. However, for the moment, these provisions vary enormously from country to country. In some important areas of industrial espionage there may be no protection at all, in others, merely partial protection whilst in rare cases there are condign punishments permissible by statute in respect of particular offences.

To the best of my information, based on intensive enquiries in many countries, no State has thus far evolved and applied a uniform and co-ordinated anti-industrial-espionage legislative programme.

Indeed, this confusion, inadequacy and lack of co-operation between different countries has produced some disastrous or ironic situations. Italy's loose laws made possible the pillage of the secrets of the Cyanamid combine. an employee of the powerful, multi-million Hoffman La Roche pharmaceutical combine in Switzerland managed to get an ex-employee, Stanley Adams, arrested and charged because he had disclosed company secrets to the European Economic Community. Yet Adam's motives in so doing were not profit, but duty; member-countries of the EEC were breaking the EEC's laws on monopoly in their relations with the Swiss concern, and although Switzerland itself was not a member of EEC (as is still the case) Hoffman La Roche's activities in that area justified investigation.

In the event, Stanley Adams found his professional career ruined, his family life disrupted and himself left a widower by the suicide of his young wife who became depressed and unnerved by the disgrace which her husband's public-spirited action had brought upon him. The whole sad story was told in great detail in a television documentary, *World in Action* on Independent Television on 12th May 1980.

Stanley Adams was charged with industrial espionage under Swiss law. He was charged because the company complaining was a *Swiss* company, and it is an offence to disclose their industrial secrets. It seems strange that the EEC did not more vigorously and quickly defend the man who was merely trying to support the laws and principles which it had promulgated. Only when Mr Adams' life had been effectually wrecked did they come up, belatedly, with any kind of compensation to him.

My approaches to the various embassies for elucidation of the laws pertaining to industrial espionage in the various member countries of the EEC (and a few other embassies besides) has revealed a certain diffidence in answering elementary questions on the subject. However, I can summarise some of the laws as they exist at the time of writing.

A list of EEC countries will be shown in the appendix. For the purposes of alphabetical convenience I propose to include in this context some countries which are not members of the EEC:

AUSTRIA

The law against unfair competition of September 26, 1923, BGBI, No. 531 penalises unauthorised use of trade secrets or abuse of documents entrusted to a person with fine or imprisonment.

BELGIUM

The law prohibits fraudulent disclosure of trade secrets by an employee or former employee to a third person by imprisonment from 3 months to three years, plus fine. Action can be taken under the Penal Code, Article 309 or under the Civil Law, Articles 7 and 20 of the Law of August 7, 1922, as reenacted July 20, 1955. The law does not apply to misappropriation of trade secrets by an employee for his own use.

FRANCE

The French Penal Code, Article 418, punishes delivery to third parties of industrial secrets by an unauthorised person by fine and imprisonment up to 5 years. If the disclosure or delivery is to foreigners or French citizens living abroad, the employee found gulty may be deprived of his civil rights for a period of up to 10 years, commencing with the end of his sentence. Under the law of July 5, 1844, patent infringement is a criminal offence.

GERMAN FEDERAL REPUBLIC

It is illegal, under both Criminal and Civil law, for a citizen, or member of a company or organisation, to tap the telephone of another. The relevant section of the Penal Code is section 201. Civil action can be taken under laws protecting the rights of the individual. There have been prosecutions for the office of telephone tapping both in 1980 and 1981.

Equally, under CF 1b of the Penal Code, the surreptitious emplacement of wired or battery-operated 'bugs' which transmit or broadcast private conversations is illegal, carrying the possible penalty of from three to five years' imprisonment. The Ministry of Posts is responsible for the implementation of laws devised to prevent tapping and bugging. And legislation is being prepared to restrict the sale of bugs in Western Germany.

The main laws which can be invoked against the securing, by surreptitious means, of secret commercial formulae, processes, patterns and projects are the relevant provisions (sections 12, 17 and 20) of the Unfair Competition Act. The use of 'lie detectors' or 'stress evaluators' for the vetting of employees is restricted by law. The securing of information by means of imposture and misrepresentation is not the subject of any written law but is illegal under Civil Case Law.

Finally, the Minister of Justice in Bonn informs me that the West German Government considers the Common Market's resolve to set up a European Patent Office in Munich will improve matters in safeguarding against the theft of Patent rights.

GREECE

I am much indebted to the Greek Embassy in London for obtaining from their Government in Athens, the following useful answers to my questionnaire:—

1. Articles 16, 17 and 18 of Law 146/1914 provide for prison sentence of up to 6 months for employees who give away company secrets, formulae etc. Those employees are also liable to pay compensation for losses or damages caused to their companies. Persons who, for competition purposes, attempt to obtain secrets by bribing or suborning competitors' employees are liable to prison sentences of up to three months.

2. Regarding telephone tapping, article 19 of the Greek constitution provides that "the privacy of correspondence and any other form of communication is absolutely inviolable". Thus article 250 of the Greek Penal Code provides that employees working for telephone companies who reveal the contents of private telephone calls are liable to prison sentences of up to three years. It is not, however, yet illegal for a citizen or member of a company or organisation to "tap" the telephone of another. This practice was unknown in Greece until recently. The Ministry of Justice has already drafted a bill, not yet passed by the Greek Parliament, which will render the practice illegal.

3. Article 370 of the Penal Code provides that persons who open sealed letters or documents or violate places where these are kept or in any other way intrude into other persons or organisations' secrets by means of reading or copying documents are liable to sentences of up to one year.

4. "Bugging" is not illegal in Greece.

5. "Intellectual property" is protected by laws 2387/1920 on "intellectual property", 2527/1920 "on patents", 1998/1939 "on trade marks" and 146/1914 "on unfair competition". In our knowledge there are no laws which can be invoked against the securing of commercial secrets by surreptitious or dishonest means.

6. We have no official comments on the EEC's proposed European Patent Office. We understand, however, that it could constitute a step towards improving matters concerning the theft of patents within the community.

7. In our knowldge there are not any legal limitations to preclude an employer enquiring into the background of a potential employee. Regarding the use of "lie detectors", "stress evaluators", etc., such devices are not common in Greece and have not therefore been the subject of any legislation.

8. Regarding the assumption of a false identity, article 415 of the penal code provides that any one who, without the permission of the proper authority, changes the name of his family or obtains for himself the name of another family shall be punished by criminal detention.

9. Unfortunately there are no statistical records of sentences imposed for the above offences.

HOLLAND

In the Netherlands the Civil Law, Sections 272 and 273, provides for fines and imprisonment for theft of proprietory information having a tangible form. By this definition it could be difficult to pursue a case of an employee being lured away from his job to another and better-paid job, because of his accumulated "know-how" — which is, in most countries, a charge difficult to establish.

ITALY

Remedies for certain types of industrial espionage may be sought under the Penal Code, Sections 622 to 623 and under the Civil Code, Section 2105. Disclosure of confidential information acquired by reason of status, office, profession or trade, or use for the employee's own benefit may be punished by imprisonment of up to two years. Italy, however, has no provision for the protection of drugs and foodstuffs but, under pressure of its Common Market partners, new legislation in this field may be expected. Italy has long been the centre of a brisk trade in stolen patents and pharmaceutical formulae — i.e. as in the notorious Cyanamid case, where stolen cultures were flown to Italy, comparable pharmaceuticals manufactured there and sold to Cyanamid's customers at greatly reduced prices.

NORWAY

There are certain statutes under which legal action may be taken, and redress sought, where trade confidentiality has been breached or information stolen by surreptitious means.

The Penal Code, Section 294, Paragraph 2 provides some relief against industrial spies. The Act of July 7, 1922, Section 1, prohibits "improper competition", such as the conveying of vital information by an ex-employee to a rival concern. Up to six months imprisonment can be incurred under the law if a person:

1. with the help of secret listening apparatus listens to a telephone conversation or other conversations between other people, or eavesdrops by whatever means on private negotiations in which he is not entitled to participate.
2. With the help of tape or other technical equipment secretly tapes conversations as mentioned in point 1, or of negotiations within a closed meeting, or gains entry to such a confidential meeting by means of deception.

   Plants any listening device, tape recording apparatus or other technical equipment for the purposes mentioned in Point 1 and 2. An accomplice in any of the acts mentioned is treated as equally culpable as the principal culprit involved.

   Prosecutions under these Statutes is not automatic; they are undertaken only if such action is considered to be in the public interest. Similarly, police will not respond to a request from a member of the public for a matter to be investigated and the alleged offender punished unless they feel that there is, *prima facie*, a case to be investigated "in the public interest".

SPAIN

The Penal Code, as amended March 28, 1963, provides, in Article

497, fines and imprisonment for disclosure of the industrial secrets of another party, while Article 499 applies specifically to the disclosure of such secrets by an employee.

There are several more recent, and very important, provisions:

1. *Article 18(3) of the Constitution of 1978* provides "secrecy of communication is guaranteed, *particularly of postal, telegraphic and telephonic communications, except in the event of a Court Order to the contrary.*
2. *The Royal Decree of 20th February 1979* lays down that this is a fundamental right which the courts must uphold as being inherent in the fundamental rights of the individual.
3. *Articles 497-499 of the Penal Code of 1973* enacts that any person guilty of infringement of copyright or of a Patent or Trade Mark is guilty of a criminal offence carrying a penalty of up to six months imprisonment, quite apart from the right of the aggrieved party under the civil laws governing copyright and Trade Marks and Patents.

SWEDEN

Swedish law offers specific protection against the defection of employees to rival concerns, and the disclosure of information entrusted to them in the course of their employment. The Swedish Act of May 29, 1951, enacts that:

"Any person in the employment of an industrial undertaking who, during the period covered by his working contract, unlawfully uses or discloses a manufacturing process . . . or the like which he knows to be a trade secret of his employer, with the intention of gaining an advantage for himself or of profiting or injuring another individual, shall be liable to a monetary fine or a term of imprisonment up to one year; he shall furthermore be liable for the damage caused."

SWITZERLAND

Very many acts relate to industrial espionage, its prohibitions, penalties and varieties of offence. A whole chapter is devoted to the subject in the *Schweizerisches Strafgesetzbuch* of 21 of December 1937 (STGB) in particular Art. 273 and Art. 179. Very many aspects of the subject are included. The protection of "intellectual property" is covered by nearly 50 acts, too lengthy and involved to list here, but obtainable for those who wish to study them from Eidgenossische Drucksachen-und Materialzentrale (EDMZ), 3000, Bern, Switzerland.

Article 273 provides for fines and imprisonment for the disclosure of industrial secrets to a foreign entity, concern or agent.

As I have endeavoured to show, within limitations which I cheerfully acknowledge and which will be apparent to the reader, the range of industrial espionage is vast, its damage beyond computing, and its social mischief — in creating a wealthy criminal elite whose influence increases in Western society — alarming to a degree.

New techniques of industrial espionage are constantly emerging, and, with the ever-increasing developments in science and industry, and the scramble for dominance in the political and economic worlds, we can expect industrial espionage to be ever more ubiquitous and even more subtle and difficult to combat.

All this constitutes a challenge to the intelligence, will and integrity of governments and industrialists everywhere, a challenge which can better be met if the extent and nature of the problem are realised.

It goes without saying that this book has many omissions and, as time goes on, may require many additions and amendments. I shall be glad to hear from any reader who has constructive suggestions to make, or who has been the victim (or perpetrator, even!) of industrial espionage, with an eye to future editions of this work.

Bibliography

ACKROYD, James E.
THE INVESTIGATOR: A PRACTICAL
GUIDE TO PRIVATE DETECTION
Frederick Muller Ltd., London
1974
ISBN 0 584 10133 3

ANONYMOUS
THE BLACK BAG OWNER'S MANUAL:
PART I — "SPOOKCENTRE"
Paladin Press, Boulder,
Colorado 1978
ISBN 0 87364 149 3

ANONYMOUS
BUGS AND ELECTRONIC IC
SURVEILLANCE
Desert Publications, Cornville,
Arizona, U.S.A. 1976
No ISBN Number
Author not stated

ANONYMOUS
THE PRINCIPLES OF INVESTIGATION
AND SECURITY
Mayday Company, Seattle,
Washington, U.S.A. 1971
No ISBN Number
No Library of Congress Catalog
Number

BARLAY, Stephen
DOUBLE CROSS
Hamish Hamilton, London 1973
ISBN 241 02423 4

BEQUAI, August
COMPUTER CRIME
Lexington Books,
Massachusetts, U.S.A. 1978
ISBN 0-669-01728-0

BEQUAI, August
WHITE-COLLAR CRIME
Lexington Books,
Massachusetts, U.S.A. 1978
ISBN 0-669-01900-3
Library of Congress Catalog
Card Number: 77-11242

BEQUAI, August
ORGANIZED CRIME
Lexington Books,
Massachusetts, U.S.A. 1979
ISBN 0-669-02104-0
Library of Congress Catalog
Card Number: 77-18574

BARRON, John
K.G.B. THE SECRET WORK OF
SOVIET SECRET AGENTS
Hodder and Stoughton, London
1974
ISBN 0 340 18904 5

BLACKSTOCK, Paul W and
SCHAF, Frank L.
INTELLIGENCE, ESPIONAGE,
COUNTERESPIONAGE AND COVERT
OPERATIONS — A GUIDE TO
INFORMATION SOURCES
Gale Research Company,

Detroit, Michigan, U.S.A. 1978
ISBN 0-8103-1323-5
Library of Congress Catalog
Number 74-55167

BLACKWELL, Gene
THE PRIVATE INVESTIGATOR
Security World Publishing Co.
Inc., Los Angeles, U.S.A. 1979
ISBN 0-913708-34-8
Library of Congress Catalog
Number: 79-4560

BROWN, Robert M.
THE ELECTRONIC INVASION
John F. Rider Publisher Inc.,
New York, U.S.A. 1967
Library of Congress Catalog No.
67-21759

BYRNE, Denis E. and JONES,
Peter H.
RETAIL SECURITY: A MANAGEMENT
FUNCTION
20th Century Security Education
Ltd., Leatherhead, Surrey,
England 1977
ISBN 0 905961 00 3

CARSON, Charles R.
MANAGING EMPLOYEE HONESTY
Security World Publishing Co.
Inc., Los Angeles, California,
U.S.A. 1977
ISBN 0-913708-27-5
Library of Congress Card
Number: 76-51836

COMER, Michael J.
CORPORATE FRAUD
McGraw Hill Book Company
(UK) Ltd. 1977
ISBN 0 07 084494 1

DEIGHTON, Suzan
THE NEW CRIMINALS: A
BIBIOLOGRAPHY OF COMPUTER
RELATED CRIME
The Institution of Electrical

Engineers, London 1978
ISBN 0 85296 446 3

FARR, Robert
THE ELECTRONIC CRIMINALS
McGraw-Hill Book Company,
New York, U.S.A. 1975
ISBN 0-07-019962-0

FRENCH, Scott
THE BIG BROTHER GAME
Lyle Stuart Inc., New Jersey,
U.S.A. 1975
ISBN 0-8184-0240-7 —
hardcover
ISBN 0-8184-0241-5 —
paperbound

FUQUA, Paul and WILSON,
Jerry V.
SECURITY INVESTIGATOR'S
HANDBOOK
Gulk Publishing Company,
Houston, Texas, U.S.A. 1979
ISBN 0-87201-664-1
Library of Congress Catalog
Card Number: 78-62615

GEISS, Gilbert and MEIER,
Robert F.
WHITE-COLLAR CRIME OFFENCES IN
BUSINESS, POLITICS AND THE
PROFESSIONS
Macmillan Publishing Co. Inc.,
New York, U.S.A. 1977
ISBN 0-02-911600-7
Library of Congress Catalog
Card Number: 76-27223

GREENE, Richard M. Jr.
(Editor)
BUSINESS INTELLIGENCE AND
ESPIONAGE
Dow Jones-Irwin Inc.,
Holmwood, Illinois, U.S.A.
1966
Library of Congress Catalog
Card No. 66-25591

HAMILTON, Peter and
KETTELL, Alison
BUSINESS SECURITY
Associated Business Press,
London 1980
ISBN 0 85227 212 X

HICKSON, Philip
INDUSTRIAL COUNTER-ESPIONAGE
Spectator Publications Ltd.,
London 1968
(Sponsored by The Institute of
Directors)
No ISBN number

HOUGAN, Jim
SPOOKS: THE PRIVATE USE OF
SECRET AGENTS
W.H. Allen, London 1979
ISBN 0 491 02266 2

HSIAO, David K.; KERR,
Douglas S.; MADNICK, Stuart
E.
COMPUTER SECURITY
Academic Press Inc., New York,
USA 1979
ISBN 0-12-357650-4

HAMILTON, Peter
ESPIONAGE, TERRORISM AND
SUBVERSION IN AN INDUSTRIAL
SOCIETY
Peter A Heims Limited, Cleeve
Road, Leatherhead, Surrey 1979
ISBN 0 9506426 0 6

INSTITUTION OF
ELECTRICAL ENGINEERS
THE NEW CRIMINALS: A
BIBLIOGRAPHY OF COMPUTER
RELATED CRIME
Compiled by Suzan Deighton
The Institution of Electrical
Engineers, London 1978
ISBN 0 85296 446 3

KRAUSS, Leonard I. &
MACGAHAN, Aileen
COMPUTER FRAUD AND
COUNTERMEASURES
Prentice-Hall Inc., New Jersey,
U.S.A. 1979
ISBN 0-13-164772-5

LEE, Fred
THE COMPUTER BOOK
Artech House Inc., U.S.A. 1978
ISBN 0-89006-058-4
Library of Congress Catalog
Number: 78-17450

LEIBHOLZ, Stephen W. and
WILSON, Louis D.
USER'S GUIDE TO COMPUTER CRIME
Chilton Book Company,
Pennsylvania, U.S.A. 1974
ISBN 0-8019-6095-9

LUIS, Ed San
OFFICE AND OFFICE BUILDING
SECURITY
Security World Publishing
Company Inc., Los Angeles,
California, U.S.A. 1973
ISBN 0-913708-12-7
Library of Congress Catalog
Number: 73-85627

MADGWICK, Donald and
SMYTHE, Tony
THE INVASION OF PRIVACY
Sir Isaac Pitman & Sons Ltd,
London 1974
ISBN 0 273 00702 5

MCKNIGHT, Gerald
COMPUTER CRIME
Michael Joseph, London 1973
ISBN 0 7181 1178 8

MARTIN, James
THE WIRED SOCIETY
Prentice-Hall Inc., New Jersey,
U.S.A. 1978
ISBN 0-13-961441-9

MITCHELL, Ewan
COPING WITH CRIME
Business Books Limited,
London 1969
ISBN 220 79936 9

NEWTON, Anne/PERL,
Kathleen
Yaskiw/DOLESCHAL, Eugene
INFORMATION SOURCES IN
CRIMINAL JUSTICE: AN ANNOTATED
GUIDE TO DIRECTORIES, JOURNALS
AND NEWSLETTERS
National Council on Crime and
Delinquency, New Jersey,
U.S.A. 1976
No ISBN Number
No Library of Congress Catalog
Number

OLIVER, Eric and WILSON,
John
PRACTICAL SECURITY IN COMMERCE
AND INDUSTRY
Gower Press Ltd., Epping,
Essex, England 1978
ISBN 0 566 02033 5

PAINE, Lauren
THE TECHNOLOGY OF ESPIONAGE
Robert Hale Ltd., London 1978
ISBN 0 7091 6832-2

PAYNE, Ronald
PRIVATE SPIES
Arthur Barker Limited, London
1967
No ISBN number

POLLOCK, Dr. David A.
METHODS OF ELECTRONIC AUDIO
SURVEILLANCE
Charles C. Thomas, Springfield,
Illinois, U.S.A. 1973
ISBN 0-398-02382-4

POWELL, William; with an
introduction by P.M.
BERGMAN
THE ANARCHIST COOKBOOK
Lyle Stuart Inc., Secausus, New
Jersey, U.S.A. 1971
ISBN 0-8184-0003X (hardcover)
ISBN 0-8184-0004-8
(paperbound)
Library of Congress Catalog
Card Number: 71-12797

ROWAN, Ford
TECHNO SPIES
G.P. Putnam's Sons, New York,
U.S.A. 1978
ISBN 399-11855-1

RULE, James B.
PRIVATE LIVES AND PUBLIC
SURVEILLANCE
Allen Lane, London 1973
ISBN 7139 0322 8

SCHABECK, Tim A.
COMPUTER CRIME INVESTIGATION
MANUAL
Assets Protection, Madison,
WI., U.S.A. 1979
ISBN 0-933708-01-7

SMITH, P.I. Slee
INDUSTRIAL INTELLIGENCE AND
ESPIONAGE
Business Books Limited,
London 1970
ISBN 220 79866 4

SMITH, Robert Ellis
PRIVACY: HOW TO PROTECT WHAT'S
LEFT OF IT
Anchor Press/Doubleday,
Garden City, New York 1979
ISBN 0-385-14288-9
Library of Congress Catalog
Number: 78-55857

SOBEL, Lester A.
CORRUPTION IN BUSINESS
Facts on File, Inc., New York,
U.S.A. 1977
ISBN 0-87196-292-6
Library of Congress Catalog
Number: 76-49186

STROBL, Walter M.
HANDBOOK FOR
INDUSTRIAL/COMMERCIAL SECURITY
FORCES TRAINING GUIDE
Training Consultants Inc.,
Knoxville, Tennessee, U.S.A.
1977
No ISBN Number
No Library of Congress Catalog
Number.

THOMPSON, Antony A.
BIG BROTHER IN BRITAIN TODAY
Michael Joseph, London 1970
ISBN 7181 0511 7

TODD, Alden
FINDING FACTS FAST: HOW TO FIND
OUT WHAT YOU WANT
Ten Speed Press, California
1979
ISBN 0-89815-012-4
ISBN 0-89815-013-2

TURNER, William W.
HOW TO AVOID ELECTRONIC
EAVESDROPPING AND PRIVACY
INVASION
Investigators Information
Service, Los Angeles, U.S.A.
1972
No ISBN No.
Library of Congress Number:
72-75216

UNITED STATES
DEPARTMENT OF JUSTICE
NATIONAL CRIMINAL JUSTICE
THESAURUS
(Descriptions for indexing law
enforcement and criminal justice
information)
National Criminal Justice
Reference Service, P.O. Box
24036, S.W. Post Office,
Washington, D.C. 1977

VAN DEWERKER, John S.
"former CIA employee"
THE ELECTRONIC SURVEILLANCE
THREAT
Ashby & Associates — no
address stated — U.S.A.
No ISBN Number given
No Library of Congress Number
stated

VAN DEWERKER, J.S.
(author) and R. BARRY
ASHBY (Editor)
THE SCIENCE OF ELECTRONIC
SURVEILLANCE
AASD Ashby & Associates,
Washington, D.C., U.S.A. 1976
No ISBN Number
No Library of Congress Number

WALKER, Bruce Jay
COMPUTER SECURITY AND
PROTECTION STRUCTURES
Dowden, Hutchinson & Ross,
Inc., Stroudsburg, Penn.,
U.S.A.
ISBN 0-470-15155-2
Library of Congress Catalog
Card Number: 76-11767

WALSH, Timothy J. and
HEALY, Richard J.
PROTECTING YOUR BUSINESS
AGAINST ESPIONAGE
Amacom, a division of
American Management
Association, New York, U.S.A.
1973
ISBN 0-8144-5311-2
Library of Congress Catalog
Number: 72-84119

WARNER, Malcolm and
STONE, Michael
THE DATA BANK SOCIETY
George Allen & Unwin Ltd.,
London 1970
ISBN 0 04 300025 8

WESTIN, Alan F.
PRIVACY AND FREEDOM
The Bodley Head, London 1967
ISBN 370 01325 5

WRIGHT, K.G.
COST-EFFECTIVE SECURITY
McGraw-Hill Book Publishing
Company (UK) Limited 1972
ISBN 07 084403 8

APPENDIX A

THE EUROPEAN COMMUNITY

The member nations of the European Community are:

Country	Population
Belgium	10 million
Denmark	5 million
France	53 million
Germany	61 million
Greece	9 million
Ireland	3 million
Italy	57 million
Luxembourg	⅓ million
Netherlands	14 million
United Kingdom	56 million

APPENDIX B

RECOMMENDED INVESTIGATIVE AND SECURITY ASSOCIATIONS

INTERNATIONAL

American Society of Industrial Security
Room 651
2000 K Street N W
Washington
DC 20006
U.S.A.

International Professional Security Association
292A Torquay Road
Paignton
DEVON TG3 2ET

Council of International Investigators
311 Oak Grove Drive
Akron
Ohio 44319
U.S.A.

World Association of Detectives
PO Box 36174
Cincinnati
Ohio 45236
U.S.A.

Internationale Kommission der Detektivverbande
Boks 46
Ljan
Oslo
NORWAY

NATIONAL

America
California Association of Licensed Investigators, Inc
PO Box 1001
Fairfield
Ca 94533
U.S.A.

Florida Assocation of Private Investigators, Inc
PO Box 2461
Tampa
Florida 33601
U.S.A.

National Association of Legal Investigators
442 Europe Street
Baton Rouge
Louisiana 70802
U.S.A.

Private Detectives Association of New Jersey, Inc
397 Jackson Avenue
Hackensack
NJ 07601
U.S.A.

Associated Licensed Detectives of New York State
161 East 35th Street
New York
NY 10016
U.S.A.

Ohio Association of Private Detective Agencies, Inc
1120 Snowville Road
Cleveland
Ohio 44141
U.S.A.

Pacific Northwest Association of Investigators, Inc
117 1st Avenue N
Seattle
WA 98109
U.S.A.

Texas Association of Licensed
 Investigators Directory
PO Box 42517
Houston
Texas 77045
U.S.A.

Virginia Security Association, Inc
PO Box 12952
Roanoke
Virginia 24029
U.S.A.

Association of Washington State
 Private Security Executives
1525 14th Avenue
Seattle
Wa 98122
U.S.A.

Argentina
C.A.S.I.P.I.
Rosario de Santa Fe 231
Piso 10° — Of "F"
Edificio de "La Boisa de Comercio"
Cordoba
ARGENTINA

Austria
Osterreichischer Detektivverband
1040 Wien
Wiedner-Hauptstrasse 50
AUSTRIA

Belgium
L'Association Belge des Détectives
Rue Jonruelle 44 (B)
4000 Liége
BELGIUM

Canada
Conseil des Agences de Sécurité et
 d'Investigation du Québec, Inc
B P 456
Mont-Royal
Montréal P G
G3P 3C6
CANADA

The Canadian Society for Industrial
 Security
PO Box 5585
Station "F"
Ottawa
Ontario
CANADA K2C 3M1

Finland
Association of Finnish Private
 Detectives
Pohjois Esplanaadinkatu 33A
00100 Helsinki 10
FINLAND

France
Chambre Syndicale Nationale des
 Détectives Privés
Boîte Postale 117 R.P.
Puteaux 92
803 FRANCE

Association Française des Détectives
 et Agents Privés de Recherches
10 Avenue Rachel
75018 Paris
FRANCE

Germany
Bund Deutscher Detektive E.V.
Lueschnerstrasse 17
D 7000 Stuttgart 1
WEST GERMANY

Zentral Verband
2000 Hamburg 36
Jungfernstieg 30
WEST GERMANY

Greece
Panhellenic Association of Private
 Detectives
Pax International
PO Box 2563
Athens
GREECE

India
Association of Investigators &
 Security Organisations of India
Monitron Security Pvt Limited
Jolly Bhaven No 2
Marine Lines Bombay 400-020
INDIA

Security Association of India
Deccan Security Consultants
8 Abhiman Apartments
5th Lane
Prabhat Road
Pune 411 004
INDIA

Ireland
Association of Irish Investigators
17 Upper Ormond Quay
Dublin 7
IRELAND

Italy
Federpol
40 via Accademia Albertina
10123 Torino
ITALY

Norway
**Nordisk Organisasjon Av Private
Etterforskere**
Box 46
Ljan
Oslo 11
NORWAY

South Africa
**The South African Council of Civil
Investigators**
3rd Floor
U B S Buildings
Oxford Street
LONDON E

Spain
**Agrupacion Nacional de Detectives
Privados**
C/Preciados 35 2° Drcha
Madrid 13
SPAIN

Switzerland
**Association Fédérale des Détectives
Privés Autorisés**
1205 Genève
58 Rue de Carouge
SWITZERLAND

**Fachverband Schweizerischer
Private-Detektive**
Buchelstr 2
9001 St Gallen
SWITZERLAND

United Kingdom
Association of British Investigators
ABI House
10 Bonner Hill Road
Kingston Upon Thames
Surrey
ENGLAND

British Security Industry Association
68 St James's Street
LONDON SW1A 1PH

Institute of Professional Investigators
9 Victoria Road
Fulwood
Preston PR2 4ND
Lancashire
ENGLAND

APPENDIX C
EXCHANGE AND MART

The following advertisements appeared in the 15th October 1981 edition of the Exchange and Mart under the Audio, TV and Video Leisure Section.

231

● **T) Miniature transmitter,** 2in. x 1in., picks up all voices and sounds with crystal clarity and transmits to any FM/VHF air band radio up to 2 miles away. **Ready to use,** only £9.95 post paid, full guaranteed, money refunded if not delighted. Phone 0273 36894 for Access/Barclaycard, COD or send cash/cheque/PO to: **Solon Electronics,** 115 Crescent Drive South, Brighton BN2 6SB.   L88

● **Brand new designs,** 15 mile transmitter to any VHF/FM receiver, tunable from 75-145 MHz, kit includes board, components, comprehensive instuctions and illustrations, size 3in. x 2½in., only £13.95, just send your name, address and cheque or PO for £13.95, made payable to: D. Mitchell and send to 66 Glenavon Road, Birkenhead, Merseyside.   P06

● **Surveillance transmitters,** 22mm x 15mm, 1.4 volts 100 hours, £14; non-printed circuit board, 1.5 volts, £10; kit, £5; low cost speciality, highly sensitive range up to 1 mile, receive on RM radio, tunable, 60-150 mhz, assembled, £4; kit, £1.50, assembled units guaranteed two years. **Radio Research,** 33 Beaumont Road, Orpington, Kent BR5 1SL.
                                                 P07

APPENDIX D

INDUSTRIAL ESPIONAGE
QUESTIONNAIRE RESULTS

In the spring of 1975, the National Wiretap Commission queried a number of corporate security officials concerning the effect electronic surveillance laws have had on industrial espionage. Has the Law (18 U.S.C. 2511-12) been effective in curbing the use of illegal electronic surveillance against the nation's businesses? Do corporate security officials feel able to cope with the dangers of electronic espionage? Should firms dealing in countermeasure services and/or equipment be licensed?

With the aid of the American Society for Industrial Security, three hundred and seventy-two officials were consulted, and one hundred and four of them chose to participate in the survey. These one hundred and four broke down into the following categories: 46 manufacturers, 23 research and development organizations, 20 sales and service organisations, 11 government contractors, and 4 miscellaneous businesses.

The questions asked and the total results were as follows:

Questions 1 and 2 involved identifying the type of firm and size.

Question 3.
Do you believe that there has been less industrial/business espionage by means of electronic surveillance since the passage of the 1968 Federal Wiretap Law?
24 Yes
32 No
48 Don't know

Question 4.
How worried are you about eavesdropping and the possible invasion of your firm's privacy?
10 Very worried
51 Not too worried
31 Fairly worried
12 Not at all worried

Question 5.
Do you believe your organization has ever been the subject of privacy invasion through electronic surveillance?
15 Yes
79 No
10 Don't know

Question 6.
If Yes, by what method?
13 Telephone Interceptions
8 Audio room interceptions
0 Video surveillance
1 Other—Government mail

233

Question 7.
Type of device used?
5 Radio
6 Hard wire
8 Don't know
1 Other—phone slug, bumper beeper

Question 8.
Authority notified?
1 Federal
0 State
1 Local
6 Telephone company
1 Other—Private investigator
8 None

Question 9.
Was an investigation of this invasion successfully pursued by your organization or a government authority?
3 Yes
11 No
2 No Answer

Question 10.
If No, why not?**

Question 11.
Do you believe that your organization can combat electronic surveillance through modern countermeasure techniques?
76 Yes
20 No
8 To some degree/don't know/no answer

Question 12.
Do you have in-house expertise for countermeasure activities?
46 Yes
58 No

Question 13.
Have you had occasion to obtain countermeasure services from a private firm or individual?
31 Yes
71 No
1 No answer
1 Now considering this step

Question 14.
Were you satisfied with the quality of those services?
24 Yes
6 No
73 No answer
1 Don't know

Question 15.
Were you recommended licensing for those engaged in countermeasure services?
82 Yes
18 No
4 No answer

** Answers to Question 10 are summarized in the section "Findings and Conclusions."

Findings and Conclusions

The results of this survey reveal that a substantial number of the consulted organizations are highly concerned about the possibility of electronic surveillance of their activities. Out of a total of one hundred and four, thirty one described themselves as "fairly worried" and ten were "very worried" about this possibility. Those concerned comprise almost 40 per cent of the manufacturers, 49 per cent of the research institutions, 20 per cent of the sales and service organizations and 54 per cent of the government contractors who participated in the survey. Forty four per cent of the organizations maintained in-house expertise for countermeasure activities, and almost 30 per cent have hired private firms or individuals to provide countermeasure services. However, one fourth of the respondents do not believe their organization could successfully combat a private invasion. The fact that 40 per cent of the respondents chose not to identify themselves presents another indication of uneasiness among the participants. Those who remained anonymous were more than 1.5 times as likely to be very or fairly worried about the problem than were those who identified themselves.

In addition to the high level of concern among almost half of the respondents, 16 of them reported actual incidents, or suspected incidents, of electronic surveillance of their companies. Thirteen of these privacy invasions involved telephone interceptions, and eight involved audio room interceptions. Five respondents indicated that both methods had been employed. Once the problem surfaced, the victims of electronic surveillance were generally reluctant to notify any authority other than the telephone company. Although four discovered the privacy invasion well after it had occurred so that investigation was not deemed worthwhile, of the remaining twelve, six notified the telephone company, and one also notified local authorities. A seventh respondent notified federal authorities, and an eighth notified a private investigator and is currently considering taking additional measures. The other four took no steps whatsoever.

Finally, the respondents' concern and uneasiness regarding problems of electronic surveillance is reflected in their replies to the more general questions posed by the questionnaire. Almost half of them feel uncertain about the effect of the 1968 Federal Wiretap Law on the incidence of industrial espionage, and 30 per cent believe the Law has had no effect whatsoever. Of the officials who participated, an overwhelming majority, about 80 per cent, recommend licensing of those engaged in providing countermeasure services.

APPENDIX E

Reproduced by kind permission of **Security Gazette**

Detection equipment for Bugging Devices

Maker/Supplier	Ref. No. or name	Specification	Price
Audiotel International Ltd., 193-195 City Road, London EC1V 1JN. Tel: 01-253-4562. Tlx: 28328 AUDINT G. Contact: Paul Ford, Sales Manager.	SCANLOCK 2000	Counter-surveillance receiver for fast detection and location of hidden radio microphones. Frequency range 10MHz-4GHz with AM, FM, and Sub-carrier demodulation modes. Scanlock 2000 also detects other devices that use standard mains cables for transmission. Unit is complete with all accessories.	£1,950.00 + VAT.
CCS Communication Control Systems Ltd., 62 S. Audley St, London W1.	Bug Detector EJ5	A miniature detection system hidden in a notebook pad. Tiny red light tells you if a transmitter is in your presence.	Not available
	Wiretap Detector B411	Gives you 24 hour protection against telephone bugs & wiretaps being placed on the telephone or telephone line.	"
	Privacy Protector	Pocket sized system that fits into a cigarett pack. A series of red lights let you know if a "bug" is in your presence & helps locate the signal.	"
	Tape Recorder Detector TRD 009	World's First pocket sized system that detects tape recorders in your presence.	"
	Counter Surveillance Receiver VL224	Professional system contained in a briefcase that does a sophisticated electronic "sweep" of premises & telephones. Detects & locates bugs & wiretaps.	"

Appendix E

237

Maker/Supplier	Ref. No. or name	Specification	Price
Diversified Corporate Services Ltd., 1 Prince of Wales Passage, 117 Hampstead Road, London N.W.1. 3EE	F.G. Mason Counter — Surveillance Receivers	Covering from 2KHz-10GHz in portable and miniaturised forms. Digital frequency read-out and sub-carrier detection capabilities.	P.o.A. (price on application)
	Microlab/-FXR — C2	Non linear junction detector. Detects both PASSIVE and ACTIVE devices. A breakthrough in search techniques.	US$20,000 ex works
Exchange Telegraph Company Ltd., (Special Products Division) 73-75 Scrutton Street, London EC2A 4TA. 01-253-4614.	Synchrotec Rover	Robust, self powered unit: — for detection of radio frequency listening devices. Operating from 30MHz to 1GHz. A.M. F.M. or S.C.	P.o.A.
	Synchrotec — Traveller	Compact, self powered unit: for detection of radio frequency, listening, devices operating from 30MHz to 1GHz. A.M. F.M. or S.C.	P.o.A.
	Teletec — Traveller	Compact, self powered unit for detection of radio or AUDIO frequency devices fitted to telephone or infinative devices on telephone line. F.M. A.M. S.C.	P.o.A.
	Maintec — Traveller	Compact, self powered unit for detection of radio frequency devices fitted to mains wiring. F.M. A.M. S.C.	P.o.A.
	Tritec	Brief case unit incorporating complete range of detection. Devices fitted neatly into brief case — giving advantages to high power output mains. Rechargeable and very robust.	P.o.A.
Merit Security Equipment Limited, 10/12 Emerald Street, London WC1N 3QX. Tel No: 01-831 7551.	ECR-1	Capacity to scan the full frequency range used by all modern eaves-dropping transmitters, between 20KHZ and 1GHZ. Both automatic and manual tune facilities are built in and the unit incorporates a 14 square inch CRT in place of the usual micro-screen. Will search for AM and FM modulation as well as sub-carrier.	Approx. £6,750.00.

Maker/Supplier	Ref. No. or name	Specification	Price
	DAR-1	A discriminated audio receiver designed to detect and locate wireless transmitting devices within strong RF signal areas. A mechanical multiplexing power line adaptor allows a full sweep of power lines to detect the presence of carrier current transmitters. Frequency range of 50 KHZ — 1300 MHX.	Approx. £1,800.00
	DAR-3	Specifications are similar to those of the DAR-1 except that the frequency range extends to 12 GHZ.	Approx. £2,850.00
	PLD-1	Determines if a carrier current transmitter is present on standard AC power lines. Plugged into any standard power point, it detects transmitters placed behind the point, or attached to lighting fixtures, lamps, electric clocks as well as the presence of RF transmitters from 5 KHZ — 1MHZ.	Approx. £625.00
Security Research, 1 London House, High Street, Ripley, Surrey GU23 6AA. Telephone: Ripley 2700 STD 048 643 2700 International (+) 44 48 643 2700 Telex: 85 95 35 Attn: SECURE	"TSR 7" electronic surveillance detector	A comprehensive "bug detector" incorporating the "TRACER" transmitter detector, and the "SR7" analyser for detecting telephone taps and wired listening devices. Supplied with detailed instruction manual for non-technical operators.	£5,250
	"SR7"	The telephone and wiring analyser part of TSR7, detects parallel and series telephone taps, hard wired listening devices, mains borne carriers, "infinity" bugs, tone activated devices.	£3,400
	"ASADAPT 1"	Available in January 1982, the latest professional surveillance detector. Microprocessor based, and of modular construction to ensure total capability throughout the 1980s. Available as a single unit or as two units, "ASADAPT 1 GF" and "ASADAPT 1 TD" (detection capabilities listed below).	£12,500

Maker/Supplier	Ref. No. or name	Specification	Price
	"ASADAPT 1GF"	Detects audio devices on mains, telephone and other wiring; concealed microphones and associated devices; triggers and detects devices activated by tone or high voltage; telephone and intercom listening devices, audio attachments, non-transmitting taps and all types of hookswitch bypasses.	£5,500
	"ASADAPT 1TD"	Detects telephone, room and mains borne RF devices. Transmitter detection covering 5KHz — 4GHz, demodulating AM, FM, SSB, USB, LSB, SC, with adjustable bandwidth and sensitivity. Digital LCD displays and a dot-matrix Spectrum Analyser, with store facility for RF scans.	£7,000
	"SSR7"	Available in early 1982, an updated version of TSR7 (described above), but incorporating "SCANLOCK 2000" and produced as a single comprehensive "bug" detection unit in a more compact carrying case.	£5,700
The Security Warehouse Company, Merton House, 70 Grafton Way, London W1P 5LN. 01-388 2051	ETD 001	Pocket sized (4½" × 7" × 1¼) 'Bug' detector, with dual mode operation for both locating 'bugs' or establishing if one has been used during a meeting. Basically a Wide Bandwidth receiver for Electroniagnotic Radiation.	£54.00 + VAT
	ETD 002	Easily installed device for determining whether a telephone line has any form of monitoring system attached. Can be used for quick 'spot checks' or left permanently installed.	£76.50 + VAT

APPENDIX F

Reproduced from **Better Buys for Business** *published by Managing Your Business Limited, Vine House, 41 Portsmouth Road, Cobham, Surrey KT11 1JQ, telephone number Cobham 7008, with kind permission.*

SHREDDERS
The different types, the different features and the individual machines compared

The fear of industrial espionage is often laughed off as a symptom of watching too much *Tinker, Tailor, Soldier, Spy*. But documents containing information about your firm's activities, products and staff can present real internal and external security risks. Although you might keep final documents in a safe or locked cabinet, don't ignore the fact that notes, shorthand pads, drafts, carbon papers or microfiche which are often openly left lying about or in the waste paper basket can also contain information which could be valuable in the wrong hands. The occasional well-publicised finds on rubbish dumps should be a reminder to those responsible for confidential papers to check out their own security procedures and potential risk points.

Shredding machines have long provided the solution in high security areas, being a clean and efficient way of destroying the evidence right where it is produced and stored. There is a wide range of shredders on the market and since prices start at around £30 this makes them worth considering by an firm with confidential papers to destroy.

Developments
Shredders have moved a long way since they merely slit the material into spaghetti-like strips, which with diligence could be reconstituted into readable form. The latest machines have been designed for many different applications in terms of degrees of security, materials that can be destroyed, and capacity.

The market for shredders in the UK is estimated to be worth about £1.75-£2 milllion, and sales in this country, and exports, are said to be healthy. The market leaders are Ofrex, Rexel and Business Aids but, as shown in our charts, several other firms offer a wide range of machines. The manufacturers' main problem appears to be in persuading potential buyers that there may indeed be a security problem in their document disposal.

Types
There are four main types of shredder: the executive desk-top or desk-side model, quiet with low capacity, taking only a few sheets of paper or card at a time; larger, faster and more powerful models with greater capacity, suitable for single or open-plan offices, taking up to 30 sheets of paper in one go (depending on shred width), card, computer printout, and some other materials; models specifically designed for the volume disposal of computer printout, with a continuous feed facility; heavy-duty semi-industrial machines, capable of handling most types of office waste.

In addition to the above there are also large truly industrial machines designed to run continuously and to dispose of all types of waste — rubber and metal products as well as paper etc. We don't cover these here but can give names of suppliers if required.

Some machines which shred paper will also shred microfilm and related materials — but the manufacturers usually make a point of stressing that they will only destroy limited amounts of microfilm at a time. Also available are specialised microfilm shredders. Some of these are disintegrators which reduce the microfilm to powder without fumes or vapour.

Choosing a shredder
Since shredding machines have a long life it is clearly vital to select at the outset a machine which can copy with both your present requirements and with your anticipated shredding needs — our survey strongly suggests that most problems experienced by users stem from the fact that the machine wasn't up to the tasks demanded of it. Check the following:
● *materials* — do you (or will you in the future) only want a machine which shreds paper and card? If you need to dispose of negatives, lithoplates and microfilm ensure that the shredder is designed to do this. Most machines these days eat up staples and paper clips, but make sure.
● *shred width* — the degree of security required will dictate the width of shred you need. Some manufacturers offer a choice of shred within a single model. For routine papers and volume material such as computer printout, a 4mm to 12mm shred width is sufficient; high security documents require between 2mm and 4mm; top security and highly confidential papers require between 0.8mm and 1.5mm. Where the most rigorous security standards are necessary, machines with a cross-cutting action are best (they cut at

right-angles across the shred, which reduces the document to tiny chips approximately 9mm × 0.8mm — or smaller).
● *width of feed or entry aperture* — how wide a document can be fed in.
● *cutting capacity* — how many sheets of a certain thickness it will take at one time.
● *speed* — how many documents or what footage of paper are cut per minute.

These features are related to the motor power of the machine, and the bigger more powerful shredders are noisier and heavier. Check the dimensions of the machine, its weight, and how noisy it is, as this will influence where it is to be sited.

Be realistic about how often the shredder will be used. If you have 500 sheets of paper each week to dispose of, the machine might give way if they are all to be shredded after 4 o'clock on Friday afternoon!

Machines come with forward, stop and reverse mechanisms, and some have an automatic reverse switch or overload release to prevent jamming, and/or thermal cut-out to prevent overheating. Automatic feed is available for volume disposal. Most machines have integral or external wastebins or plastic bags to take the waste.

Our survey
84 firms responded to our questionnaire designed to discover what people thought about their particular shredding machine. The main findings appear to be that shredders are generally long lasting machines which are easy to use and very reliable — about three-quarters of respondents said that their machine had never broken down. Of those who had experienced breakdowns many were honest enough to admit that the main cause was overheating due to excessive use. Several people complained that their machine frequently jammed but, again, it was suggested that this was largely due to misuse — i.e. the machine was fed with materials it wasn't intended to take or too many sheets at a time. What emerges from this is the importance of choosing the right machine for your particular requirements.

Other problems isolated by respondents concerned slow speed, noise and the fact that machines need frequent lubrication.

Recommendations

Inevitably, given the large number of machines available, we don't have reports from users on all of them. Of those we received mentions on, the **Emgee Desktop** (£34.86 from Spicers) at the very bottom end of the market seems well liked. It is, though, only suitable for firms with very limited shredding requirements. The **Scimitar** (£405 from Business Aids) received the most favourable reports amongst the ordinary small-capacity machines but Rexel's **Versishred Compact** (£320) and **Versishred 9** (£620) seem worth a look too. On the next rung up the **Intimus 407** (£995 from Davies and Medhurst) was warmly recommended by two users.

KEY

 M *indicates those suppliers who also offer machines for microfilm only.*

1 P = paper B = cardboard/light board C = computer printout S = continuous stationery
Pl = metal plates (e.g. litho and addressing plates) L = plans, large drawings, blueprints M = microfilm

2 Size of feed aperture

3 Width of shredded materials CC = cross cut

4 Approx. no. of paper sheets (or other materials where indicated) machine will take at one time. Alternatives relate to shred widths.

5 Approx. length (cms) and/or weight where indicated (kg) of material shredded per minute. M = manual, speed depends on operator.

Supplier*	Model	Price (RRP exc. VAT)	Materials¹	Width of feed (mm)²	Shred widths (mm)³	No. of sheets⁴	Speed or capacity⁵	Comments
Z. Brierley Ltd., Ferry Farm Rd., Llandudno Junction, N. Wales LL31 9SF. 0492 81777	Document Shredder	£29.75	P	220	3.2	1-3	M	Very simple machine which clips onto desk. No user response.
Business Aids Ltd., 3 Whitby Avenue, Park Royal, London NW10 7SQ. 01 965 9821	Plus 4	£129	P,B	188	4	3-4	660	7 not very enthusiastic **Plus 4** users considered it compact and very easy to use but disappointed by limited capacity — needs to rest after 15mins work. 11 out of 20 **Scimitar** users warmly recommend — performs well, easy to operate and reliable but some problems with paper jams. 6 users considered capacity too limited. 3 satisfied users of **Scimitar Super**. No user response on other machines. Scimitar models have automatic reverse facility.
	Popular	£235	P,B	213	4	7-8	660	
	Sentinel	£285	P,B	213	2/4/6	5/7/10	660	
	Executive/ Executive 2000	£295/ £325	P,B	213	2/4/6	5/7/10	660	
	Scimitar Secura	£365	P,B,Pl,M	228	2/4/6	9/13/17	960	
	Scimitar	£405	P,B,Pl,M	228	2/4/6	14/21/25	1,200	
	Scimitar Super	£620	P,B,S,L,M	310	2/4/6	20/28/32	1,800	
	Scimitar XC	£625	P,M	310	11 × 1.4CC	6	720	
	Data 5000	£745	P,C,S,Pl,L	420	3/6	20/30	2,400	
	Microplus Destructor	£845	P,M	127	0.6 × 3CC	3 films/1 fiche	320 (film) 16 (fiche)	
	Datashred 6000	£895	P,C,S,Pl,L	420	3/6	24/30	3,100	
	Supershred	£1,250	P,B,C,S, Pl,L	310	2/4/6/8	25/35/40/45	1,800	
	Servant 4101	£2,225	"	410	3/6/9	40/70/100	3,000	
	Servant Super 4102	£2,750	"	410	3/6/9/12	65/100/130/150	3,000	
Davies & Medhurst International Ltd., Intimus House, 20 Bridport Rd., Thornton Heath, Surrey CR4 7RG. 01 689 0526 **M**	Intimus Simplex	£239	P	220	1.9/3.8	6-7/9-11	356	1 fairly satisfied user of **Intimus 203** but stresses only suitable for small quantities. 2 users of **Intimus 407**, both recommend warmly — high capacity machine with good performance and good reliability record but considered rather pricey. No user response on other machines. Intimus **407** and **007** have automatic reverse facility.
	Intimus 203	£419	P	220	1.9/3.8/5.7	10-14/14-18/ 20-25	1,220	
	Intimus 304/306	£459	P,C	300	3.8(304) 5.8 (306)	12-15 16-18	1,220	
	Intimus 405	£599	P,B,S,L	450	5.8	10-12	3,000	
	Intimus 407	£995	P,B,C,S, Pl,L	407	5.8	40-45	1,980	
	Intimus 444	£1,595	P,B,L	432	3.8 × 40CC	40-50	3.3kg	

Supplier*	Model	Price (RRP exc. VAT)	Materials[1]	Width of feed (mm)[2]	Shred widths (mm)[3]	No. of sheets[4]	Speed or capacity[6]	Comments
Davies & Medhurst contd.	Intimus 007S	£1,699	P,B,C,S	330	0.7 × 9.5CC	12-14	2,130 (6.4kg)	
	Electronic 500	£4,250	P,B,C,S, Pl,L	450	3.8/7.8/3.8 × 3.8CC	300	6,000	
EBA Systems Ltd., 20 Broadway Thatcham, Berks. RG13 4HX. 0635 63208 Also imported and distributed by Tarnator Ltd., 1 High St., Thatcham, Berks RG13 4JG	Sympathetic 100	£270	P,C,S,Pl,L	220	1.9/3.8	5-8/10-14	910 (3.8 width)	**1 TE4** user who was very happy with it but wished capacity was greater. No response on other machines.
	Allround 200	£425	P,C,S,Pl,L	220	1.9/3.8/5.7/ 1 × 15CC/ 2 × 18CC	6-10/12-17/20- 27/2-3/4-6	910 (5.7 width)	
	Sympathetic 200	£456	P,C,S,Pl,L	220	1.9/3.8	5-8/10-14	910 (3.8 width)	
	Allround 410	£600-£800	P,C,S,Pl,L	450	4	15-20	1,370	
	TE4	£610/£675 CC	P,C,S,Pl, L,M	220	1.9/3.8/5.7 1.2 × 15CC/ 2 × 18CC	7-11/16-20/20- 30/2-4/4-8	1,520 (5.7 width)	
	Agent 004	£1,455	P,C,S,Pl,L	444	4/8	20-30/40	1,830	
Gestetner Ltd., Gestetner House, 210 Euston Rd., London NW1 2DA. 01 387 7021	Shredder	£293	P,C	220	4	8-10	1,060	No user response.
Lawtons Ltd., 60 Vauxhall Rd., Liverpool L69 3AU. 051 227 1212	Executive Paper Shredder	£89	P	152	4	3-4	590	No user response.
Ofrex Ltd., Ofrex House, Stephen St., London W1A 1EA. 01 636 3686 **M**	Fordishred Diplomat 210D	£150-£160	P	222	4	7-8	152-180	**4 Fordishred 246** respondents considered it OK — very easy to use and fairly reliable. Complaints though of noise and frequent jams. 3 fairly satisfied users of **Fordishred 13** — easy to operate and reliable. 1 said noisy especially when shredding card. Models 9 and 13 have optional feed funnel for wider input.
	TT90	£197	P,B	216	4	6-8	1,050	
	Fordishred 246	£249	P	216	2/4/6	6-8/8-12/12-16	1,050	
	Ambassador 400	£319	P	222	2	6-8	1,050	
	Fordishred 9	£530	P,B,S,Pl,L	222	0.78/1.5/3.2/6	5-6/10-12/ 15-18/20-22	2,700	
	Fordishred 13	£664	P,B,S,Pl,L	330	0.78/1.5/3.2/6	5-6/12-14/ 18-20/24-26	2,700	
	Fordishred X9	£740	P,B	215	0.78 × 9CC	5	1,830	
	Computershred 1600	£844	P,B,C,S,L	406	6.4	25-30	3,350	
	1600 HS	£919	P,B,C,S,L	406	6	17	5,790	
Ofshred Ltd., Firth St., Huddersfield, Yorks HD1 3AH. 0484/34214	Executive 642 (standard)	£299	P	229	2/4/6	9		No user response on Ofshred models. Other versions of Executive 642 and Milldale 3000 available for continuous stationery.
	Milldale 3000 (standard)	£565	P	311	3/6/9	20		
	Midway 16	£775	P,C,Pl	406	3/6/9	15		
Perforag (Sales) Ltd., Greaves Way, Stanbridge Rd., Leighton Buzzard, Beds LU7 8UD. 0525 376743 **M**	Mini	£168.52	P	220	1.9/3.8	6-7/9-11	1,500	These Taifun machines from W. Germany only imported since 1979. No user reports.
	Junior	£478.50	P	300	3.8/5.8	12-15/16-18	1,500	
	Datex	£602.56	P,S,L	440	5.8	10-12	3,000	
	Boy	£638	P,Pl	240	3.8/7.6	20-22/28-30	1,500	
	Minex 1	£705.34	P,B,S,L	330	0.7 × 9.5CC	13-15		
	Minex 2	£1,240.56	P,B,S,L	330	0.7 × 9.5CC/ 1.4 × 9.5CC	13-15/23-25		
	Master	£1,205.10	P,B,Pl	330	3.8 × 40CC	50-60		
Plandale Micrographics Division, Office Equipment (John Dale) Ltd., Winchester Wharf, Clink St., London SE1 9QD. 01 403 0818 **M**								

Supplier*	Model	Price (RRP exc. VAT)	Materials[1]	Width of feed (mm)[2]	Shred widths (mm)[3]	No. of sheets[4]	Speed or capacity[6]	Comments
Portable Factory Equipment Ltd., 48 Smith Street, Hockley, Birmingham B19 3EW. 021 554 7241/3	Shredminor Model D	£124	P,B	225	3	3	610-760	No user response for PFE machines. **Shredtamer Model 111** has automatic reverse facility.
	Shredmaker Desk Top	£225	P	225	2/4/6	12/18	1,050	
	Shredmaker Model 1 Console	£262	P	216	2/4/6	8-10/12/25	420	
	Shredmaker Model 1 Executive	£336	P	216	2	8	420	
	Shredmaker Model 11	£514	P,C	248	0.78/1.5/ 3.2/6.4	5/10/16/22	2,438	
	Shredmaker Model 111	£648	P,C	330	2/3/6/12	20	2,990	
	Shredmaker Model 1V	£780	P,C	406	6	20	1,830	
	Shredtamer Model 1	£965	P,B,C,S, Pl,L	406	6	35-40	1,830	
	Shredtamer Cross Cut	£1,485	P	406	4 × 25CC	25-30	1,830	
	Shredtamer Model 453	£1,498	P,B,C,S, Pl,L	437	3/6/9/12	30-40	1,830	
	Shredtamer Model 111	£2,418	P,B,C,S, Pl,L	508	3/6/9/12	90	8.5kg	
Rexel Ltd., Gatehouse Rd., Aylesbury, Bucks HP19 3DT. 0296 81421 **M**	Versishred Discreet	£130	P,B	225	3	3	152	1 user of **Versishred Discreet** found it very easy to operate and fairly satisfactory but only suitable for very small volumes. Of the 9 users of the **Versishred Compact** 4 recommended it warmly. All said it was easy to operate and reliable. Complaints re its inability to cope with thicker materials and staples. 2 users of the **Versishred 9** both warmly recommend. Shreds very satisfactorily, easy to operate and reliable. 1 complained that paper dust was difficult to remove. 2 users of **Versishred 13** felt it was reliable and adequate. 1 user of the **Versishred Destroyer** said he wouldn't be without it! However, he considered it rather slow. No response on other machines.
	Versishred Desktop	£260	P,B	220	4	8-10	1,060	
	Versishred Compact	£320	P,B	220	2/4/6	5-6/6-9/10-12	1,060	
	Versishred Executive	£380	P,B	220	2	6-7	1,060	
	Versishred 9	£620	P,C,S,Pl,L	230	1/2/3/6	3-5/6-8/ 11-12/15-20	2,400	
	Versishred 13	£780	P,B,C,S, Pl, L	330	2/3/8	20-25	2,400	
	Versishred Destroyer	£820	P,B,C,S, Pl,L	230	2/3/6		2,400	
	Versishred 16	£910	P,B,C,S, Pl,L	400	8	25-30	3,350	
Sharpenset Engineering Ltd., Dashwood Works, Dashwood Ave., High Wycombe, Bucks HP12 3ED. 0494 30177	Shredway Mark 5	£325	P,C	275	1/1.5/3/6	6-8/12-15/ 19-25	0.6kg (1.5 mm cut) 0.08kg (3mm)	No user response.
Spicers Ltd., (Office Services Division), Sawston, Cambridge CB2 4JG. 0223 834555	Emgee Desktop Shredder	£34.86	P	210	3	3	M	2 users considered it excellent value for money with adequate performance.
Volumatic Ltd., Taurus House, Kingfield Rd., Coventry CV6 5AS. 0203 84217/9	700	£3,300	P,M	229	Dust	8-10/5 films/ 8 fiche		Disintegrator will not take film spools.
	1012	£7,000	P,C,Pl,M	305	Dust	100 fiche	2.27kg	

EPM PARABOLIC MICROPHONE

The EPM Parabolic Microphone is to sound recording what the telephoto lens is to film.

The EPM Parabolic Microphone comes in two basic versions: the EPM Electronic and the P-200. For ultra-critical sound recording, such as voice recording, the Electronic (EPM-E) is recommended. For less critical work, such as close surveillance or nature recording, the P-200 is the economical route.

Catalog Nos. P-200 & EPM-E

The Electronic operates from two easily obtainable 9V transistor radio batteries. Its built-in modular circuitry produces amplification of the signal and is fed to the high-efficiency monitoring headset which is included. Virtually flat response from 250 Hz to 18,000 Hz is accomplished by the internal electronics. The effective recording range, under ideal conditions, is up to ¼ mile. This unit has been used in numerous wildlife movie sound track recordings. Ideal for nature study. The Electronic comes with its shielded output cable "pigtailed."

The physical characteristics of the P-200 are identical to the Electronic. The P-200 has no electronics. Sound output from the specially designed and focused microphone module is fed directly to the "pigtailed" output cable. The P-200 may be wired for high or low impedance.

Sound monitoring from the P-200 must be done from the input device, since there is no provision for direct headset monitoring as in the Electronic.

Specifications:

Microphone: Controlled dynamic with large diaphragm
Frequency Response: Electronic: 250-18,000 Hz +5dB — P-200: 300-10,000 Hz +5dB
Cable: High quality, 100% shielded. Terminated in "pigtailed." May be wired for balanced/or unbalanced output as required by user.
Shield: Diameter 18 3/4 (47.6 cm). Made of non-resonant transparent, high-impact plastic. Temperature range from -10 to 105 F. **Headset:** Electronic model only: EPM-E)
High quality, lightweight, high efficiency. Cushioned earcup to seal out extraneous noise.

Carrying Case: High density styrofoam. Vinyl covered.
Weight: Electronic (EPM-E): 5½ lbs. (2.5 kilograms) — P-200: 3½ lbs. (1.6 kilograms)
Delivery Time: 3 weeks

Problem: Sie benötigen eine Kombination von Sender und Empfänger für den professionellen Einsatz in Miniaturausführung mit hoher Leistung.

Lösung: Die Professionell-Kombination PK 815 + PK 835 (Nur für Export)
Beide Geräte sind im Frequenzbereich von 150 MHz bequarzt. Durch diese hohe Sendefrequenz werden extrem gute Reichweiten in dicht bebauten Regionen erzielt. Die Kombination bietet hohe Empfindlichkeit und große Reichweite.
Technische Daten: Sender: Abmessungen: 80 x 55 x 20 mm. Gewicht: 120 g. Stromversorgung: Mallory Quecksilberbatterie 9 V. Bequarzung: 1 Kanal. Ausgangsleistung: 75 mW. Reichweite: 3000 m. **Empfänger:** Abmessungen: 90 x 60 x 25 mm. Gewicht: 160 g. Stromversorgung: 9 V Akku. Kanäle: 4. Bequarzung: 1 Kanal. Eingangsempfindlichkeit: 2 µV. Zubehör: Ohrhörer, Schleppantenne.

Problem: You need a combination of transmitter and receiver in miniature design for professional use and with a high output.
Solution: PK 815 plus PK 835. The Professional Combination (for export only)
Both units are equipped with a crystal for the 150 MHz range. This high frequency guarantees an extremely good range in regions of high buildings.
Specifications: Transmitter: Channel: 1 with crystal. Dimensions: 80 x 55 x 20 mm. Weight: 120 grams. Power Supply: Mallory mercury battery 9 V. Output: 75 mW. Range: 3000 m. **Receiver:** Dimensions: 90 x 60 x 25 mm. Weight: 160 grams. Power Supply: 9 V battery. Channels: 4. 1 crystally controlled. Input sensitivity: 2 µV. Accessories: Ear-set, trailing antenna.

Problem: Sie müssen einen Raum elektronisch überwachen. Es ist nicht möglich, den zu überwachenden Raum zu betreten. Ein Sender oder elektronisches Stethoskop kann nicht eingesetzt werden.

Lösung: Laser-Abhörgerät PK 1035
(Nur für Export)

Dieses neu entwickelte Abhörsystem bietet ungeahnte Möglichkeiten. Durch die beim Sprechen auftretenden Schallwellen werden die im Raum befindlichen Scheiben in leichte Schwingungen versetzt. Ein Laserstrahl, der auf die Fensterscheibe gerichtet ist, wird reflektiert, empfangen und über einen elektronischen Converter in Sprache umgesetzt. Ein direktes Abhören bzw. eine Aufzeichnung ist bis zu einer Distanz von 500 m möglich.

Technische Daten: Abmessungen: ⌀ 150 x 250 mm. Gewicht: 12 kg. Stromversorgung: eingebauter 12-V-Akku.

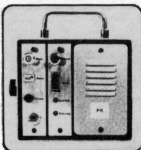

Problem: You have to monitor a room electronically. It is impossible to enter this room. A transmitter or an electronic stethoscope cannot be used.

Solution: Use the PK 1035 Laser Listening Device
(for export only)

PK 1035 is a new development in the field of listening equipment and can be used in a surprising number of ways. The window panes are caused to vibrate slightly by sound waves which arise from speaking. A laser beam pointing at the window pane is reflected, received and translated into speech by an electronic converter. Direct listening and recording is possible up to a distance of 500 m.

Specifications: Dimensions: ⌀ 150 x 250 mm. Weight: 12 kg. Power Supply: built-in 12 V accu.

Problem: Sie benötigen einen möglichst gut getarnten Sender mit einer extrem guten Reichweite.

Lösung: Professionell-Filzschreibersender PK 585 (Nur für Export)
Dieser normale voll funktionstüchtige Filzschreiber beinhaltet einen kompletten Miniatursender mit einer Spannungsversorgung von 9 V, bei einer Stromaufnahme von 14 mA. Die hieraus resultierende Leistung wird über das eingebaute, speziell hierfür entwickelte Antennensystem abgegeben. Die Aufnahmeempfindlichkeit übertrifft die des menschlichen Ohres erheblich.
Technische Daten: Reichweite: 300 m. Betriebsdauer: 6 Std. Stromversorgung: 6 x 1,5-V-Knopfzellen. Abmessungen: ⌀ 11 m x 135 mm. Gewicht: 25 g. Mikrofon: Elektret-Kondensatormikrofon.

Problem: You require a well camouflaged transmitter with an extremely good transmitting range.
Solution: PK 585 Professional Felt Pen Transmitter (for export only)
This Felt Pen which is fully functionable incorporates a complete miniature transmitter with a power supply of 9 V at a consumption of 14 mA. The resulting output power will be emitted through the built-in antenna system, specially designed this purpose. The receiving sensitivity is better than the sensitivity of the human ear.
Specifications: Range: 300 m. Operating time: 6 hours. Power Supply: 6 x 1.5 V button cells. Dimensions: ⌀ 11 mm x 135 mm. Weight: 25 grams. Microphone: Electret-capacitor-microphone.

Problem: Polizei-, Jagd- und Werkschutzhunde müssen abgerichtet werden
Lösung: Elektronisches Fernsteuerdressurgerät PK 990
Mit Hilfe dieser elektronischen Einrichtung ist jeder Hund dressierbar. Ob der Hund 30 oder 300 Meter entfernt von seinem Herrn läuft, mit PK 990 können Sie jederzeit auf ihn einwirken. Die Anlage besteht aus einem Empfänger (mit einem Lederhalsband am Hund befestigt) und einem Sender. Durch den Sender wird am Empfänger ein elektrischer Impuls ausgelöst. Jeder einzelne Impuls läßt sich in seiner Stärke auf das Verhalten des Hundes abstimmen. Die Anlage ist für sämtliche Hunderassen geeignet. **Technische Daten:** Sender: Abmessungen: 11 x 6 x 3 mm. Gewicht: 320 g. Antennenlänge: 110 mm. Stromversorgung: Akku 6 V. Frequenz: 40,68 MHz. Modulation: 5000 Hz Ftz-Nr. (postalische Zulassungsnummer): Q-70/72. — Empfänger: Abmessungen: 2 Kästchen je 7,2 x 3,5 x 4,4 cm. Gewicht: 372 g. Antennenlänge: 20 cm. Stromversorgung: Akku 4,8 V. Sonstiges: spritzwassergeschütztes Gehäuse. Impulsdauer: 1/1000 sec.
Problem: Police, sporting and working dogs have to be trained.
Solution: Use the PK 990 Electronic Remote-Control Training Device
By using this electronic device every dog can be trained. It doesn't matter if the dog is 30 or 300 m away from his owner. PK 990 sets you in the position to reach the dog whenever you want. The unit consists of a receiver and transmitter.
Specifications: Transmitter: Dimensions: 11 x 6 x 3 mm. Weight: 320 g. Length of Antenna: 110 mm. Power Supply: Accu 6 V. Frequency: 40.68 MHz. Modulation: 5000 Hz Ftz-No. (postal licence number): Q-70/72. — Transformer: Dimensions: 2 boxes, each 7,2 x 3,5 x 4,4 cm. Weight: 372 g. Length of Antenna: 20 cm. Power Supply: Accu 4,8 V

Problem: Sie müssen entfernt geführte Gespräche oder Geräusche aufnehmen.
Lösung: Richtmikrofon PK 375
Dieses hochempfindliche Richtmikrofon wurde für die professionelle Anwendung entwickelt. Die leisesten Geräusche werden hiermit aufgenommen. Nebengeräusche, die nicht in der Aufnahmerichtung liegen, werden absorbiert. Dieses wird durch einen Parabolspiegel mit eingesetztem Richtcharakteristikmikrofon und einem nachgeschalteten rauscharmen, stufenlos regelbaren Verstärker erreicht. Die empfangenen Signale werden über einen Kopfhörer übertragen oder von einem Tonbandgerät aufgezeichnet. **Technische Daten:** Abmessungen: ⌀ 600 x 300 mm. Gewicht: 1,2 kg. Stromversorgung: 2 x 1,5 V Batterien. Betriebsstunden: 75 Std. Verstärkung: 90 dB. Anschlüsse: Tonbandbuchse, Kopfhörerbuchse.
Problem: You have to record conversations or sounds over a considerable distance.
Solution: Use the PK 375 Directional Microphone
This highly sensitive directional microphone was developed for professional use. Hereby the smallest sounds are picked up. Background noises which are not within the pick-up range are absorbed. This effect is achieved by a parabolic reflector with an inserted directional diagram microphone and a connected lownoise variably adjustable amplifier. The received signals are transmitted by headphone or recorded by a tape recorder.
Specifications: Dimensions: ⌀ 600 x 300 mm. Weight: 1.2 kg. Power Supply: 2 x 1.5 V batteries. Time of Operation: 75 hours. Amplification: 90 dB. Terminals: Tape socket. headphone socket.

Problem: Sie suchen ein Gerät, mit dem Sie unbemerkt Gespräche aus größerer Distanz aufnehmen können.
Lösung: Richtmikrofon PK 385
Bis zu 75 m weit lauscht dieses Richtmikrophon. Nebengeräusche die nicht in der Aufnahmerichtung liegen, werden absorbiert. Dieses wird durch ein Spezial-Richtcharakteristik-Mikrofon und einen hochempfindlichen, rauscharmen Verstärker erreicht. Die akustische Übertragung erfolgt über einen Kopfhörer. Die Lautstärke ist stufenlos regelbar. Für eine Aufzeichnung sind unsere Tonbandgeräte PK 630 oder PK 650 anschließbar. **Technische Daten:** Abmessungen: ⌀ 80 x 650 mm. Gewicht: 600 g. Stromversorgung: 2 x 1,5 V Batterien. Betriebsstunden: 75 Std. Verstärkung: 80 dB, 10.000fach, stufenlos regelbar. Anschlußbuchsen für Tonband und Kopfhörer.
Problem: You are looking for a device to record conversations held at a considerable distance.
Solution: Use PK 385 the Directional Microphone
The directional microphone picks up even the smallest sounds. Background noises which are not in the recording area are absorbed. These qualities are provided by a special pick-up pattern microphone and a highly sensitive noiseless intensifier. The acoustic transmission is performed by a headphone. The loudness level is variably adjustable. For recording, use our PK 630 or PK 650 tape recorders.
Specifications: Dimensions: ⌀ 80 x 650 mm. Weight: 600 g. Power Supply: 2 x 1.5 V batteries. Time of Operation: 75 hours. Amplification: 80 dB, 10.000fold, variably adjustable. Sockets: For tape and for headphone.

Problem: Sie benötigen für Geld oder Schmuck-Transporte einen stabilen Koffer mit eingebauter Nebelpatrone und akustischer Alarmvorrichtung.
Lösung: Sicherheitskoffer PK 045
Unser Sicherheitskoffer schützt das Geld beim Transport und verringert die Gefahr einer Verletzung des Trägers bei Überfällen auf ein Minimum. Dieser Koffer eignet sich für alle Geschäftssparten, ob Löhne geholt werden oder Einzelhandelsgeschäfte mit Schmuck beliefert werden. Wenn PK 045 dem Träger entrissen wird, aktiviert sich die eingebaute Nebelpatrone und zusätzlich wird ein akustisches Signal ausgelöst. **Technische Daten:** Abmessungen: 45 x 33 x 7,5 cm. Gewicht: 4 kg. Inhalt: 9000 cm³. Die Farbstoff- und akustische Alarmvorrichtung ist auch einzeln erhältlich.

Problem: For your money or jewelry transports you need a stable suit-case with a built-in fog cartridge and an acoustical alarm device.
Solution: Use The PK 045 Safety Case
In our safety case your money is well protected against robbery during transport. The danger that the bearer will be hurt by aggressors is reduced to a minimum. The case is suitable for all branches where wages have to be fetched from the bank or e. g. retail shops have to be delivered with jewelry. If PK 045 is torn away from the bearer the built-in fog cartridge is activated immediately. At the same moment the acoustical signal is released.
Specifications: Dimensions: 45 x 33 x 7,5 cm. Weight: 4 kg. Contents: 9000 cm³. The colour and the acoustical alarm device are both seperately available.

VEHICLE/CARGO TAILING SYSTEM

Vehicle/cargo tailing is one of the toughest phases of investigative work. The VCTS System can make it one of the easiest. Aegis Electronics has recently developed a new concept in a fully crystal controlled tailing system with a unique computerized vector proximity feature. With a crystal controlled system the transmitter and receiver are virtually locked together eliminating constant tuning for a lost signal, common with all non-crystal controlled systems.

Small enough to fit in the palm of your hand, the tracking transmitter powered by a standard 9 volt transistor radio battery punches out a signal that will satisfy most tailing needs in metropolitan and rural areas. With the constant fear in mind of loosing an expensive piece of equipment we have priced the transmitter accordingly. The pulse tone receiver will operate from any 12 volt negative ground vehicle electrical system, using a cigar lighter plug and power cable for easy power take off. The signal from the transmitter is translated to an audio tone and is pulsed at a rate of approximately 3 beats per second and diminishes to a steady tone with the transmitter is in close proximity to the receiver. Any standard vehicle radio antella fully extended to 3 feet or more will serve well for most tailing applications, eliminating the need for specially installed antennas which usually identifies the vehicle as containing special radio equipment. Comes with complete, easy to follow instructions.

Specifications:
RECEIVER-VR
Size: 2¼ x 5½ x 8'' (5.7 x 14 x 20.3 cm)
Weight: 3¼ lbs. (1.5 kilograms)
Power: 12 Volts negative ground
Audio Output: 3 Watts

Speaker: 4 Ohms Built-in
Adjacent Channel Rejection: 50 dB
Sensitivity: 0.3 uV 20 dB quieting
Includes: under dash mounting bracket & hardware, variable tone and pitch control

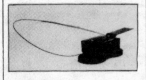

TRANSMITTER-VT
Size: 4 x 1-3/8 x 1'' (10.2 x 3.5 x 2.5 cm)
Weight: 6 ounces (170 grams) with battery
Power Requirements: 9V
Operating Life: Approximately 17-20 hours with mercury battery.
Antenna Length: 12 inches
Range: 1½ miles, in cities to line of sight, some rural areas 2 miles.
Comes with two powerful disc magnets

Catalog Nos. VCTS
(Transmitter = VT)
(Receiver = VR)

EXTERNAL BATTERY SUPPLY

Special magnet bar and powerful disc magnets couple with either an Eveready -2356 or RCA -VS-330 battery for extension of transmitting time to one full week. Comes with proper battery clip connectors and Eveready -2356 battery.

Catalog No. EBS

Size: 6 x 2-3/16 x 1-9/16''
(15.5 x 5.5 x 4 cm)Weight: 1 lb 6½ ounces with battery (687 grams)

MINI-MIKE

The model 2M is a new design offering excellent sensitivity and transmission. It is a self-contained unit operating on a 1.3 volt mercury battery. The microphone picks up the slightest sounds and transmits these sounds through your FM radio. There is no wire connection between the microphone and the radio. Under ideal conditions you can hear anything that the microphone picks up through your FM radio positioned up to 300 feet away, outdoors, and up to 100 feet, indoors. The unit is tuneable to any blank spot on your FM radio dial between 88 and 108 MHz. Ideal for patient altert, public speakers, stage shows, baby alert and classrooms.

Catalog No. 2M
Specifications:
Size: 2¼ x 3/4 x ½'' (5.5 x 2 x 1.3 cm)
Weight: Approximately 1 ounce (27 grams)
FCC Approval:Type WM-155
Modulation System: FM
Frequency Range: 88-108 MHz
Covering Distance: Up to 300 feet (open area)
Battery Life (continuous use): 60-80 hours.
Detailed operating instructions furnished
Field Strength: 50 uV/M at 50 ft.
Battery Information: 1.3 volt (furnished)
Commercial numbers: Mercury — MP675,PX 675 or RM 675R. Available at most electronic/radio parts stores.

Guarantee: This microphone is guaranteed against manufacturing defects. Any claim for adjustment or refund must be made within ten days after receipt of merchandise.

'PLUG' TYPE MONITOR TRANSMITTERS

These are miniature monitor/transmitter devices housed within a standard electrical plug casing. The microphone picks up sounds within the 'target' room and relays them, via a radio signal, to a remote surveillence point with either an FM/VHF or Air Band receiver.

The advantage of the 'Plug' bugs is that their presence within the room is unlikely to arouse suspicion. The more expensive devices, such as the PM 001 (below) can be used as normal electrical fittings, though the lower-priced models cannot.

PM 001 — 'Plug' Type Monitor Transmitter
A highly sophisticated unit with a micro-transmitter built into a standard 2-Way 13 Amp adaptor socket. The device is indistinguishable from the real thing — indeed, it is the real thing, and it can be used as a fully functioning 2-Way adaptor.

Special care has been taken to ensure that the mains current does not interfere with the radio signal, and the PM 001 does have an exceptional clarity of transmission.

The unit is powered from the mains electrical supply, and once in place it can be left for an indefinite period and requires no further attention.

Size: as per a standard 2-Way 13 Amp adaptor plug.
Frequency: about 115 MHz Air Band.
Receiving Medium: any radio with an Air Band.
Range: maximum of 1,000 yards, though this could be substantially reduced in practice.

PM 002 — 'Plug' Type Monitor Transmitter
The principle is the same as that of the PM 001 (above) except that the budget priced PM 002 is housed in a normal 13 Amp mains plug, is battery powered, and cannot be used as an operational electrical fitting. Moreover, both the positive and negative pins have been removed from the plug and thus, if removed from the mains socket it could arouse suspicion.

The PM 002 is, nonetheless, a well made and reliable unit, providing clear signals for transmission. In practice it is obviously suitable for applications where the installer might not be able to regain access to the 'target' premises, even after the surveillance has been called off.

Size: as per a standard 13 Amp plug.
Battery: PX625 camera type.
Battery Life: 300 to 400 hours typically.
Frequency: set on 104 MHz but adjustable from 80-110 MHz on FM/VHF.
Receiving Medium: any radio with an FM/VHF band.
Range: maximum of 200 yards.

PM 002/BS — 'Plug' Type Monitor Transmitter
Identical to the PM 002 (above) except that an external booster is added to enormously increase the transmission range. The booster unit is typically housed in a device such as a mains recharger unit for a calculator — something that would not arouse suspicion if seen in the room — and the wire runs from the basic unit to the booster.

The booster increases the range up to ten (10) times, giving a range up to 2,000 yards maximum — an impressive distance for a device of this price.▶

TELEPHONE MONITOR TRANSMITTERS

These are units whose sole purpose is relaying telephone conversations, via a radio transmitter, to a remote surveillence point with either an FM/VHF or Air Band receiver. The units themselves are placed either inside the telephone, or somewhere along the line. They monitor both sides of the conversation.

Many of these units are powered from the telephone line itself, with the advantage that once in place they require no attendance. However, care has to be taken not to draw off too much power from the line or the quality of the telephone itself will suffer, with the possibility that this could lead to detection, either by the 'target' or by telephone engineers called in to check the 'fault'. Consequently range of the transmitter is somewhat limited. This may not be a problem, but if greater range is required a device with a separate battery power source is the answer.

TT 001 — Telephone Monitor Transmitter

A miniature transmitter which can be fitted inside the telephone, or at some convenient point along the line — e.g., at a junction box or jack point or, because it is weatherproof, it can be fitted outside, on a telegraph pole, or in an external junction box.

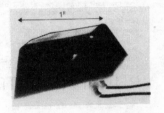

The 001 will also work on multiple extension systems. There are just two (2) wires to clip on and installation should take less than one minute. The unit is powered from the telephone line so, once installed, no further attention is required.

Size: 1 x ¾ x ½ ins.
Power Source: direct from the telephone line.
Frequency: factory set at 114 MHz (other frequencies to order).
Receiving Medium: any radio with an Air Band.
Range: 500 yards maximum.

TT 002 — Telephone Monitor Transmitter

Similar in operation to the 001 (above) but battery operated, allowing much greater transmitter power, and a maximum range of 2 miles.

TT 003/AB — 'Drop in'-Type Telephone Monitor Transmitter

This transmitter takes the form of a replacement capsule which is fitted in place of the standard Post Office item in the Telephone Hand Set. Installation should take less than one minute.

The 003/AB is powered from the telephone line so, once installed, no further attention is required. It is identical in appearance to the standard Post Office unit and visual detection is almost impossible.

Note: The 003/AB is for use with standard type telephones only, and will *not* fit the Trimphone type. For alternatives use the TT 001 unit (above).

Size: as per standard Post Office telephone hand set unit.
Power Source: direct from the telephone line
Frequency: factory set at 110 MHz (other frequencies to order).
Receiving Medium: any radio with an Air Band.
Range: 500 yards maximum.

TT 003/VHF — 'Drop in'-Type Telephone Monitor Transmitter

Identical to TT 003/AB (above) except that this unit operates on the FM/VHF frequency and is factory set at 104 MHz.

P.U.I. 3103 CIGARETTE LIGHTER TRANSMITTER

High sensitivity subminiature transmitter with high
sensitivity mini-microphone installed in a table lighter.
This elegant chrome housed cigarette gas lighter
transmits all conversations and other noises clearly
and distinctly.
It also lights cigarettes!
Switched on by laying it on its side and switched off
by returning it to normal position.
To change the batteries, the baseplate is removed.

APPLICATION:
The room must be accoustically controlled.
The monitoring transmitter should not be
conspicuous and you require high receiving
sensitivity.

SPECIFICATIONS:
* Frequency Range: 88-108 MHz — adjustable with
trimming screw.
Transmitting Range: up to 300 m., according to local
conditions.. Power Supply: 9 V battery.

Time of Operation:
  By an ordinary battery: 60 hours.
  By a Mallory MN 1604 battery, approx. 250 hours.
  By a Mallory Tr-146 X, approx. 400 hours.
Dimensions: 85×53×32 mm.
Weight without battery: 140 grams.
Housing: Chrome and plastic material.

For Export Only.

P.U.I. 3104 ASHTRAY TRANSMITTER

This beautifully shaped ceramic ashtray, with a
built-in micro-transmitter, serves serious monitoring
functions.
This article cannot be recognised as a listening
device. All conversations may be supervised
through its built-in dynamic high sensitivity microphone, which broadcasts with extreme clarity.
The battery-inserted device is effected by a built-in
mercury switch which is disconnected by turning
and connected by putting up again.

APPLICATION:
For the requirements of a surveillance transmitter
which should be inconspicuous and in the right
place when the conversations takes place.

SPECIFICATIONS: Transmitting Range: up to 350 m.,
according to local conditions.
* Frequency Range: F.M. 88-108 MHz — adjustable
with trimming screw.
Time of Operation: 100 hours (up to 14 days —
special order).
Power Supply: 9 V battery. Weight: 300 gr. approx.

For Export Only.

P.U.I. 3105 CIGARETTE CASE TRANSMITTER

This is a standard cigarette case — functions
normally. The case has a false bottom in which a
highly efficient transmitter with battery is installed.
APPLICATION:
When an absolutely inconspicuous transmitter,
which is always at hand, is required.
SPECIFICATIONS:
Transmitting Range: up to 350 m., according to local
conditions.
* Frequency Range: F.M. 88-108 MHz — adjustable
with trimming screw.

Power Supply: 9 V battery. Time of operation:
By standard 9 V battery — 60 hours.
By a Mallory TR 146 X — 250 hours.
Dimensions: 100×61×22 mm. Weight: 65 grams.

For Export Only.

---

* The device can be received on any ordinary F.M.
  Radio.
  Also available with Special Frequency 130-150
  MHz (2 meter band) not being received with an
  ordinary radio. Reception then possible with our
  special receivers.

  All specifications are subject to manufacturers changes.

APPENDIX H

'THE LAW THAT MIGHT BE'

Reproduced by kind permission of the Law Commission

In October 1981 the Law Commission published a 240 page report on the Breach of Confidence. As one of the appendices was included a draft of the Breach of Confidence Bill as follows:

DRAFT

Breach of Confidence Bill

ARRANGEMENT OF CLAUSES

Preliminary

11. Plaintiff's claim liable to fail unless upholding of confidentiality is in public interest.
12. Defences

Remedies

13. Remedies in proceedings for breach of confidence: general.
14. Damages.
15. Adjustment orders.
16. Remedies in respect of future use of information which is no longer subject to an obligation of confidence.
17. Special provisions as to county court.

Transmission of benefit of obligations of confidence

18. Transmission of benefit of obligations of confidence.

Operation of Act in relation to proceedings in contract

19. Operation of Act in relation to proceedings in contract.

General

20. Interpretation.
21. Supplemental.
22. Application to the Crown.
23. Citation, commencement and extent.

EXPLANATORY NOTES

Clause 1.

1. This clause concerns the relationship between the provisions of the Bill and the present law as to breach of confidence. The first recommendation in the report, which appears in paragraph 6.5, is that the existing law as to breach of confidence should be abolished and replaced by a new statutory tort. Subsection (2) of this clause accordingly effects, as the prerequisite of such replacement, the abolition of the existing substantive law. However, subsection (3) of the clause makes clear that the abolition of the present law relates only to breach of confidence as such and not to certain related areas of law which may have a bearing on obligations of confidence.

2. *Subsection (1)(a)* refers to four later clauses, 3 to 6, which concern the creation of obligations of confidence in various situations. Clauses 3, 4 and 5 relate respectively to the initial creation of an obligation of confidence arising by virtue of (i) an undertaking on the part of the recipient of information not to disclose or use it, (ii) the acquisition in certain circumstances of information disclosed in or for the purposes of legal proceedings and (iii) the improper acquisition of information. Clause 6 imposes, subject to certain conditions, a duty of confidence upon a third party who acquires information which has already been impressed with an obligation of confidence. Clause 8, to which clause 1(1)(a) also refers, sets out the duties comprised in an obligation of confidence that has arisen under any of clauses 3 to 6.

3. *Subsection (1)(b)* provides for the replacement of both the existing law and its remedies by the new obligations of confidence and the remedies for their breach laid down in later provisions of the Bill.

4. (*a*) *Subsection (2)* abolishes the existing law, which is wholly non-statutory, on breach of confidence. The present remedies for breach of confidence are abolished by the subsection (to be replaced by the range of remedies referred to in clauses 13 to 17), since the principles now governing the subject may be viewed as relating either to substantive rights or to procedural remedies.

(*b*) The effect of the reference to subsection (3) is explained in paragraphs 5 and 6 below.

5. Where an obligation of confidence takes the form of a contractual undertaking, proceedings for breach of contract may be brought in the event of such obligation being broken. *Subsection (3)(a)* preserves the right to bring such proceedings notwithstanding the general abolition of the present law on breach of confidence. The point is explained in paragraph 6.128 of the report. The Bill does, however, affect to some extent the law concerning contractual undertakings not to disclose or use information: see clause 19.

DRAFT

OF A

BILL

TO

Impose obligations of confidence giving rise to liability in tort on persons acquiring information in certain circumstances and otherwise to amend the law of England and Wales as to civil liability for the disclosure or use of information and for connected purposes.

BE IT ENACTED by the Queen's most Excellent Majesty, by and with the advice and consent of the Lords Spiritual and Temporal, and Commons, in this present Parliament assembled, and by the authority of the same, as follows:—

Preliminary

New statutory obligations of confidence.

1.—(1) The provisions of this Act have effect for the purpose of—

(*a*) providing for obligations of confidence, within the meaning of section 8, to be imposed on persons acquiring information in the circumstances mentioned in sections 3 to 6; and

(*b*) providing for proceedings to be brought under this Act in respect of breaches of such obligations, and for the remedies available in those proceedings.

(2) In consequence of the provisions of this Act, any principles of equity or rules of the common law by virtue of which obligations arise in respect of the acquisition of information in circumstances of confidence, or by virtue of which relief may be granted in respect of the disclosure or use of information in breach of confidence, are (subject to subsection (3)) abolished.

(3) Nothing in subsection (2) has effect in relation to—

    (*a*) contractual obligations to treat information confidentially so far as enforceable by proceedings for breach of contract; or

    (*b*) proceedings for contempt of court.

formation to
ich the Act
plies.

2.—(1) An obligation of confidence can arise under this Act only with respect to information which is not in the public domain; and references to information in any of sections 3 to 6 are accordingly references to such information.

(2) Information in the public domain includes information which is public knowledge or accessible to the public (whether or not on payment of a fee or subject to any other restriction); but, for the purposes of this Act, information which is capable of being extracted from any matter in the public domain (whether a document, product, process or anything else) is not in the public domain on that ground alone if such extraction would require a significant expenditure of labour, skill or money.

(3) For the purposes of this Act, information not already in the public domain which is orally disclosed in such a way as to be generally available to those present at the proceedings of any court—

    (*a*) does not come into the public domain if the court is sitting in private; but

    (*b*) comes into the public domain if the court is in open session and publication of the information is not prohibited in the circumstances by any statutory provision or by an order or direction of the court (having the power to make such an order or direction).

(4) In subsection (3) "court" includes a judge, tribunal and any person exercising the functions of a court, judge or tribunal; and the reference to a court sitting in private includes a court sitting in camera or in chambers.

Circumstances in which obligations of confidence arise

3.—(1) A person who has acquired information from another person shall owe the other an obligation of confidence under this section with respect to the information if—

(*a*) he has expressly undertaken to the other to treat the information, or a description of information within which it falls, confidentially; or

(*b*) an undertaking by him to the other to that effect is, in the absence of any contrary indication given by him to the other, to be inferred from the nature of any relationship between the parties or from his conduct in relation to the other.

(2) A person who has acquired information on behalf of another person shall, if either paragraph (*a*) or (*b*) of subsection (1) is applicable, owe to the other person an obligation of confidence under this section with respect to the information.

(3) For the purposes of this section it is immaterial whether the undertaking given by a person (expressly or by inference) was given at the time when he acquired the information in question or at some other time, whether before or afterwards.

(4) A person who has acquired information from another person and is, or in all the circumstances ought to be, aware that the information was supplied by the other on behalf of a third person shall be treated for the purposes of this section as having acquired the information from that third person as well.

(5) It is declared that subsection (1) applies in relation to the following, namely—

(*a*) the acquisition by a person from another person of information supplied to him by the other in accordance with any requirement to do so imposed by or by virtue of any statutory provision, or so supplied in connection with an application under a statutory provision for the grant of any benefit or permission;

(*b*) an undertaking within paragraph (*a*) or (*b*) of subsection (1) which is an express or implied obligation of a contract.

4.—(1) Where information, or any document or other matter containing information, is required to be disclosed to a person for the purposes of any legal proceedings (pending or otherwise)—

(*a*) by an order or direction of a court, or

(*b*) by rules of court,

then, on acquiring the information as a result of it or the matter containing it being disclosed in pursuance of that order or direction or those rules, that person or any other person to whom the disclosure is made on his behalf shall owe an obligation of confidence under this subsection with respect to the information to the person required to make the disclosure.

(2) Where information is disclosed in legal proceedings—

(*a*) at a time when the court is sitting in private otherwise than in chambers, or

(*b*) if this subsection applies to that disclosure in accordance with subsection (3), at a time when the court is sitting in chambers,

any person who thereupon acquires the information shall owe an obligation of confidence under this subsection with respect to the information to the person making the disclosure.

(3) Subsection (2) applies to a disclosure of information at a time when the court is sitting in chambers in the following cases, namely—

(*a*) where the proceedings relate to a breach of an obligation of confidence under this Act or to a breach of a contractual obligation to treat information confidentially and the information disclosed is material to the proceedings;

(*b*) where the proceedings relate to any secret process, knowhow, discovery or invention and the information disclosed is material to the proceedings;

(*c*) where it appears to the court proper that the information disclosed should be protected by means of an order under this paragraph and the court accordingly by order directs that subsection (2) is to apply to the disclosure.

(4) If a person acquiring information as mentioned in subsection (1) or (2) is or in all the circumstances ought to be aware that the person in whose favour an obligation of confidence arises under that subsection made the disclosure in question on behalf of a third person, the person acquiring the information shall owe an obligation of confidence under that subsection with respect to it to the third person as well.

(5) In this section "court" has a meaning given by section 2(4); and the reference in subsection (2)(*a*) of this section to a court sitting in private includes a court sitting in camera.

(6) Nothing in this section prejudices the exercise by any court of any power to prohibit or punish contempt of court (whether in relation to its own proceedings or otherwise).

Improper
acquisition of
information.

5.—(1) Subject to the provisions of this section, a person who improperly acquires information from another person shall owe an obligation of confidence under this section with respect to the information—

(*a*) to the person from whom the information is so acquired, and

(*b*) if that person is at the time when it is so acquired holding it on behalf of some other person, to that other person as well.

(2) For the purposes of this section a person acquires information improperly if—

(*a*) he acquires it as a result of doing any of the following acts without authority (express or implied), namely—

   (i) taking, handling or interfering with any document, record, model or other thing containing the information,

(ii) taking, handling or interfering with anything in which any such thing as is mentioned in sub-paragraph (i) is for the time being kept,

(iii) (without prejudice to the generality of the fore-going) using or interfering with any computer or data retrieval mechanism,

whether, as regards any such act, the absence of authority relates to his doing it at all or only to the manner or purpose in or for which he in fact does it; or

(b) he acquires it as a result of using any violence, menace or deception; or

(c) he acquires it while somewhere where he has no authority (express or implied) to be; or

(d) he acquires it by means of the use of—

(i) a device made or adapted primarily for the purpose of surreptitiously carrying out the surveillance of persons, their activities, communications or property, or

(ii) subject to subsection (3), any other technical device capable of being used for carrying out such surveillance, whether surreptitiously or overtly,

provided that (in either case) he would not in the circumstances have acquired the information but for his use of the device in question.

(3) A person's acquisition of information by means of the use of a device within subsection (2)(d)(ii) is not improper for the purposes of this section if a reasonable man in the position of the person from whom the information is acquired would have appreciated the risk of, and taken precautions adequate to prevent, its being acquired by means of the use of a device of the kind in question; and nothing in that sub-paragraph is to be read as referring to a device designed to bring vision or hearing so far as possible up to a normal standard.

5(4) Any person interfering with a device mentioned in subsection (2)(*a*)(iii), any person by or on behalf of whom the information was supplied to the device shall be regarded for the purposes of subsection (1) as a person from whom the information is acquired (and subsection (1)(*b*) accordingly does not apply).

(5) Where two or more persons ("participators") have jointly participated in the acquisition of information from another person, any participator—

(*a*) who has personally acquired the information from the other person, and

(*b*) whose acquisition of it was not improper under subsection (2) apart from this subsection,

shall nevertheless owe an obligation of confidence under this section to the other person with respect to the information as from such time as the participator is aware, or ought in all the circumstances to be aware, of any act done by any other participator in connection with the acquisition of the information which, if done by the former participator, would have rendered his acquisition of the information improper under subsection (2).

(6) In any case where a person's acquisition of information falls within subsection (2) but the information was acquired by him—

(*a*) in the course of the lawful exercise by him of any official function to acquire information for the purposes of protecting the security of the State, or of preventing, detecting or investigating crime, or

(*b*) in pursuance of any statutory provision,

nothing in this section or section 6 imposes on him or on any other person directly or indirectly acquiring it from him any liability under this Act in respect of the disclosure or use of that information in so far as it is disclosed or used—

(i) for any such purposes as are referred to in paragraph (*a*) of this subsection or for the pur-

> > (ii) for any purpose expressly or impliedly authorised, in relation to information acquired in pursuance of the statutory provision referred to in paragraph (*b*) of this subsection, by that or any other such provision.

sition by
party of
nation
t to an
tion of
ence.

6.—(1) If, while an obligation of confidence under section 3, 4 or 5 is owed by any person ("the original acquirer") to another person with respect to any information—

> > (*a*) the information is acquired from the original acquirer (by whatever means and whether directly or, through successive acquisitions, indirectly) by any third person, and

> > (*b*) the third person becomes aware, or ought in all the circumstances to have become aware, of the material facts or circumstances giving rise to the obligation of confidence owed by the original acquirer or otherwise that an obligation of confidence has arisen with respect to the information under the preceding provisions of this Act,

then, as from the relevant time under subsection (2), the third person shall owe an obligation of confidence under this section with respect to the information to the other person mentioned above.

(2) The relevant time referred to in subsection (1) is whichever is the later of the following, namely the time when the third person acquires the information and the time when he becomes, or ought to have become, aware as mentioned in paragraph (*b*) of that subsection.

(3) Where a person dies (or, if not an individual, ceases to exist) while owing an obligation of confidence under section 3, 4 or 5 with respect to any information, then, unless that obligation of confidence thereupon ceases to have effect in accordance with subsection (2) of section 9, the information shall for the purposes of this section continue to be subject to that obligation of confidence, as if it were still owed by that

person, until such time as that person would have been released from it by virtue of subsection (1) or (2) of section 9 if still alive or (as the case may be) still in existence.

No obligation of confidence where information acquired in course of work merely enhances personal skills, etc.

7. Nothing in the preceding provisions of this Act has the effect of imposing an obligation of confidence on any individual with respect to any information which—

(*a*) is acquired by him in the course of his work (whether under a contract of employment or as an independent contractor or otherwise), and

(*b*) is of such a nature that the acquisition of it by him amounts to no more than an enhancement of the personal knowledge, skill or experience used by him in the exercise of his calling.

Obligations of confidence

Duties arising out of an obligation of confidence.

8.— (1) For the purposes of this Act an obligation of confidence owed under any provision of this Act with respect to any information shall, subject to subsections (3) and (4), impose the following duties on the person who owes the obligation, namely—

(*a*) a duty not to disclose or use the information except to the extent (if any) to which he is for the time being expressly or impliedly authorised to do so by the person to whom the obligation is owed; and

(*b*) a duty to take reasonable care to ensure that the information is not disclosed or used except to the extent mentioned in paragraph (*a*).

(2) Accordingly, any reference in this Act to a breach of an obligation of confidence is a reference to an act or omission in breach of one or other of the duties subsisting with respect to the information in question in accordance with subsection (1).

(3) Nothing in subsection (1)—

(*a*) prevents a person who owes an obligation of confidence under section 3 with respect to information supplied as mentioned in subsection (5)(*a*) of that section from disclosing or using it to such extent as is, in relation to information supplied in pursuance of the statutory provision in question, expressly or impliedly authorised by or by virtue of that or any other statutory provision;

(*b*) prevents a person who owes an obligation of confidence under subsection (1) or subsection (2) of section 4 from disclosing or using the information in question for the purposes of the proceedings referred to in that subsection; or

(*c*) prevents a person who owes an obligation of confidence under section 6 with respect to information directly or indirectly acquired from a person such as is referred to in paragraph (*a*) or (*b*) of this subsection from disclosing or using the information to the extent to which the latter may do so by virtue of that paragraph.

(4) Where a person owing an obligation of confidence under section 3, 4 or 5 with respect to any information has been expressly or impliedly authorised by the person to whom the obligation is owed to disclose or use the information to any extent, nothing in subsection (1) of this section prevents a person who owes an obligation of confidence under section 6 by virtue of that obligation of confidence from disclosing or using the information to an extent which will not result in a more extensive disclosure or use of the information than has been so authorised.

Termination of obligations of confidence. **9.**—(1) A person who, under any provision of this Act, owes another person an obligation of confidence with respect to any information shall cease to owe the other person an obligation of confidence with respect to the information—

(*a*) if he is expressly or impliedly released by the other person from such an obligation; or

(*b*) in so far as an order of the court under section 15(2) has the effect of releasing him from such an obligation; or (*c*) if the information comes into the public domain.

(2) Where in the case of an obligation of confidence under section 3 the relevant undertaking within subsection (1)(*a*) or (*b*) of that section was given, expressly or by inference, for a particular period of time (including a period expiring on the occurrence of any event), that obligation of confidence, and any obligation of confidence owed under section 6 by virtue of it, shall cease to be owed at such time as that period expires.

(3) For the purposes of subsection (1)(*c*) of this section it is immaterial whether the person responsible for the information coming into the public domain was the person to whom the obligation of confidence was owed, the person who owed it or some other person.

(4) Subsections (1) and (2) of this section are without prejudice to—

    (*a*) any claim in respect of a person's breach of an obligation of confidence which was committed before, or as a consequence of which, he ceased to owe that obligation in accordance with this section;

    (*b*) the power of the court to grant relief in respect of such a breach in the circumstances mentioned in section 16.

Proceedings for breach of confidence

Proceedings for reach of onfidence.

10.—(1) A breach of an obligation of confidence owed under any of the preceding provisions of this Act is a tort and, subject to the following provisions of this Act, proceedings may be brought in respect of such a breach by any person to whom the obligation is owed in like manner as any other proceedings in respect of a tort.

(2) Proceedings brought by virtue of this section are referred to in this Act as proceedings for breach of confidence.

Appendix H

11.—(1) A defendant in proceedings for breach of confidence shall not be liable to the plaintiff in respect of any disclosure or use of information by the defendant in breach of an obligation of confidence if—

(a) the defendant raises the issue of public interest in relation to that disclosure or use in accordance with subsection (2); and

(b) the plaintiff is unable to satisfy the court that the public interest relied on by the defendant under that subsection is outweighed by the public interest involved in upholding the confidentiality of the information.

(2) For the purposes of subsection (1) a defendant raises the issue of public interest in relation to a disclosure or use of information if he satisfies the court that, in view of the content of the information, there was, or (in the case of an apprehended disclosure or use) will be, at the time of the disclosure or use a public interest involved in the information being so disclosed or used.

(3) A public interest may be involved in the disclosure or use of information notwithstanding that the information does not relate to any crime, fraud or other misconduct.

(4) When balancing the public interests involved for the purposes of subsection (1) the court shall have regard to all the circumstances of the case, including—

(a) the extent and nature of the particular disclosure or use in question as compared with the extent and nature of the disclosure or use which appears to be justified by the public interest on which the defendant relies;

(b) the manner in which the information was acquired by the defendant and (in the case of an obligation of confidence under section 6) the manner in which it was acquired by the original and any subsequent acquirer of it; and

(c) the time which has elapsed since the information originally became subject to the obligation of confidence owed by the defendant or (in the case of an obligation of confidence under section 6) became subject to the obligation of confidence by virtue of which that obligation arose.

Defences.

12.—(1) In any proceedings for breach of confidence in respect of a disclosure or use of information it is a defence to prove—

(a) that, at the time of the defendant's acquisition of the information which gave rise to the obligation of confidence in question, he was already in possession of the information, or

(b) that he subsequently came into possession of it by independent means,

and, in addition, that at the time he disclosed or used the information the defendant did not, in connection with his previous or (as the case may be) subsequent awareness of the information, owe any other obligation of confidence of which that disclosure or use constituted a breach.

(2) In any proceedings for breach of confidence in respect of a disclosure or use of information it is a defence to prove that the disclosure or use was required or authorised to be made by or by virtue of any statutory provision.

(3) In any proceedings for breach of confidence in respect of a disclosure of information it is a defence to prove that the disclosure was made on such an occasion as attracts, for the purposes of the law of defamation, an absolute privilege in respect of statements made thereon.

(4) Without prejudice to the generality of subsections (2) and (3) it is a defence in any proceedings for breach of confidence in respect of a disclosure of information to prove that the disclosure was required to be made by a court in pursuance of any power to order the disclosure of information.

(5) Defences generally available in tort proceedings are, in accordance with section 10(1), available in proceedings for breach of confidence.

Remedies

13.—(1) The following relief may be granted by the court in proceedings for breach of confidence—

Remedies in proceedings for breach of confidence: general.

    (*a*) an injunction restraining the defendant from any apprehended breach of an obligation of confidence (with or without, in a case to which section 15(1) applies, an adjusttment order under that subsection providing compensation for the defendant);

    (*b*) damages in accordance with section 14;

    (*c*) an account of the profits derived by the defendant from the breach;

    (*d*) an adjustment order under section 15(2) regulating the respective rights and liabilities of the plaintiff and the defendant in so far as the defendant is not to be restrained by injunction;

    (*e*) an order for the defendant to deliver up or destroy anything in which the information to which the breach relates is contained.

(2) With the exception of paragraph (*b*), the relief mentioned in subsection (1) is at the discretion of the court.

(3) Nothing in this section prejudices any jurisdiction of the court to grant ancillary or incidental relief.

Damages.

14.—(1) The damages which may by virtue of section 13(1)(*b*), be awarded to a plaintiff in proceedings for breach of confidence are, subject to the provisions of this section, damages in respect of either or both of the following matters, namely—

    (*a*) any pecuniary loss suffered by the plaintiff in consequence of the defendant's breach of an obligation of confidence owed to him; and (*b*) any mental distress, and any mental or physical harm resulting from such distress, suffered by the plaintiff in consequence of that breach.

(2) The court shall not in respect of the same breach of an obligation of confidence both award the plaintiff damages under subsection (1)(*a*) and order that he shall be given an account of the defendant's profits therefrom.

(3) The court shall not award the plaintiff any damages under subsection (1)(*b*) unless it appears to the court that a person of reasonable fortitude in the position of the plaintiff would have been likely to suffer mental distress in consequence of the defendant's breach.

ment   **15.**—(1) Where in any proceedings for breach of confidence—

(*a*) the court proposes to grant an injunction against a defendant restraining him from an apprehended breach of an obligation of confidence owed under section 6, but

(*b*) it appears to the court that, prior to the time when he became subject to that obligation, he incurred any expenditure in connection with exploiting the information to which the breach relates,

then, if the court thinks fit, it may (in addition to granting the injunction) make an adjustment order under this subsection requiring the plaintiff to make to the defendant such contribution towards that expenditure as appears to the court to be just and equitable.

(2) Where in any proceedings for breach of confidence the court has power to grant an injunction against a defendant restraining him from an apprehended breach of an obligation of confidence but considers that it would be inappropriate in all the circumstances to do so to any extent, the court may, if it thinks fit, make an adjustment order under this subsection for the purpose of regulating, as regards such future exploitation by the defendant of the information in question as it is not

proposing to restrain, the respective rights and liabilities of the plaintiff and the defendant.

(3) An adjustment order under subsection (2) may require the defendant to pay to the plaintiff one or other of the following namely—

    (*a*) such sum in lieu of an injunction as appears to the court to be appropriate in all the circumstances, or

    (*b*) a royalty in respect of the future use by the defendant of the information in question calculated on such basis as appears to the court to be appropriate, the defendant's use of the information being for such period and on such terms as the court may specify in the order,

together with (in either case) such contribution as appears to be just and equitable towards any expenditure which the plaintiff has already incurred in connection with exploiting the information in question and which is likely to become wasted expenditure as a result of the defendant being allowed to exploit the information in future.

(4) The court may in any adjustment order under subsection (2) determine any incidental question relating to the extent to which either of the parties is to be free to exploit the information in question.

(5) In any case where the court proposes to make—

    (*a*) an award of damages under section 14(1)(*a*) in respect of the defendant's breach of an obligation of confidence, and

    (*b*) an adjustment order under subsection (2) of this section in respect of future exploitation by the defendant of the information to which that breach relates,

the court, when determining whether to make the plaintiff an award under subsection (3)(*a*) or (*b*) of this section, and if so the amount of any such award, shall take such account of any element of that award of damages which reflects future loss to the plaintiff as it thinks appropriate for the purpose of doing justice between the parties.

(6) Any reference in this section to expenditure incurred by a person in connection with exploiting information includes expenditure incurred by him in connection with acquiring it.

Remedies in
respect of
future use of
information
which is no
longer subject
to an
obligation of
confidence.
16.—(1) The court may, if it thinks fit in the case of a defendant in proceedings for breach of confidence who has committed a breach of an obligation of confidence under this Act, grant relief under this section in respect of the future use by him of the information to which the breach relates notwithstanding that such use will occur at a time when the information has, or is likely to have, come into the public domain (and accordingly ceased to be subject to an obligation of confidence).

(2) The relief which may be granted by the court under this section in the case of such a defendant is—

(a) an injunction for such period and on such terms as appear to the court to be necessary to prevent the defendant from enjoying an advantage in the exploitation of the information in question over persons able to exploit it only as from its coming into the public domain (granted with or without, in a case to which section 15(1) applies, an adjustment order under that subsection); or

(b) an adjustment order under section 15(2), but only in respect of such period of future use by the defendant as, in the view of the court, the defendant is likely (in so far as not restrained under paragraph (a) from exploiting the information) to enjoy an advantage in its exploitation over persons able to exploit it only as from its coming into the public domain.

(3) Section 15 shall in its operation for the purposes of this section have effect as if, in each of subsections (1) and (2) of that section, for the words "an injunction against a defendant restraining him from an apprehended breach of an obligation of confidence" there were substituted "an injunction under section 16(2)(a) against a defendant who has committed a breach of an obligation of confidence".

17.—(1) A county court may in proceedings for breach of confidence grant the plaintiff an injunction or a declaration notwithstanding that he does not seek any relief other than an injunction or a declaration.

(2) A county court may in proceedings for breach of confidence make an adjustment order under subsection (1) of section 15 whatever the amount required to be paid by virtue of it by the plaintiff, but shall not have power to make an adjustment order under subsection (2) of that section by virtue of which the defendant is required to pay such a royalty as is mentioned in subsection (3)(*b*) of that section.

special
provisions as
to county
court.

Transmission of benefit of obligations of confidence

18.—(1) Subject to subsection (2), nothing in this Act prevents the benefit of an obligation of confidence under this Act from being assigned to a person other than the person in whose favour the obligation of confidence has arisen in so far as it is, in any particular case in view of the nature of the information to which the obligation of confidence relates, capable of being so assigned in accordance with the general law as to the assignment of rights.

(2) No proceedings for breach of confidence shall be brought in respect of mental distress, or mental or physical harm resulting from such distress, suffered by any person other than a person in whose favour an obligation of confidence has arisen under this Act.

(3) Any reference in this Act (whether express or implied and however worded) to the person to whom an obligation of confidence is or was owed includes (subject to subsection (2) and so far as the context so permits) a person to whom the benefit of the obligation of confidence has been assigned.

(4) In this section references to assignment include assignment by operation of law.

Transmission
of benefit of
obligations of
confidence.

Operation of Act in relation to proceedings in contract

tion of
relation
ceedings
tract.
19.—(1) Section 11 (plaintiff's claim liable to fail unless upholding of confidentiality is in pubic interest) shall have effect in relation to proceedings for breach of contract in respect of a breach of a relevant contractual undertaking as it has effect in relation to proceedings for breach of confidence, but with the following modifications, namely—

(*a*)   any reference to an obligation of confidence shall be read as a reference to a relevant contractual undertaking;

(*b*)   the referencce in subsection (1)(*b*) to upholding the confidentiality of the information shall be read as a reference to upholding the contractual undertaking in question; and

(*c*)   subsection (4)(*b*) and so much of subsection (4)(*c*) as relates to an obligation of confidence under section 6 shall not apply.

(2) Subject to subsection (1), any relevant contractual undertaking may be enforced by proceedings for breach of contract in all respects as if this Act had not been passed.

(3) In this section "relevant contractual undertaking" means an express or implied contractual undertaking not to disclose or use information.

General

retation.
20.—(1) In this Act, unless the context otherwise requires—

:. 22.
"the court" means the High Court or, subject to section 17(2) of this Act and section 39 of the County Courts Act 1959 (which contains financial limits on jurisdiction), a county court;

"proceedings" includes proceedings by way of counter-claim, and references to a plaintiff or defendant in proceedings shall be construed accordingly;

3 c. 30.

"statutory provision" means any enactment, whenever passed, or any provision contained in subordinate legislation (as defined in section 21(1) of the Interpretation Act 1978), whenever made.

(2) References in this Act to information in, or coming into, the pubic domain shall be construed in accordance with subsections (2) to (4) of section 2.

(3) References in this Act to an obligation of confidence shall be construed in accordance with section 8, and references to the person to whom such obligation is owed shall be construed in accordance with section 18(3).

plemental.

21.—(1) Sections 3 to 6 have effect in relation to acquisitions of information taking place before the commencement of this Act as well as to those taking place thereafter, but an obligation of confidence under section 6 shall not be owed in respect of an acquisition of information taking place before that commencement unless it would have been owed in respect of that acquisition if this Act had at all material times been in force.

(2) Section 19 has effect in relation to contractual undertakings given before or after the commencement of this Act.

(3) Sections 10(1) and 19(1) have effect, however, only in relation to a disclosure or use of information taking place after the commencement of this Act; and accordingly nothing in this Act affects any cause of action accruing before this Act comes into force.

0 c. 58.

(4) The Limitation Act 1980 shall apply in relation to a claim for damages in respect of mental distress suffered as mentioned in section 14(1)(*b*) of this Act as it applies in relation to a claim for damages in respect of personal injuries within the meaning of that Act (references to "injury" and cognate expressions in that Act being construed accordingly).

4 c. 41.

(5) Nothing in this Act affects the operation of section 1 of the Law Reform (Miscellaneous Provisions) Act 1934 (surviv-

al of causes of action against, or for the benefit of, a deceased's estate).

Application to the Crown, 1947 c. 44.

22.—(1) This Act shall bind the Crown, but as regards the Crown's liability in tort shall not bind the Crown further than the Crown is made liable in tort by the Crown Proceedings Act 1947.

(2) Without prejudice to the generality of section 21(1) of that Act (nature of relief in proceedings by or against the Crown), references in sections 15 and 16 of this Act to the granting of an injunction restraining a defendant in proceedings for breach of confidence shall, in relation to the Crown where it is a defendant in such proceedings, be read as references to the granting of such equivalent declaration with respect to the rights of the parties as the court is empowered to grant by virtue of proviso (*a*) to the said section 21(1).

Citation, commencement and extent.

23.—(1) This Act may be cited as the Breach of Confidence Act 1981.

(2) This Act shall come into force at the end of the period of three months beginning with the day on which it is passed.

(3) This Act extends to England and Wales only.

Appendix H

THE BREACH OF CONFIDENCE REPORT
(A Counsel's Opinion)

Introduction

I have been asked to consider the draft Bill included in the above and in particular to say:

i) Would the Bill protect a company from one of its employees 'stealing' a secret and endeavouring to dispose of it to a third party?

ii) Is there sufficient protection to safeguard a company against the activities of, say, a spy who gains access to premises using a pretext, albeit quite lawfully and who thereafter photographs documents or equipment?

iii) Would the Bill provide a sufficient safeguard against the obtaining of information at false job interviews and the like?

In order to answer these questions, I propose to refer to the scope of the draft Bill and the 'scheme' of the Bill before discussing each of these three points and stating my conclusions.

1. Scope of the Bill

The description of the Bill in its preamble is:

'A Bill to impose obligations of confidence giving rise to liability in tort on persons acquiring information in certain circumstances and otherwise to amend the law of England and Wales (N.B. not Scotland) as to civil liability for the disclosure or use of information and for connected purposes.'

In other words, the Bill would displace and replace any principles of equity or rules of the common law by virtue of which obligations arise in respect of the acquisition of information in circumstances of confidence other than contractual obligations to treat information confidentially (Cl. 1(2)).

This suggests that the decisions in *B.S.C. v Granada Television* (1980) (the 'mole' case), *Seager v Copydex Ltd* (1967) (protection for pre-contract information divulged) and the protection in respect of discovery ordered under what the lawyers call 'the *Mareva* jurisdiction' (see most recently *Z Ltd v A-Z and AA-LL* but earlier the thalidomide case, *Distillers Co (Biochemicals) Ltd v Times Newspapers Ltd* (1975)) could cease to be of effect.

The Bill specifically deals with 'information', a word not defined in the Interpretation section. It is reasonable to suppose that the Courts, especially while Lord Denning remains Master of the Rolls, will go out of their way to extend the scope of protection of, for instance, fiduciary relationships (solicitor-client; doctor-patient; confessor-penitent and trusteeship are the most obvious examples). Such a two-pronged approach might well aid those fighting industrial espionage.

Indeed, the note to Cl. 1 of the draft specifically underlines that 'subsection (3) of the Clause makes clear that the abolition of the present law relates only to breach of confidence as such and not to certain related areas of law which may have a bearing on obligations of confidence'.

2. The Scheme of the Bill

The Bill works on the concept of an 'obligation of confidence' ('the Obligation'). Cl. 3 sets out the circumstances under which the Obligation would arise. Failure to carry out the Obligation creates a statutory tort (Cl. 8) which enables the person to whom the Obligation is owed to bring proceedings for any of the usual remedies available against tortfeasors (Cls. 10 & 13).

These remedies include the taking of an account and orders for delivery up and/or destruction, as occurs in passing off actions.

So that the full might and majesty of the civil law can be brought into operation against both those who acquire the information and those to whom it is passed on.

But we must look at this practically, which may mean cynically. Regard for the law is not what it was and whilst many corporations would think twice before incurring the liability described in Cl. 6(1), there will always be some who will think it commercially worthwhile to do so. Moreover, many individuals may be tempted to breach their Obligation by the offer of large rewards, especially if they feel that by the time the law catches up with them, they will have enjoyed and used up the money. One can also foresee agents of foreign corporations which may be mere shells causing litigation to be protracted. And a number of unsatisfied judgments.

I enter these caveats for your consideration. Had the Bill sought to create a criminal offence (or offences), as is the case in some of the United States, 'commercial profit' considerations could, perhaps, have been more easily set aside.

3. Employees

Where relevant, all employees ought always to have a term requiring confidentiality in their contract of employment (which is required by law to be in writing). However, I am satisfied that an Obligation would be implied under Cl. 3(1)(*b*) when read with Cl. 3(2).

4. The Industrial Spy

Cl. 5(1)(*a*) establishes the Obligation wherever a person 'improperly acquires information from another person'.

Cl. 5(2) gives examples of 'improper acquisition'. Surprisingly, it refers to 'taking, handling or interfering with' but does not mention photographing or copying, both of which I would have considered prime methods of industrial espionage.

But Cl. 5(2)(*b*) covers acquisition 'as a result of using any . . . deception'.

I would underline '*a* result' and '*any* deception'. The deception need not therefore be the proximate cause of the acquisition.

A private investigator, spy, or indeed a salesman for example, who obtains access using a pretext does so by deception and the obtaining would be *a* result of that deception. I think that the Courts would hold a photograph of a document recording information to be itself information. Whether it would hold the like in the case of a photograph of equipment, must surely depend on the nature of the equipment. A photograph of, for example, a piece of equipment in respect of which claims are made in a patent specification, must, it seems to me be information. Similarly, a photograph of a 'slab' of machinery could well be information if the purpose of the photograph were to show location or siting. So that, prima facie, the activity would be caught under Cl. 5.

Further, Cl. 5(*d*) ii) deals with acquisition by means of 'a technical device capable of being used for carrying out the surveillance of persons, property etc'. Clearly, a camera comes within this definition.

5. False job interviews etc.

I understand these to be interviews in which the interviewee attends in answer to an indication, usually by way of advertisement, that a job is available, whereas the interviewer has no intention of offering a job and is merely pumping the interviewee for information.

It seems to me that any information received in the course of such an interview is likewise covered by Cl. 5(2)(*b*) (acquiring by deception) and is therefore actionable.

For the interviewer must be aware of the Obligation to which the interviewee is subject (else he would not have called him to the interview) and is therefore caught by Cl. 6.

Exactly similar considerations apply to what I gather is meant by the 'etc'.

6. Statutory defences

A defendant in proceedings for breach of confidence can raise the defence of 'public interest' (Cl. 11). This is an importation from Restrictive Practices legislation. Once that defence has been raised, it would be for the Plaintiff to satisfy the Court that the public interest relied on by the defendant is outweighed by the public interest involved in upholding the confidentiality of the information (11 (1)(*b*)).

It is difficult to see this defence succeeding in an industrial espionage case, except possibly by virtue of the 'time elapsed' criterion imported under Cl.11 (4)(*c*).

I ought perhaps to underline that another criterion (Cl. 11(4)(*b*)) is 'the manner in which the information is obtained'.

The note in the report relating to this provision (6.79) reads as follows:

'We think that in assessing the public interest in protecting the confidentiality of information, the Court should take all the circumstances into account, including the manner in which the information was acquired'.

Maybe. But how? Is the industrial spy who walked in through an open door to be treated differently from one who bound and gagged a night watchman and then broke into the premises? Both obtain identical information, which is what the Bill is all about.

I can, however, see our photographer praying in aid of the defence suggested under Cl. 5(3). He might well say: 'Any reasonable man ought to have realised that I, or someone like me, might come in and take the photograph and it was up to you to prevent it'.

7. Conclusions

So far as the Bill is concerned, I feel it provides sufficient protection against the 'stealing' employee and the false job interview. I can see difficult and interesting litigation in the case of a spy and his photograph if he does *not* use a pretext but simply walks boldly and unhindered into wherever the thing he wants to photograph is to be found openly available and clicks his camera.

And I can foresee many cases in which the financial loss to the owner of the confidential information will far outstrip any damages he may recover.

APPENDIX I

'THE LAW THAT NEVER WAS'

Industrial Information Bill

ARRANGEMENT OF CLAUSES

Clause

1. Offence of misappropriation of industrial information by direct commission.
2. Offence of misappropriation of industrial information by indirect commission.
3. Definition of industrial information.
4. Penalties.
5. Civil liability.
6. Proceedings in civil and criminal courts.
7. Definition of rightful owner and possessor.
8. Savings.
9. Short title, commencement and extent.

Industrial Information

A

BILL

To provide for the protection of industrial information.

Presented by Sir Edward Boyle
supported by
Sir Derek Walker-Smith,
Sir Arthur Vere Harvey, Mr Longden,
Mr Kirk, Mr Moonman,
Mr Richard Wainwright, Mr Tom Boardman,
and Mr Silvester

Ordered, by The House of Commons,
to be Printed, 27 November 1968

LONDON
Printed and Published by
Her Majesty's Stationery Office
Printed in England at St. Stephen's
Parliamentary Press

A

BILL

TO

Provide for the protection of industrial information.   AD

B E IT ENACTED by The Queen's most Excellent Majesty by and with the advice and consent of the Lords Spiritual and Temporal, and Commons, in this present Parliament assembled, and by the Authority of the same as follows:

1. A person shall be guilty of the offence of misappropriation of industrial information, as hereinafter defined, who without the consent of the rightful owner and possessor thereof:

Offence of misapprop of industri informatio direct commissio

> (*a*) reads, copies, receives or records such information with any photographic and/or electronic device, or

> (*b*) obtains such information from any computer, data bank, memory core, laser beam, satellite, or from any cable telephonic or television system.

2. A person who aids, abets, counsels or procures the commission of the said offence by another person, or who with knowledge of such misappropriation receives, uses, handles, sells, or otherwise disposes of such information shall likewise be guilty of the said offence.

Offence o misappro of industri informatic indirect commissic

3. Industrial information shall include unregistered or in-complete patent, trade mark, or design information, know-how, research and technical data, formulae, calculations, drawings, results, conclusions, costings, price structures, con-tracts, lists of suppliers or customers, and private business discussions, or memoranda of the same.

Definition industrial informatic

4. Any person found guilty of the commission of such off-ence shall be liable on summary conviction to a fine not exceed-ing £100 or to a sentence of nine months imprisonment, or to both, or on conviction on indictment to a fine not exceeding £1,000 or to a sentence of two years imprisonment or to both.

Penalties.

ability.   **5.**   Any person committing an offence under section 1 or 2 of this Act shall also be liable in damages to the rightful owner or possessor of the information.

dings in   **6.**   Any person adversely affected by the commission, or
ıd criminal   threatened commission, of the said offence may apply forthwith in the civil courts for interim relief by way of injunction and/or declaration notwithstanding that proceedings are either in contemplation or in being in the criminal courts, in which event the civil claim for preparation shall stand over until after verdict in the criminal proceedings.

ion of   **7.**   For the purposes of this Act the rightful owner or posses-
l owner   sor shall mean respectively any person who at the time of the
ıssessor.   alleged misappropriation had a bona fide de jure claim, and de facto control of access to, such information; save that in relation to receiving or recording private business discussions the rightful owner or possessor shall be deemed to be all parties to such discussion.

s.   **8.**   This Act shall not apply to duly authorised investigation by the police or to investigation undertaken with ministerial authority, or to investigation undertaken in the interests of national security.

itle,   **9.**—(1) This Act may be cited as the Industrial Information
ıncement   Act 1968.
tent.
              (2) This Act shall come into force at the expiration of the period of one month beginning with the day on which it is passed.

              (3) This Act does not extend to Northern Ireland.

Index